MW00652477

Go, Little Book, and since there is
so great diversity in English and
in writing of our tongue, I pray God,
No one will miswrite or mismeter
you through ignorance of language,
And wherever you may be read, I pray God,
you may be understood.

From the Canterbury Tales
Chaucer's Plea, end of "Troilus."

The
Zoo-hire
Family Cookbook

For

Todd and Jamey

Made with love by

Mom and The Cats

ZOO-HIRE INK ♥ KENMORE, WA

Cover design and graphics: Malia Bryan

Book design: Isabel Gates, Apple Tree Graphics

Copyright © 1995 by Janet L. Rider-Zerhire

All rights reserved. No portion of this book may be
reproduced--mechanically, electronically,
or by any other means, incuding photocopying--
without written permission of the publisher.

ISBN: 0-9649010-0-5

Published by:
Zoo-hire Ink
P.O. Box 82811
Kenmore, WA 98028-0811

Printed and bound in the United States of America

This book is lovingly
dedicated to

Todd and Jamey

This book is yours, for long after I am gone, so that I will never be far away. You will just have to pick it up, open its pages, and once again feel my love for you, which fills my heart to overflowing. Remember that you were the center of my being, and I love you *both* more than life itself. You are what life, for me, is all about.

May you, as I hope many others shall, be able to travel through these pages recalling a favorite meal, remembering a group of friends we had over for an unexpected treat or two—not quite sure who would be staying with us for the night, maybe more. Remember all the laughter, a few tears, the ups/downs of life, and your mommy—unlike anyone else's. Would you really have changed very many things?

So, here goes, my fellas: your cookbook, with a *little* bit more!

God keep you.

Mom

Table of Contents

Preface
Welcome to Our Home: a place to feed your tummy and fill your soul ix
*A little about me • The importance of family, and an introduction to mine •
Loving each other over the kitchen table •*

Acknowledgements xiii

Introduction
About the Cookbook 1
The Heart of the Book • A Note About the Ingredients • Recommended Cookware

Hors d'oeuvres
Those little bites to nibble on that give everyone a chance to unwind 5
*Dips and Spreads • Canapés and Finger Foods • Hot Hors D'Oeuvres •
Liqueurs and Party Drinks*

Soups, Salads and Sauces
Family favorites, from comforting to "just what I feel like" 55
Soups • Salads • Salad Dressings • Sauces

Main Courses and Side Dishes
Great dishes and a place to gather round 101
Meat Dishes • Poultry • Seafood • Pasta • Vegetable Dishes

Excerpts from The Empty Book
My daddy's tribute to the art of living 181

Bread and Breakfast Sampler
What smell is more welcoming than that of freshly baked bread? 211
Quick Breads • Yeast Breads, Rolls and Muffins • Pancakes and French Toast

Desserts and Delectables
Too much of a good thing can be wonderful 239
Cakes • Cookies and Bars • Pies and Pastries • Candies and Confections

Helpful Hints
Trade secrets from the Zoo-hire Family kitchen 307
*Cleaning Tips • Laundry Tips • Gardening Hints • Stain Helps • Equivalents
and Substitutions • Quantities for Parties*

Index 317

Welcome To Our Home

A Place To Feed Your Tummy and Fill Your Soul

For men and women are not only themselves,
they are also the region in which they were born,
the city, apartment or the farm in which they
learned to walk, the games they played as children,
the old wives tales they overheard, the food they ate,
the schools they attended, the sports they followed,
the poets they read, and the God they believed in.
It is all these things that have made them what they are,
and these are things that you can't come to know by hearsay,
you can only know them if you have lived them.

W. Somerset Maugham from "The Razor's Edge"

The recipes in this cookbook have been lovingly put together over many years now, and it is with much joy that I share the four things in these pages that I am truly passionate about: great food and wonderful quotes that are timeless in their wisdom and inspiration, my family and my friends. I can hardly remember a time when I haven't met every day with: "I am so blessed, let's see what today brings." What I didn't do yesterday I will try to do today, and there is always tomorrow… I always have time to sit down with a friend. The way I celebrate my love for family and friends is to draw them together with wonderful food. When a dish is prepared with love, the food nurtures both the body and the soul. Two sayings I have found true: "The way to a man's heart is through his stomach," and

After a good dinner, one can forgive anybody,
even one's own relations.

Oscar Wilde

♥ A Little About Me

I began my life on the Aurora Bridge in the back seat of a car. Afterward, my parents turned around and returned home, where I was handed into the arms of my older sister, Joy (10) who thought I was for her and showed me to my brother Bill (12). Perhaps when you begin life in such a way, it is only natural that your life will turn out a bit like a story, each day like a page turning in a book…isn't this actually true for all of us?

♥ A Gift of Love

Houses are made of brick and stone
Homes are made of love alone.

I was adopted at nine months of age by Carl and Edith Rider through Dorothy Alber, my biological father's sister. Aunt Dorothy lovingly intervened on my behalf and arranged for

Carl and Edith Rider to see me. Dad always told me I was chosen, and that they could have had any baby, but when they saw me, they knew I was meant for them. Dorothy remained Edith's best friend for the rest of her life and shared her family with me. I was always told the truth about the adoption and therefore was able to later meet Joy and Bill. Around the time I was five, I would go on bank trips with dad and mom, where I was also introduced to Julie and Tom, who were born three and five years after me and adopted out also. Throughout the years us "kids" have found we all love to cook and that brother Bill became a chef!

♥ My Father's Legacy

The night shall be filled with Music
and the cares that infest the day
shall fold their tents like the Arabs
and, as silently, steal away.

Henry Wadsworth Longfellow

I was raised as an only child after the adoption of Julie fell through for my parents. Because of this, I am sure, books became my life-long companions. It helped that Dad told wonderful stories in that great English accent of his and he had such a gift for bringing the characters in a book to life. Our lives were very quiet with little entertaining, unless it was to sit and listen to his music with guests and look out across the lake he so loved to sail on with his boat, the Voyager. Music always filled the air and wound itself around you from the vast selection of records he kept beside his chair. Throughout his life he would write stories, poems and notes, some he would record. As I look back, I realize I owe a huge debt of gratitude to my father, for instilling in me my deep love for the written word, beautiful music and good food on the table.

♥ For Better or Worse...

There is one advantage in being married.
You can't make a fool of yourself
without knowing all about it in detail.

I met my future husband, Bill, in Junior High. He was quiet, soft spoken, and drop dead gorgeous. It was only after high school that we got together. Over the years, we have found our "fit" together. Dad always told us that marriage was 70-70. You both had to give a little more. The years have flown by: 33 last anniversary. He is still full of surprises, and I tell everyone he is 16 in a 54-year-old body. The title, "Grandpa," is his crowning glory with Riley Jordan Zerhire, age 2.

♥ The Gift of My Sons

What can I say? Todd and Jamey are my life, my reason for being. Oh, I know, parents are supposed to want to be free of their kids, but we have been so lucky and had so much fun with them, that I tend to be a bit of a pest and want more time joining in on their activities. They have such great friends and do so many fun things. They are best of friends and are always there for each other. (Were we ever kids or always just parents–since we wed so young?) I try for Sunday dinners–every Sunday if I can, and we all call each other up at the last minute and say: "Want to meet us at…?" With the addition of our daughter-in-law Lisa to the family and the birth of our first grandchild, Riley, we couldn't be more blessed.

♥ Our Open Door Policy

Perhaps being adopted has made me more sensitive to people in need, but I have nurturing in my soul. So many kids and friends have come into our lives, searching for love and the listening ear and respect that might be missing in their own lives. As my parents opened their door to me, so it is with our home. The many people that have lived with us over the years – some still do – have learned to obey the house rules, and in return they know that even if their point of view differs from ours, God blesses those differences.

♥ The Cats

The cat paws meandering through this book are those of our four Himalayan-Welsh cats: Jasmine, the mom, and her children Bandit, Buddha and Muffin, who were fathered by Tuffy, the Liliac Siamese across the street. Buddha has more than just his paws in this cookbook: he is quite my favorite so his face is around a lot, too! Not a day goes by that doesn't find him checking on me, sitting in my lap while I make my lists or following me around the room. Jasmine, his mother, was brought to the house by Denise, who was crazy about Todd at the time. He wasn't home, so she asked Bill if he would hold her until Todd showed up. The kitten was in a wicker basket with a fancy bow and was barely bigger than Bill's hand. She had a face only a mother would love. Make that father. But oh my, did she ever turn out beautiful. By the time Todd got home, she was Daddy's cat and still is. In the summer, the cats help us weed the yard, when they are not napping or overseeing the goings-on in the kitchen!

♥ From Zerhire to Zoo-hire

There has always been *a lot* of activity at our house with live-in Grandma, kids, animals and our friends who have gathered here over the years. Definitely a zoo. Danny Law grew up, as Todd did, working at the Sirloin Inn Restaurant with me in Lake Forest Park. He was the one who officially changed our name to "Zoo-hire" after Peanuts, Todd's Shetland pony, followed Todd into the house and into his bedroom, where she was quite happy to stay. We finally got her onto the front porch, but it took us 3 to 4 days to get Peanuts back through the house and back to her corral! The name "Zoo-hire" stuck, and even now with the kids grown, we still get mail from their friends addressed to that name.

♥ Into the Kitchen

I have always loved to cook, but my interest was peaked when Oscar and Frances Fodor got a Cuisinart and demonstrated all it could do. Bill bought me one and it came with free lessons which were taught by Mauny Kaseburg. I found my niche. Mauny taught me a whole variety of new cooking methods, and after she branched out to new things, Beverly Gruber came into my life, both as good friend and mentor. She runs The Everyday Gourmet, her cooking school, from Larry's Market in Bellevue. Shortly after working with Mauny and

Beverly, I joined the **International Association of Culinary Professionals,** and have been a member since 1984.

With people wanting me to cook for them, asking for my recipes, often when I was busy, I began to put my favorite ones down in a book for my dearest and closest friends. Not enough time to do everything brought about the writing of this book. Now I have created a monster. Riley and Grandma must do a book for him and his friends and maybe—with my big new kitchen—cooking classes.

Everyone always wants to be in my kitchen. Although it has been very crowded on many occasions, we are now adding on a family room so I have room to move about, yet I must admit the kitchen is where I am happiest. Along with my friend Suzanne M., who makes handmade chocolates and Scandinavian cookies, we have formed the Home Spun Fun Bazaar for crafters to get together during the holidays and for me to sell my cookbooks—first my Holiday sampler and now this one. Come join us!

Life continues to move on and each day finds me with my lists, Buddha on my lap, coffee in hand, the phone ringing, and something else needing to be done. We are so blessed! I hope that each of you who read and cook from this book feel as if you have joined me and mine. You're invited... God Bless.

Janet L. Rider-Zerhire (Mom)

Acknowledgements

One evening during the 1954 Oscars, *Frank Sinatra*, in his acceptance speech for Best Supporting Actor, said, in essence: "I share this Oscar with all of you out there who try very hard and give it your all, even when no one acknowledges the fact. Don't give up! You've got it now! The Oscar will be at my house, but it will be ours!" Thank you, Mr. Sinatra. I have often looked back to you for a source of strength and encouragement, when I have needed a push to pick myself back up and keep going. Polish it one time for me!

Thank you to the most important beings in my life—my sons, *Todd and Jamey*, and their dad, *Bill*, who let my world come full circle. I love you so much! Love always to my daughter-in-law *Lisa* (Jamey's wife) who is what every mother wishes in a wife for her son and who gave us the greatest gift of all—our first, and hopefully not only—grandson, *Riley Jordan Zerhire*– who is *exactly* like his father. How very much he is loved.

And of course, deepest, sincerest thanks to my mom, *Edith (Granny Rider)* who was more than willing to adopt a scrawny, little baby, and who has given so much love to me, Bill, and, in time, to my sons and who now finds that in watching Riley, life is still sweet at age 91-1/2.

I want to thank my father, *Carl (Bobba) Rider*, who instilled in me my deep love for the written word, beautiful music and good food. His legacy for me—the Empty Book filled, is in the center of this cookbook: words to fill your soul and for you to share and pass on too.

To my sisters *Joy* and *Julie* and my brother *Tom:* let's get together and cook!

Much thanks and love to *Uncle Dougie* for buying me a laser printer to help this cookbook on its way. Thanks to *Lynn DeVaney* for keeping me calm and answering all my Macintosh questions through so many long distance phone calls to California. And thanks to *Lizzie,* for your help in putting the Holiday Sampler together with me–not only did it sell 600 copies but it inspired me to begin this one. Many thanks also to *Maggie Marshall*, who has always been there for me as a teacher and confidant, guiding me to reach for my goals, long after I was no longer her student. A *very dear* friend to share a glass of champagne and stimulating conversations with and who has a great passion for life. God bless you.

Sincere thanks to *Mauny Kaseburg*, who in teaching a Cuisinart Beginners class, made everything easy, taste wonderful and put me on the path to here. And to *Beverly Gruber*, always so willing to share her expertise in the world of good food, through the "Everyday Gourmet," our IACP commitments, or a phone call. Thank you to *all my very dear friends*, who have shared the road of life—and many of their own recipes–with me. You are too many to name, and I am so rich in your love. God bless you all.

♥ Special thanks to: *Susannah Ortego*, my editor, for being so detail-oriented and pulling this enormous volume of work together, gathering it all with expertise. Heartfelt thanks. To *Malia Bryan* and *Ethan May* for listening and bringing to the cover what I had always seen in my mind's eye–even all the colors. You're marvelous! And to *Isabel Gates*—Issy, who saw the layout of the book as if she were my other self, and lovingly pulled together the graphics and finishing touches as if I did it all myself. Deepest gratitude.

The
Zoo-hire
Family Cookbook

Introduction

The Heart of the Book
There is a Center or "Heart" of this cookbook which is dedicated to my father, Carl H. Rider ("Bobba" to his grandsons). He was a man who could repeat from heart *all* of Shakespeare, told stories of Ancient Greek mythology and filled a room with his presence. He was well known for his beautiful, soul-searching stories and poetry. He felt that the house we still live in and share with my mother Edith in Lake Forest Park was Heaven on Earth. Every time I drive up the winding road that leads to the top of the hill overlooking Lake Washington and home, I feel as if I can still see him walking down the street with Gizmo, his Airedale dog at his side, lost in thought, wandering in his mind with other people's written words, places and times.

In his last year, due to ill health, I gave my father "The Empty Book" to fill with the treasures of his life, the words he'd lived by. They are a very special legacy, and I pass on these timeless wisdoms to you in this book's heart, to fill your soul and bring peacefulness to you and yours.

A Note About the Ingredients
As you read through this cookbook, please take the time to read through each recipe once, and maybe a second time, so you have all your ingredients out on the counter when you're ready to cook. My recipes specify the brand name ingredients I prefer to use. I have found so often in giving a recipe to someone that she/he didn't use the same products and it would taste different and they would be disappointed. So look for Mazola, Morton's Nature's Seasoning, Baker's Joy, use butter, etc. But of course, please feel free to use the products that work best for you! Taste buds belong to you, as does your heart and body. I believe that you'll have more success in recipes that include wine, if you use a vintage you would also drink. And I use all-purpose flour and granulated white sugar and *dark* brown sugar, unless otherwise specified.

Recommended Cookware
I use nonstick pans for browning or to sauté and Le Creuset for saucepans and roasting. I have Corning Ware, Revere Ware and an extra pan here and there. I really think in most cooking that it's the "Food Product" you use that makes the difference and the cooking temperature, along with the methods. For my candy making, I use a large Club Aluminum saucepan with a long handle: it's heavy and candy comes out perfectly. A *good* candy thermometer is also a must.

Helpful Hints
I have also added a section of helpful hints, which features measurement equivalents and product substitutes, because I am always needing it, too–right, Shirley?–and I hate to look and look and look for that one cookbook that has it! It also includes some helpful cleaning tips, hints for stain removal and other useful "How To's."

One Last Thought
No part of this book is meant to plagiarize anyone else's words, thoughts or ideas. I hope those who go named or unnamed, will understand that including your contribution was not meant to copy for credit, but rather to praise you for your wonderful gift. It is my hope that your words will inspire my readers, as they have me and mine. Thank you!

Hors d'oeuvres

Be not forgetful to entertain strangers:
For thereby some have entertained angels
unawares.

Hebrews 13:2

Baked Green Chile Dip - Melissa B.

4-oz. can chopped green chiles, drained
10-oz. pkg. frozen chopped spinach, thawed/drained well (squeeze out)
1 cup mayonnaise
1 cup fresh grated Parmesan cheese
6-oz. jar marinated artichoke hearts, drained (save oil for greasing pan)

Melissa mixes all these ingredients in a large bowl, but I chop mine up in the Cuisinart to a chunky consistency, leaving the chiles until last.

Pour ingredients in an oiled dish of your choice. (To oil it my way: Rub the dish with a mixture of melted garlic butter and the drained artichoke oil. It just gives it a touch more flavor.)

Bake at 350° for 20 minutes until top is golden brown and heated through.

Serve with fresh tortilla chips of your choice.

♥ *Variation*

My friend Janeen Harris likes to add at least one cup of fresh crab meat to this dip mixture, and uses water-packed instead of marinated artichokes—chopped medium.

Darling, ladylike, soft-spoken Melissa is the mother of five, and a grandmother. Once in our youth, angry over not being driven to my house six miles away, she walked there in cotton-thonged shoes which were in shreds by the time she arrived three hours later. My mom then called her mother to say she was safe...as she had called earlier. Mr. and Mrs. Barney drove right out and took her home. Life was so unfair. She should have been able to stay after that ordeal! Right? Neither of us remember why she wasn't allowed to come over. Probably because we were together too much. In those day kids were expected to stay home and enjoy family things, instead of hanging out with each other all the time!

Baked Bean Dip - Mom's Way

Our Krysy has had great success with this at parties. It's always a must-have or "please bring request.

2 16-oz. cans refried beans
1-1/2 lbs. ground beef (you might want a bit more)
1/2 cup chopped red onion (use more if you like, or other onions)
2 4-oz. cans chopped green chiles and—if you want it hot—some
    chopped jalapenos, too!)
2 2-1/2 oz. cans of sliced, black olives
2 large ripe tomatoes chopped
12 oz. (or more*) of taco sauce of your choice—hot, medium, mild
1 cup grated medium Cheddar cheese
1 cup grated Monterey Jack or (for added zip) Pepper Jack cheese
16 oz. sour cream

*If I have fresh salsa, I use a lot.

First, rub bacon grease all over the bottoms and sides of a 9' x 13" pan and spread the refried beans over the bottom of the dish.

Cook and then drain the ground beef. Put it over the beans.

Sprinkle all the remaining ingredients—*except the cheeses and sour cream*—in layers over the ground beef.

Now mix the cheeses and sour cream together and spread the mixture carefully over the top of the layered dish with a spatula.

Bake at 350° for 35 to 45 minutes, edges will start to brown.

Serve with tortilla chips or others of your choice.

♥ Variation

Heat at 350° for ten minutes, on foil, flour tortillas, lightly buttered.

Toast on a cookie sheet with a bit of garlic butter, if you wish to dip with them.
If there are any avocados around, we dice those up and put on just before serving.

This can really be a fun dinner with a salad. It can be reheated or frozen.

Hummus - Mauny K.

 Bring on the toasted Pita bread, slathered with garlic butter and dusted with grated cheese! Son Todd uses medium Cheddar, and here we go to the Desert Country!

3 large cloves garlic
1/4 cup red wine vinegar
1/2 tsp. Morton's
1/2 tsp. Dijon hot mustard
1/2 cup Mazola oil
3 green onions, chopped
1/4 cup fresh chopped parsley, if you have it, or 1 Tbs. dry
1 drop of sesame seed oil (Don't overdo!)
15-oz. can garbanzo beans, drained and rinsed

Put all the ingredients in a blender or Cuisinart and blend thoroughly. Let the hummus marry for an hour in the refrigerator. It is most flavorful served at room temperature, so leave it out a bit before serving.

Dip in the toasted pita bread or *ak-mak* crackers and enjoy. Robin likes it as a dip with veggies: Cucumber, jima, celery, carrots, zucchini, broccoli, cauliflower, radishes, mushrooms, etc.

This keeps in Tupperware, refrigerated, for at least two weeks. Of course… not around here!

Jezebel Dip - Lynn D.

I know: doesn't this sound just awful!? But this recipe is so tasty that the crackers just disappear! Take it to a party and let them guess what's in it. It will be the hit of the party! Lynn and I discovered this dip at the Waldorf Wilkerson when we were setting up for a Boat Cruise Feast. To be honest, I really didn't want to taste this at all. But boy, was I surprised! For a moment I was afraid I might make a Pig out of myself... Now, I just read in a cookbook, from down South, that they use this for a sauce on their meats. If ever I win any money, I would love to travel through the South to take in all the beautiful stately homes, gardens and the people, who seem so warm and inviting. And I would love to take Lynn along on that adventure--because she talks to everybody, too, and I know we would have a ball eating our way through the cultures.

18-oz. jar apple jelly
18-oz. jar pineapple/apricot preserves
2-oz. can plus 1 heaping Tbs. dry mustard
4-oz. jar prepared horseradish
1 Tbs. ground black pepper

Mix all the ingredients together well. If you're using a mixer, blend it for at least three minutes to marry all the flavors. In a Cuisinart, it takes at least one and a half minutes.

Put in glass container and let sit at least a day in the refrigerator.

When you're ready to serve, pour the sauce over a block of soft cream cheese and put it out with a paté knife and wheat thins, or crackers of your choice, or combine the sauce with the cream cheese and serve it as a dip.

These proportions make quite a bit, so use it for gifts, or treats when you drop by to see one of your friends. It also keeps for up to four months in the refrigerator, but I can't see it not being used up. Great for late night TV.

♥ ♥ ♥

Hot Shrimp Dip - Lynn D.

Robbie T. finds that the more people he has at his parties, the larger the portions of this recipe he has to make—as it is otherwise one of the first things gone! It's great for large parties, as it can be made so far in advance and just put in a Crockpot and forgotten about. It's nice not to have to fuss when you're so busy pulling everything else together in those last few minutes before a party.

2 8-oz. pkgs. cream cheese
2 cloves minced garlic
1 small yellow onion, diced, or about 1/2 cup
1 medium tomato, diced, or about 1 cup
4-oz. can slightly drained, chopped green chiles
1/2 tsp. dry crushed or fresh minced hot red pepper
3 small cans of shrimp, drained and patted dry, or
    two cups fresh, peeled shrimp

Melt the cream cheese down over low heat with all the rest of the ingredients, *except* the shrimp. Make sure everything is well blended.

Now add the shrimp.

This is better done the day before, or in the morning so flavors have a chance to marry.

Put in glass container in refrigerator until ready to serve. Take out what you wish. Save the rest for later use. It will keep up to four days.

This is good hot or cold. To serve it hot, reheat in microwave or on low. Put either on hot plate or in a fondue pot to keep it warm.

Serve with plain crackers or those of your choice. Baguette slices are also nice.

Hot Pepper Jelly and Cream Cheese - Robin R.

Robin uses Certo liquid fruit pectin for this recipe. This is easy, easy, to make, and gosh darn handy to have around if someone drops by. I sent a jar of this jelly home with my friend Joan D. once. A few days later she had unexpected company and no supply of cream cheese. So she mixed the jelly with sour cream and served it with tortilla chips. It was a real hit. Hot and sour!

2 medium bellpeppers (I use any color)
12 fresh jalapeno peppers, destemmed
1-1/2 cups white vinegar
6 cups white sugar
1 6-oz. pkg. liquid fruit pectin - Certo
Green food coloring (I don't use)
Prepared 8-oz jelly jars (or whatever size you have on hand)
Paraffin for sealing
Block(s) of cream cheese

Remove the stem and seeds from the bellpeppers and put them in a blender or Cuisinart.

Destem the jalapenos. If you want a *mild* jelly, remove all the seeds. If you prefer a *medium-hot* taste, remove *some* seeds. If you want your jelly *hot*, throw the jalapenos in *whole*, as I do! Put it in with the bellpeppers.

Purée both the peppers with the vinegar, pour it into a large pan, and set it on the stove.

Stir in the sugar and bring the mixture to a rolling boil. Stir occasionally.

Remove it from the heat and let it stand for ten minutes. Skim off the top.

Add the pectin and food coloring (if used). Mix well and let it stand for another ten minutes.

Pour the mixture into prepared canning jars of your choice and cover with melted paraffin.

To serve, get out that block of cream cheese that you always keep on hand and let it sit until it reaches room temperature. Spread the jelly over the block and provide it with a paté knife and crackers—or tortilla chips like we do. Dick S. puts it on his morning toast.

♥ *Helpful Hint*

When making jams or jellies, hang a piece of string over the edges of the glass before pouring in paraffin. This makes it easier to remove the paraffin when opened for table use.

Man Keeper Dip - Liz B.

This just does not last at this house, or any party I've ever taken it to. Bill and Todd don't even wait for the nuts. This has been a must-have recipe for both Michael D. and Krysy, and you too will set this one aside to use and use and use. I would really suggest that you double this—and get the Margaritas ready, or the Cervasa!

2 8-oz. pkgs. cream cheese, brought to room temperature
1 pkg. Uncle Dan's Original Dressing
2 heaping Tbs. of canned jalapenos (preferably the ones that come with
    carrots and onions)
2 tsp. at least, of reserved jalapeno juice (optional)*
Chopped, dry roasted peanuts for topping

*We like our dip very hot, and this dip will get hotter as it marries. So
    adjust the amount accordingly. For when I say hot, I mean *hot*! (If
    you want yours *firmer*, though, just eliminate the jalapeno juice.)

Put all the ingredients together in a Cuisinart, mixer or blender and blend well.

Put it in the refrigerator and bring it out 15 minutes before company arrives.

Roll the mixture into a ball with the nuts, or make two logs and dust them with nuts.

Serve with tortilla chips of your choice and Robin's Margaritas (*see* page 51).

No-Avocado Guacamole - Lynn D.

I must remember to try this on my friend Sara T. to see if she can tell the difference. How she hates peas! Lynn says you can't tell at all. We'll see!

1 jalapeno pepper, canned
1/4 cup extra virgin olive oil
2 tsp. lemon juice
1 lb. fresh or 1 10-oz. box frozen sweet peas, cooked and drained
1/4 tsp. cumin
Salt to taste
1/4 piece of medium red onion, chopped just a bit
1 small tomato cut in quarters

Remove the seeds from the jalapeno. Now don't touch your eyes!

Then, *in the order shown*, process the pepper, olive oil, lemon juice, peas, cumin and salt in a food processor with a cutting blade until the mixture is smooth.

Add the onion and quartered tomato and process just long enough to leave the guacamole with a chunky consistency. This takes just a flip of the off/on switch.

Chill thoroughly in an airtight container.

Will keep for many days without turning dark.

♥ *Helpful Hint*

For less tears, cut off the root end of the onion. Chill first. Bite a toothpick?

♥ ♥ ♥

Spinach Dip -
Marilyn A.'s Ten-Star Recipe

1 box *Knorr's* Leek Soup
1/2 cup chopped green onion
1 cup sour cream
1 cup mayonnaise
11-oz. pkg. chopped frozen spinach, thawed and drained well
8-oz. can sliced water chestnuts, chopped
Morton's to taste
1 loaf of round French or Italian bread
Baguette, sliced for dipping

Combine and refrigerate all the ingredients except the bread(s).

Marilyn hollows a deep pocket out of a large round loaf of French or Italian bread to contain this truly *delectable* dip, and serves it with baguette slices. She sometimes toasts her leftover bread pieces for dipping, too.

It's so easy to throw everything in the Cuisinart and blend well. If using your mixing bowl, just remember to chop the water chestnuts first. (You knew, of course, not to throw in the bread, right?)

Refrigerate to marry all of the flavors. Later on, put the dip into the bread pocket just before leaving home (if you're taking it as a treat to someone's house) or just before your guests arrive.

It is such fun to watch the reaction when this is put out on a table. Once people taste it they tend to just stand there and dip...and dip...and dip...until it's all gone!

The dip itself is also good in omelettes with a bit of chopped ham, some shrimp, or crab, and it can keep for up to two *weeks*. If we hadn't lost a container of this in our refrigerator one time, we may never have *known* this—as it never lasts when it's right in front of you! In California, Uncle Dougie even puts it on his meatloaf sandwiches!

If I'm smart, I make *two* batches at a time.

*Resolve to keep happy, and your joy and you
shall form an invincible host against difficulties.*

Helen Keller

Salsa - Mark C.

🐾 *Bill had raved about this salsa for over a year and a half before he finally managed to sneak a taste home to me after one of their office parties—as there was never any left, it was so popular. When Bill told Mark how much I loved it, Mark sent a small jar home. I would really like to thank him for allowing me to share a recipe with you that's been enjoyed by his family for generations. It was passed down from his great-great grandmother's mother.*

I have doubled the recipe. Cut it in half for a quart jar.

20 Serrano chiles
1/3 cup chopped white onion
2 large buds of fresh garlic
1/4 cup of fresh cilantro leaves
1/2 tsp. salt, to taste (I use Morton's)
2 28-oz. cans peeled whole tomatoes* or equivalent amount of chopped
**   fresh tomatoes**

*I substitute one of those cans with a can of peeled tomatoes with purée, as I like my salsa a little thicker.

Toast the chiles at 400° until just black. Watch. It takes 15 to 20 minutes. Shake the pan every now and then so they don't stick and turn over to toast on all sides. Let cool and cut off stems.

In a blender or a Cuisinart add the onion, garlic, cilantro, toasted chiles and salt.

Blend it well. I mince it.

Add the tomatoes last so the salsa maintains a chunky consistency.

Store in the refrigerator.

This recipe makes two quart jars of salsa. If this seems too much—wait until you taste it! You may discover that you won't be able to leave it alone! This has such an addictive taste that I keep two jars full, as one jar could empty at a sitting.

My friend Sonia tells me that whenever she and her husband Larry want to lose some weight, they eat salsa and chips—baked chips, of course! Well I can surely see how a diet of this could make it easier!

Sweet and Sour Mustard - Robin R.

 2 oz. dry mustard
1 cup apple cider vinegar
3 large eggs
Dash salt
1 cup sugar

Whisk the mustard and vinegar together in a small bowl and let the mixture stand on the counter, covered with plastic, for about eight hours.

Beat together the eggs, salt, and sugar and add to the mustard mixture.

Mix everything well with a whisk.

Pour into saucepan and cook over medium/low heat until it thickens, in about ten minutes. Stir constantly, so it won't burn or stick.

Now, Robin likes to bake spinach balls to dip into this mustard. I love to put it on roast beef, ham, or shrimp—with a touch of sesame seeds, too. It's also great with deep fried fish and chips, chicken—and did I say *pork*? It's just a *very* versatile sauce!

Keep it in the refrigerator.

Robin is one of my favorite people to "get busy with." She's always involved with some project, yet always ready to set aside some time to enjoy a glass of champagne, a snack or two and a little gossip. Did I say gossip? Well, we're ladies: we call them "selective subjects." She is a dear friend who shares my love of cooking and went back to school after 13 years of married life and a divorce and got her degree. She reaffirms the value of having goals and going for it, i.e.: it only gets done when you do it! I'm grateful for the little bits of time—but quality time—that Robin feels free to share with me—between getting Rosa and Andy raised, handling a full-time job and going for a Master's.

Hawaiian Cheese Roll - Liz B.

2 8-oz. pkgs. cream cheese, softened
1/2 cup chopped sweet green pepper
3 Tbs. chopped onion
1 tsp. seasoned salt
1 8-oz. can crushed pineapple, well drained
3/4 cup chopped fresh parsley
1 cup chopped, toasted pecans

I put first five ingredients—everything except the parsley and pecans— in my Cuisinart and Liz does hers in a mixing bowl or blender. Mix well and then wrap in plastic. Refrigerate to marry flavors.

When ready to serve, roll the cheese mixture in parsley and pecans.

Serve with crackers of your choice or on sliced French bread.

Salmon Party Ball

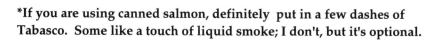

1/2 cup coarsely chopped toasted pecans (see below)
2 Tbs. butter
16 ozs. kippered, regular canned, or smoked salmon
8-oz. pkg. cream cheese, softened to room temperature
1 Tbs. lemon juice
2 tsp. grated white onion
1 Tbs. prepared horseradish
1/4 tsp. Morton's
2 Tbs. chopped parsley
Dash of Tabasco* if you like it with a bite

*If you are using canned salmon, definitely put in a few dashes of
Tabasco. Some like a touch of liquid smoke; I don't, but it's optional.

First, toast the pecans. Melt the butter and mix it with the pecans. Spread the nuts
on a cookie sheet and bake them at 350° until brown, shaking occasionally to toast.
Or do it fast—like I do—and under the broiler. (Watch carefully and shake often). Remove and
chop.

Combine everything in a Cuisinart, except the pecans and parsley. Mix well. Put in plastic
wrap and refrigerate so flavors can marry.

When you are ready to serve, or to take it to someone's home, roll the mixture into the chopped
parsley and then pecans. (Sometimes, I do *two* logs—one for each side of the room, so guests
don't have to get up so often and can just reach for a cracker and a dab!)

♥ Variation

You can make this recipe with tuna instead. To the other ingredients, also add 1/4 chopped
English cucumber and half of a chopped boiled egg. Put in plastic wrap-lined mold, chill,
unmold on plate and top with other half of (finely) chopped egg and chopped parsley. Some
chopped black olives would be tasty, too.

Frogs are smart. They eat the things that bug them.

Grape Leaves
- Michael D.'s Ten-Star Version

I just can't tell you how great these are! They have such an unusual filling—not just the typical rice and nuts, and we just can't stop eating them. At a glance this recipe may look a little hard and complicated, but actually it's just a bit time-consuming. But I can tell you: it's worth it!

♥ Lamb Mixture

1 lb. ground lamb or 2 to 3 lamb shanks
Olive oil (I use Extra Virgin)
3/4 cup *minced* yellow onion
8-oz. can tomato sauce
1/8 cup *minced* parsley
1/8 cup lemon juice
1/8 cup grape jam or currants (we use jam)
1/4 cup pine nuts, toasted first in butter for more flavor
1/4 tsp. cinnamon
1/2 tsp. paprika
1/4 tsp allspice
2 cups beef broth
1 large jar of grape leaves (about 50)

In a roasting pan, brown the meat and onions in the olive oil. (If using shanks, remove the meat first and brown both the meat *and* the bones with the onion.)

Add the tomato sauce, parsley, lemon juice, jam, nuts and spices to the lamb mixture and simmer with the beef broth in the oven—uncovered— for 2 1/2 hours at 325°. Watch so that all the liquid doesn't evaporate on you. Stir occasionally.

♥ Risotto

2 Tbs. butter
1/4 cup brown rice
1/2 cup wild rice
1 cup beef broth (use canned if you can't get to Larry's Market for their homemade version)

Mix the rices together, add the butter and stir constantly over medium heat. Slowly add the beef broth so that the rice stays moist and absorbs it. Turn the heat down to low, cover the rice pot, and let it simmer for 25 minutes.

When the rice is done, put it in a large bowl.

Remove the bones (if used) from the meat mixture in the roasting pan. If you did use the shank meat taken from the bones, remove the meat from the roaster, chop it up medium to fine and return it the the pan. Heat the mixture and stir it up a bit so you can get all the crumbs blended in for better flavor.

Combine the meat mixture with the risotto and refrigerate the filling for about four hours so the flavors can marry.

♥ *Assembly*

Remove the grape leaves from the jar and rinse them well.

Lay them out in rows and put one tablespoon of the meat/risotto filling on each leaf until they are all filled, then roll them up and lay them seam side down on a platter.

Cover the dish with plastic and refrigerate until serving.

These are best eaten at room temperature.

To serve: Dip in plain yogurt with parsley and slices of fresh lemon.

He who works with his hands is a Laborer.
He who works with his hands and his head is a Craftsman.
He who works with his hands, his head, and his heart is an Artist.

Hamet

 Robin R. brought this recipe back from Ohio, where she was visiting her sister, Gayle. They serve "Hamet" in the cocktail lounges. I changed it just a bit because I thought it was a bit bland. Now, it costs more money to make. Oh, well....

2 10-oz. cans water-packed artichokes, rinsed and drained
1/2 cup mayonnaise
1/2 cup sour cream
1 cup Parmesan or Parmano (1/2 cup Parmesan and 1/2 cup Romano)
1/2 cup sharp Cheddar cheese, grated

Put all the ingredients in the Cuisinart and chop up. Leave a bit chunky, by adding artichokes last.

Garlic butter the bottom and sides of a 7" x 11" x 1/2" deep glass dish and pour in the filling.

Bake at 350° for 30 minutes, or make ahead of time, cover and refrigerate, and then bake.

Serve hot with *ak-mak* (Armenian bread) crackers, French bread or crackers of your choice.

I keep on a warming tray so it retains its heat. It also reheats well in the oven or microwave.

♥ ♥ ♥

♥ Helpful Hint

Butter edges of cut cheese before storing so it won't harden. A damp cloth with vinegar wrapped around cheese will also prevent drying out. Cheese freezes, so buy in larger quantities; grate/slice and keep rest in freezer for further use.

Bacon-Wrapped Water Chestnuts – Dolores S.

3 5-oz. cans whole water chestnuts, drained
1 lb. lean bacon, cut in half (It will shrink as it cooks.)
Box of wooden toothpicks (soak in water 1/2 hour, so they don't burn up).
1/4 cup soy sauce
1/2 tsp. of fresh grated ginger
1/2 tsp. of fresh chopped garlic

Wrap each whole chestnut in a half strip of bacon and hold with toothpicks. Put the chestnuts in a large oblong glass dish or in a heavy-duty plastic bag, carefully, and set it in a pan.

Combine the soy sauce, grated ginger, and chopped garlic in a bowl. Pour this over the wrapped chestnuts in the plastic bag or the pan, and let the chestnuts marinate for several hours or overnight (covered, if you're marinating them in a pan.)

Shake the marinade off the chestnuts and spread them on a large, Pam-sprayed cookie sheet—with edges to catch drippings.

Bake, uncovered, at 450° for ten minutes. Shake occasionally so that all the bacon browns. *Watch carefully* as the marinade tends to burn easily.

Serve on a warming tray on a platter to catch the drips.

*This marinade can be saved and used within a week on more chestnuts and bacon. *Don't use the same marinade on meat or chicken, however, or it may make you sick.* What do you mean you don't have company twice in one week?

♥ *Helpful Hint*

To peel off cold, uncooked bacon, roll up the bacon like a jelly roll, starting from the short side. Reverse and roll again. Slices will not tear.

Meat Log - Via Ron at Linda/ Michael D.'s

1 large French bread, sliced down the middle horizontally
1 cup mayonnaise
1/4 cup Miracle Whip
1/4 cup Sandwich Spread
2 Tbs. of Thousand Island dressing
2 Tbs. Dijon mustard
Thinly sliced roast beef, ham, and salami
Sliced Cheddar, Swiss, Mozzarella, and Provolone cheese
Sliced black olives and tomatoes
Shredded lettuce
Sliced or chopped dill pickles

Mix together the mayonnaise, Miracle Whip, Sandwich Spread, Thousand Island and mustard.

Spread the mixture on the cut bread and layer it with alternate slices of meat and cheese: roast beef, Cheddar, ham, Swiss, turkey, Mozzarella, salami, Provolone. Top with shredded lettuce, tomato slices, black olives and sliced dill pickles.

Hold with toothpicks at approximately every two inches and cut finger-sized sandwiches for your guests. Or have it at home on a Sunday, when everyone is watching TV and you're not supposed to talk while the show is playing.

Serve with potato chips, of course. And for us this wouldn't be complete with the one beverage our household can't live without: Classic Coke!

Spicy Asparagus Spears
- Doug and Lois B.

This is a ten-star recipe, and I usually make enough to fill at least two dozen canning jars, since I and my little helpers—by this I mean my family and friends, not the cats!—can't stay out of them.

4 lbs. fresh asparagus
2 quarts water
2 quarts white cider vinegar
1/2 cup salt
4 large fresh garlic cloves, peeled
1/2 red bell pepper chopped up in small chunks—more if you like it stronger
Sesame seed oil—a drop

Wash the asparagus thoroughly and cut off the tough part on the bottom. It isn't necessary to blanch the asparagus before canning. I like it crunchy.

Drain and pack in jars, tip down, laying jars on their sides while packing, for neatness of product. Allow for 1/4 inch of space at the top.

In a saucepan, bring the water, vinegar and salt to a boil.

Split the garlic cloves and add them to the upright jars with chopped red pepper chunks (or red pepper flakes—1/4 teaspoon—if you want it fiery hot) and a drop or two of sesame seed oil.

Pour the boiling seasoned water over the spears to within 1/4 inch from top, but covering the asparagus.

Wipe the edge of the jar and put on lid. Tap to remove bubbles. Adjust screw caps, not too tight.

Process ten minutes in boiling water bath. Remove from bath and let settle until cool on counter.

Adjust the lid, by tightening when cool, and little bubble on top is down to tell you they are correctly sealed. You will notice that the asparagus has shrunk in cooking.

Let the asparagus marry for three months for the best flavor—but if you can't wait that long, you *can* start eating them after a month.

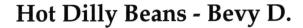

Hot Dilly Beans - Bevy D.

I usually do two cases: not only because they make great gifts but because Bill will start plowing into them within a month and can eat a jar at one sitting. And though I sometimes think, "Well, darn it—they take a bit of time to do—the Rat", I admit that they're made for him and not for me to look at, for all my labor. So I've learned to say, "Enjoy"—and also to get him to help with the supply and demand!

2 lbs. trimmed fresh green beans
1/4 cup salt
8 large cloves of fresh peeled garlic
8 heads of dill flower—available in your green grocers' produce section
2 tsp. cayenne pepper or red pepper flakes
2-1/2 cups water
2-1/2 cups apple cider vinegar

Pack the beans lengthwise into wide-mouth jars which are hot and sterilized from the dishwasher or a canning pot. Leave 1/4" room at top. I turn the jars on their side and place rows of beans in, as it's neater looking when done.

To each (upright) jar, add 1/4 tsp. cayenne or red pepper flakes, one head of dill and one large clove of garlic—split for more flavor.

Combine the rest of ingredients and boil.

Pour the *hot* seasoning over the beans, wipe the edge of the jar and put on the lid.

Tap the lid to remove the bubbles. Adjust the screw caps—not too tight—and process for ten minutes in a boiling water bath. Remove from bath and let settle on counter until cool.

Adjust lid by tightening when it's cool and the little bubble on top is down—to tell you they are sealed correctly.

Let the beans marry for at least three months.

Tuna Salad Sandwich - Mom

On the day both my boys were born, I had to have this sandwich! On those days I, who could keep nothing down, would just chow out on these and then find out I was in labor. Oh well, it must have helped: Four hours with Todd, and only 45 minutes with Jamey. My friend Sara just loves these sandwiches, too. When we're reclining on the patio (honest folks, Seattle does have its share of sunshine) and she suddenly suggests: "Maybe, we should have a little lunch", I know exactly what she wants! These tuna fish sandwiches are best served with potato chips between slices of bread—right Todd? This is, of course, a Lake Chelan "must have" in every picnic hamper.

6-1/2 oz. can oil- or water-packed tuna (my Aunt Marie insists that
    Bumble Bee brand is the best!), well drained
3/4 cup mayonnaise
Morton's to taste
1/2 cup chopped English cucumber
1/2 cup chopped celery
1 large chopped kosher dill (I use Farman's)
1/4 cup chopped white onion (If I have red, or yellow only, I use them instead)

Mix all these ingredients together well, and if you like a bit more mayonnaise, go ahead! We put more on our bread, with butter first on one side.

When Sara and I are being fancy and there is a leftover boiled egg, we throw that in too. Sometimes, if "he" feels like it, my son Todd adds crisp bacon pieces or some of the real pieces from Hormel, in the small can.

♥ Variations

If it's *canapé time,* I'll add a half teaspoon of curry powder and cut the bread into little squares, circles, fingers and diamonds. (Remember, your leftover bread is great for making croutons— or that wonderful stuffing on holidays and those special occasions that often arrive at the drop of a hat.)

For open-faced sandwiches I add a sprig of parsley on top.

Don't shy away from trying different breads. Tuna fish is great on pita, Broadmoor (a special Seattle bread), French, and all the different kinds of rye, etc.   And oh dear, I almost forgot to add my *favorite*—the one with sesame seeds or poppy seeds. I love two different types of bread per sandwich, too—if I have it. Yes, Nanny Rider's white bread (see the Bread and Breakfast section) works great!

Deli Delights - Linda D.

These tidbits are a favorite of mine because they look fancy and are very simple to make!

From the deli nearest you, buy those *thin*—not shaved—slices of:

Roast beef
Ham
Pastrami
Turkey

Combine:

3 oz. whipped cream or regular cream cheese with 1 Tbs. cream
1/2 tsp. hot Dijon mustard - or the kind with jalapenos
1/4 cup chopped fine green onions, white and tops
1/4 cup grated sharp Cheddar cheese— or blue cheese, for more flavor
Grated dill pickles

Spread this mixture on one side of each meat slice. Roll up the slices and refrigerate them, covered in plastic, until the company arrives.

To serve: Cut the meat rolls into little bite sized pieces and set them out on lettuce leaves. This makes such pretty little spirals it will seem as if you've been working in the kitchen forever! When in fact, you could have just made them the night before and then sliced them just before your company arrives.

I would just throw this together if someone dropped in and I had any leftover meat.

♥ Variations

Chop or grind that leftover chicken. Use guacamole dip and spread it on some processed cheese squares—American, Monterey Jack or Swiss. Put chicken down on one end. Hold with toothpicks and cut into spirals. Roll up the cheese to make spirals.

You can also roll the meat and mixture around small baby Kosher Dills. Or, put in some black or green olives, in a row. Leave a green onion whole and press filling around the end.

Happiness is like potato salad. When you share it with others...It's a picnic!

Egg Salad Sandwiches - Mom

Imagine my surprise when Sara said, "You do have your egg salad in "The Cookbook", don't you?!, as we ate them one night on bread from her new Bread Maker—which she leaves at our house, so that when she stays over she awakens to fresh hot bread. And here my Mom is the best bread maker in the world...But Sara hates to bother her and sometimes it's late when she decides to stay overnight, and Granny's asleep, so she cheats ! I must say to Sara and Mr. McCutchan with their bread machines...My Mom's is so much better! Of course she's had at least 75 years' head start on their machines. There are some things a machine will never, ever, get just right! But have your fun, if you don't have Nanny handy!

4 large eggs boiled, shelled and rinsed
3/4 cup Best Foods or other real mayonnaise of your choice
Morton's to taste
1/2 tsp. French's mustard - regular
1 Tbs. of Farman's or other kosher dill liquid of your choice

Mix together well. Add more mayonnaise if you wish.

Let sit together for a while, not too long or refrigerate, to marry flavors.

I always butter the bread, too, and I think that adds to the good flavor.

I sometimes add chopped up Farman's kosher dill pickle to this salad.

When one has tasted it (Watermelon)
He knows what the Angels eat.

Mark Twain

Deviled Eggs

*Hardly anybody goes to the trouble of making deviled eggs anymore, I guess! But what I know is that when it's offered, some of our friends have been known to eat a whole plate of these by themselves—right, Colleen? No **wonder** everyone starts hovering around the table when they come out!*

♥ *The Eleanor Roosevelt Boiling Technique*

I don't remember where I read this—probably in one of her son's murder mysteries—, but this technique has been attributed to Mrs. Roosevelt, and it works perfectly!

Use at least **two dozen large eggs**. They just disappear.

Carefully place all the eggs in a large pot with enough water to completely cover them. Add *a* **teaspoon of salt**. Sister Julie and I add **two tablespoons of cider vinegar** as well. Bring the water to a boil and cover.

Turn off the heat, leaving the pot on the burner, and set your timer for 20 minutes.

When the timer goes off, put the eggs under cold water, making sure the pot becomes cold and the eggs are left in cold water to stop them from overcooking. Otherwise the yolks will become kind of brownish and ugly. Peel right away so the shells don't stick.

I always rinse off the eggs afterwards, to double check for those tiny little pieces of shell we sometimes miss. (Don't you just *hate* biting into shell?) And then I pat them dry.

Cut the eggs in half and put the yolks in a blender or Cuisinart.

Mix together or combine:

3/4 cup mayonnaise (You might need more to taste, so keep the jar handy!)
1 Tbs. dill pickle juice
Morton's to taste
1 tsp. mustard of your choice

Stuff the egg whites with this mixture or any of the variations and decorate them any way you want: with parsley, dill, a piece of shrimp or crabmeat. Bacon bits are good, too.

Let the flavors marry for at least an hour in the refrigerator, covered.

♥ *Variations*

♥   We add some chopped up Farman's home-style dill pickles, if it's just family.

♥   Sometimes we add a little curry powder and serve the eggs with a drop of chutney on top for something a little more exotic!

♥   My friend Kimberly likes hers topped with caviar!

Deviled eggs are great at BBQ time with hot dogs, potato salad, and baked beans; with grilled salmon, steaks, or chicken; as an appetizer; or with— really—*any* kind of meal.

I like to make them on Friday or Saturday and Sunday mornings—when everyone, except me, is in a hurry. And on Christmas morning they are a must with Nanny's Brunch Cake and tiny little sausages—browned, strawberries and whipped cream, coffee and champagne...Sigh.

Garlic Almonds

1 lb. blanched almonds, skinless
2 Tbs. Mazola oil
Garlic salt, garlic powder (with parsley), or crushed fresh garlic to taste*

Preheat the oven to 350°.

Put the almonds into a bowl, and coat them with the oil and garlic salt or powder.

Spread them on a cookie sheet or in a large, shallow pan. Toast them until they're nice and brown. Shake, so they brown evenly and don't burn.

*Fresh garlic *does* have a tendency to burn, so if you want to use fresh garlic, bake the nuts first a while in the oil, adding the garlic at the end, so you don't have to worry about burning. I do it both ways, depending on my mood and how much time I have available to fuss with it.

In preparing a dish for bedtime, champagne makes the best tenderizer!

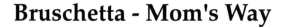

Bruschetta - Mom's Way

This must be the all-time ten-star recipe among all the other ones! When Todd's friends are over it calls for a double recipe. Along with the Spinach Dip the flight attendants and Kevin B. have called from all over the U.S. and Mexico for this recipe so they can make in their travels. Great eating!

1 long thin baguette, cut in 1" slices
2 sticks butter, softened
1 jar marinated artichokes, drained
3 cloves garlic
2 cups whipping cream
1 cup fresh grated Parmano (1/2 Parmesan / 1/2 Romano)
3 Tbs. butter

In blender or Cuisinart, blend the butter, artichokes and garlic.

Take the bread slices and cover all sides and bottom/top with artichoke/garlic butter mix.

Arrange the slices on a large cookie sheet with *sides*, to contain the drippings. Brown both sides under the broiler, or bake the bread at 350° for ten to twelves minutes. Turn the slices over, browning both sides.

In a saucepan, mix the whipping cream with the cheese and butter. Heat through, and stir until all the cheese is melted.

Pour the cheese/cream sauce mix over the toasted bread.

Bake at 350° for 15 to 20 minutes, or until the sauce begins to bubble and brown.

This is similar to a fondue.

We serve it as an hors d' oeuvre, but it can be a main course with a salad or soup before, and a glass of wine.

It's a dish we just can't stop eating until it's all gone.

Crab-Filled Won Tons - Jim R.

1 pkg. of won ton wrappers
3-oz. pkg. cream cheese, room temperature
2 tsp. lemon juice
1 tsp. Worcestershire sauce
2 drops Tabasco
1 cup fresh or 6 oz. canned and drained crab meat (check for shell bits)
2 Tbs. chopped green onions

Mix the cream cheese, lemon juice, Worcestershire sauce, and Tabasco.

Add the crab meat and green onions.

I put everything except the crab into my Cuisinart, adding it last so it doesn't become too mushy.

Take the won ton wrappers and lay them out in rows.

Put one tablespoon of the filling on each one, brushing water on the edges, folding over, pressing with fork tongs to seal. (Seal leftover wrappers in a plastic bag for later use.)

Fry won tons in hot oil at 365° for 1-1/2 minutes, a few at a time. You want them lightly browned. Watch that they do not get *too* brown.

Keep warm in oven until time to serve. These are best served on a warming plate. I find that nice round and oblong grills, covered with foil, also work great!

Chinese hot mustard, catsup, and sesame seeds are good dipping condiments to set out on the side. France's Sweet and Sour sauce (see the sauce section of this book) is also great for people who like to dip into something sweet.

When you are right, no one remembers. When you are wrong, no one forgets.

Stuffed Mushrooms - Ellen H.

These are good as a second vegetable—not only as an appetizer. It's a bit rich, but no one seems to mind. They disappear too fast! My Jamey loves these. Todd eats the filling. Kids...

12 large fresh mushrooms, washed and patted dry
1/4 cup butter
1/2 cup finely chopped yellow or white onion
Morton's to taste
Cream sherry (optional)
Garlic salt (I use garlic powder with parsley)
1/2 cup whipping cream
1 Tbs. flour
1/4 cup Jarlsberg cheese, shredded
Bacon bits or 1/2 lb. fresh—cut in quarters, fried crisp, or done in the microwave and crumbled

Remove stems from the mushrooms and set the buttons aside. Chop the stems up fine.

Place the mushroom buttons bottom up in garlic-buttered baking dish, of choice.

In frying pan on medium, sauté the onion and stems in butter with Morton's. Can put in a splash of cream sherry, like I do, if you want.

Remove onion and stems when cooked and turn down burner to low heat.

Add whipping cream to the frying pan and slowly add the flour, whisking in until blended and not lumpy. Add a touch of the garlic salt or powder.

Put a dab of grated cheese in the mushroom caps. Stuff the onion/stem mixture on top. Pour the cream sauce over filling.

Sprinkle top with bacon bits.

Bake 15 minutes at 350°. I usually let it get bubbly and brown.

Mushroom Squares

Make pastry for two 9" pies. Roll out to fit in a medium cookie sheet with a 2" rim coming up the sides to contain the filling.

Bake the crust at 350° for ten minutes. Cool. Paint with an egg wash. (of whites, whipped with a splash of water) and let it dry so the filling doesn't soak through the crust and make it soggy.)

Mix together:

1 large egg, slightly beaten
1/4 cup minced white onion
2 Tbs. chopped fresh parsley
1/2 cup grated Jarlsberg cheese
10-1/2 oz. can Cream of Mushroom soup, undiluted
1/4 cup cream sherry (use a good brand)
1/2 cup chopped Black Forest ham or whatever kind you have (can use
    crab or shrimp instead)
1/2 lb. sliced mushrooms, sautéed in butter with a dash of Morton's
1 medium clove minced garlic
1/2 cup grated Parmesan cheese
1 tsp. of lemon juice

Carefully pour this mixture into the prepared crust and top it with a touch more grated Parmesan. (If I have some sharp Cheddar I also add 1/2 cup to 1/4 cup, of that too.)

Bake for 20 to 25 minutes at 400°. Check for doneness. You don't want this to be either runny or too firm.

Serve hot, cut in squares. Can be served at room temperature, too.

This *could* be a main course—with a salad, soup, or a cup of fruit and a nice glass of wine.

♥ *Helpful Hint*

If parsley is washed with hot water instead of cold, it retains its flavor and is easier to chop.

Mushroom Turnovers

I have made this for cooking classes and it has always been very successful.

♥ Dough

8-oz. pkg. cream cheese
1/4 cup butter, softened
1 cup flour
1/8 tsp. salt

In a Cuisinart or mixing bowl, blend the cream cheese and butter.

Add the flour and salt, and mix until it begins to form a ball.

Chill, wrapped in plastic, for one hour. While waiting, make the filling.

♥ Filling

4 Tbs. butter
2 Tbs. Mazola oil
12 medium mushrooms, washed, dried, chopped in pieces
Morton's to taste
1/8 tsp. + garlic powder (I use the one with parsley)
1 bunch fresh spinach - washed, destemmed and chopped medium
Squeeze of fresh lemon - or about 1 Tbs.
Splash of cream sherry - or about 1 Tbs.
3 oz. Feta cheese
1/8 tsp. oregano
1 whisked egg white (for glaze)

Sauté the mushrooms in the butter and *one tablespoon* of the oil for three minutes over medium heat. Stir occasionally.

Season lightly with Morton's and garlic powder. Remove the mushrooms to a bowl.

In the same pan, add the *remaining* butter and oil, and sauté the spinach with the lemon juice and cream sherry for three minutes. Stir occasionally.

Sprinkle with a touch of Morton's and more garlic, to taste.

Add the crumbled Feta cheese and oregano. Blend with mushroom pieces and let cool.

♥ *Assembly*

Roll out the dough to approximately 9" x 12". Cut it into 2" squares. Put two tablespoons of filling on each half, fold the dough over and seal it with a fork, pinching the dough shut around the edges.

Place on a lightly sprayed baking sheet and brush the tops with whisked egg white for a glazed, finished look.

Bake at 425° for 20 minutes until golden brown. Serve hot.

A modern girl is one who dresses fit to kill and cooks the same way.

Rolls and Breadsticks in the Tube

🐾 *For this recipe I use Butterflake rolls and breadsticks that come in a tube— from the refrigerated section of the grocery store near the cheeses and butters. They are just so great for a quick "someone important has dropped by" moment when I need something now! that I try to keep a supply of the tubes on hand.*

♥ *Breadsticks*

Separate the breadsticks and roll them on a cookie sheet drizzled with good olive oil.

Brush each stick with Dijon mustard, sprinkle some poppy seed, and lay over some thin strips of *Black Forest* ham and Jarlsberg cheese.

Roll the sticks around into spirals and top them with a dab more of Dijon and another sprinkle of poppy seeds.

Bake the breadstick spirals at 350° for 15 to 18 minutes, or until golden brown.

♥ *Butterflake Rolls*

Separate the rolls, and lay them out about an inch apart on an oiled cookie sheet or put them in small, oiled muffin tins.

Spread or fill them with a tablespoon of filling of your choice. Here are some suggestions:

♥ Combine about six ounces of canned tuna, or fresh or canned shrimp or crabmeat together with a tablespoon of chopped green onion tops, a cup of grated Jarlsberg cheese, 1/2 cup mayonnaise, 1/4 teaspoon of curry, 1/2 teaspoon of salt, 1 teaspoon of lemon juice, and an 8-ounce can of sliced water chestnuts, drained. Blend all these ingredients to a chunky consistency.

♥ Try a dollop of tuna salad topped with a slice of cheese with an interesting shape. Add curry to this for an extra "bite".

♥ Drop a little bit of mustard and mayonnaise mixture into about 1/2 tablespoon of homemade paté. (Be sure to reseal the paté with melted butter to keep it fresh before you put it back in the refrigerator.)

♥ Combine finely chopped leftover chicken, ham or roast beef with grated sharp cheddar cheese, chopped dill pickle and white or red onion. Or, for a variation on this, substitute *hot pepper* cheese and chopped *sweet* pickle.

Bake the rolls at 400° for six minutes or until golden brown.

Remove, sprinkle with chopped parsley, and serve immediately or put them on a warming tray.

NOTE: You can use any of the fillings suggested here to stuff puff pastry.

Greek Bread

For years—every time I got the chance to visit my friend Uncle Doug—I'd have him take me to the Spin a Yarn Restaurant in Fremont, California for the original version of this bread. Back home I would try everything I could think of to capture the wonderful taste I had enjoyed over there—but to no avail. It took about ten years for me to finally find someone who, upon hearing my plight, was able to suggest just the right ingredients. Good luck on getting a second piece of it if you have company. Today only one loaf of this bread doesn't satisfy six people here!

1 large loaf of heavy French bread*
1 stick of butter, softened
2 to 3 garlic cloves (to taste)
1 small jar of marinated artichokes, with oil (optional)
8-oz. package of creamy feta cheese (Don't use the drier ones—not enough flavor)
1/8 cup milk might need a dash more
1/4 cup chopped fresh parsley

*They use sour dough, I don't, but go ahead.

Use only *fresh* garlic and *real* butter. Crush the garlic and mix or mash it into the softened butter. I like to add chopped marinated artichokes, and some oil from the same jar.

Cut the bread in half and cover each side well with the garlic butter.

Place the bread halves, buttered side up, on a cookie sheet and bake at 350° for about five minutes or more, until the edges begin to brown. *Watch*, and don't let them burn. In the meantime:

Pour the milk into a sauce pan over medium heat and crumble up the feta cheese, stirring until it is a lumpy, creamy consistency in a sauce form. Just heat it through.

Remove the bread from the oven and pour the feta sauce over top. Put the bread back in the oven for at least five minutes, or until the cheese begins to firm up and absorb into the bread. Remove the bread from the oven, and sprinkle it with the parsley.

Cut it into wedges and serve immediately.

Stuffed Sausage Bread - Linda D.

♥ *Bread Dough*

You can make your own bread dough for this recipe (see Granny Rider's recipe in the Bread and Breakfast section), or use quick and easy frozen dough from the freezer compartment at your grocery store. If using the latter, just follow the directions on the back of the package up to the point where you're ready to form the loaves to put in the oven.

Roll the bread dough out flat and spread the following filling to just within a half-inch from the edges.

Mix together:

1 10-oz. pkg. chopped frozen spinach, drained and squeezed to get rid of moisture
1 lb. sautéed and drained sausage of your choice. Can use Italian hot.
16 oz. grated Mozzarella cheese
1/4 to 1/2 cup grated Parmesan cheese
1/4 cup+ Romano - I like more cheese
1/2 tsp. garlic powder - or sauté some fresh garlic with the sausage instead
1-1/2 tsp. oregano
1/8 to 1/4 tsp. red pepper flakes
Basil to taste - she uses lightly, so it doesn't overpower
1/4 cup chopped parsley

After spreading this mixture over the dough, roll it up jelly roll style. Lay the seam down on a *greased* cookie sheet.

Bake in oven according to the directions on the bread dough wrapper or at 375° for 45 minutes.

When it's done, remove the bread from the pan and slice. Serve hot or at room temperature.

You can also cut and form the dough into small spiral rolls and cook the bread for a shorter time. I don't know which way is best, as it depends on how much time you have available to spend on this.

Today, well lived, makes yesterday a dream of happiness,
and tomorrow a vision of hope.

Hot French Bread - Bonnie

1 loaf plain or sourdough French bread
1/2 cup butter
3 green onions, chopped
French's mustard, regular
Toasted sesame seeds

Split bread lengthwise.

Soften butter. Mix in green onions.

Spread over halves of bread.

Top with layer of French's mustard.

Sprinkle with sesame seeds.

Bake at 350° for eight to ten minutes until it starts to brown.

Cut in slices and serve hot.

♥ *Helpful Hint*

Grating a stick of butter softens it quickly–you can also invert a small heated pan over it. Dip spoon or cup into hot water before measuring butter or shortening and it will slip out easily without sticking.

Pizza/Bread Sticks - Robin R.

I cannot count the times I have just thrown this together, and it always turns out. The smell wanders through the house as we collect our pillows, blankets and rented videos, all claiming our favorite place in the living room to watch TV while we "pig out" on pizza and Classic Coke. This is so easy with a Cuisinart. I've used it more than once for unexpected visitors during the dinner hour. You can make the pizza from whatever you have on hand: Pineapple, Canadian bacon and Ragu pizza sauce. Or, pepperoni, salami—hey, go for it! My favorite: olive oil, minced garlic, raw deveined prawns, Feta cheese, Parmesan, a touch of sharp Cheddar, fresh chopped tomatoes, and a pinch of Italian spices. Yum! The smell is so wonderful your guests will not be able to help being impressed as they sip their wine and watch—or help!

♥ *Pizza*

2 pkgs. fast-acting or 2 oz. fresh yeast
3 to 3-1/2 cups all-purpose flour
1 Tbs. sugar or honey
1 tsp. salt
1/4 cup Mazola or olive oil
1-1/4 cups *warm* water

Combine in Cuisinart: 1-1/2 cups of the flour, salt, yeast, and gradually add the oil. (I use Extra Virgin olive oil.)

Pour in the warm water and beat for two minutes.

Add the rest of the flour, slowly, until the mixture is just a bit sticky.

Let it stand in the machine for about 15 minutes, until it rises to double.

Divide the dough in half. To form a the pizza crust I put the dough on an olive-oiled pizza pan, and push it out to form the crust, with my hands oiled, too. You can use the other half to make another crust, or form breadsticks with the other half for tomorrow's dinner, cover and bake later.

Bake pizza at 300° for 25 minutes. For crunchy crust, bake it on the bottom rack of the oven.

♥ *Breadsticks*

Using oiled hands, pinch off pieces of the dough and roll out between the palms until you have a stick. Coat in an egg wash (one egg white and one tablespoon of water) to hold sprinkles of poppy seeds or sesame seeds.

Or, add any combination of the following to the dough for fancy, fancy: 1/2 cup grated Cheddar, Monterey Jack, or Parmesan cheese; Italian spices; jalapeno pieces; pepperoni pieces; leftover ham.

Bake the breadsticks at 300° for about 15 minutes or until brown.

Crab Logs

3/4 lb. Velveeta or 2 jars Kraft Old English cheese
1-1/2 sticks or 3/4 cup butter, softened
6-1/2 oz. crab meat, fresh or canned, rinsed and drained (check for shells)
1-1/2 cups sesame seeds, toasted
1 loaf of bread of your choice, sliced
Another 1-1/2 sticks butter, melted for dipping
Chopped green onions (optional)

Over low heat, melt the first 1-1/2 sticks of butter and add the cheese. Mix together, and stir until melted.

Add the crabmeat and let the mixture cool.

Remove crusts from the bread and roll the slices carefully out flat. Spread the cheese/crab mixture on the bread.

Sprinkle chopped green onion over the tops if you like. Roll the slices up tight, so that they look like little logs.

Pour the melted 3/4 cup of butter into a deep saucer and dip the logs in the butter, then roll them in sesame seeds.

Cut the stuffed bread rolls into small, bite-size pieces. Place on *ungreased* cookie sheets.

Bake at 500° for eight to ten minutes, or until starting to brown.

Serve on warming plate. These are best served hot. But you can also freeze in logs, in Ziploc bags on cookie sheets and bring out as needed for company.

Serve in slices or in full log, topped with chunks of avocado, tomato and a glass of wine.

Chicken Wings - Gloria S.

These are simply the best! Easy to do and fast, they will not last at parties. Once tasted , they vanish!

5 lbs. fresh or frozen chicken wings or drummettes*
1 cup of Burgundy (some friends use scotch or tequila)
1 cup white sugar
1 cup soy sauce

*We like to use drummettes, as they're called—without the wing tip. These are so much nicer, as most people don't think to save the tips for soup and they wind up getting thrown away. If you're using a sack of frozen wings/ drummettes, thaw them in the bag so you can snip off the corner and pour in the marinade later on.

Mix the wine, sugar and soy sauce and heat together in a sauce pan until sugar dissolves completely. Let it cool.

Now pour the sauce over the thawed chicken in the sack and seal it tightly with a clothespin, or over the fresh chicken in a sealable plastic bag.

Put the sack or bag in a 9" x 13" pan to marinate for at least four hours or overnight. Turn occasionally.

Put the chicken wings, drained, in a large, Pam-sprayed baking pan, and pour a little of the sauce over them. (Put the leftover sauce in glass jar and use, *within a week*, for other chicken *only*, or do another batch of these wings, as I am sure just one batch won't be enough!)

Bake at 300° for at least 1-1/2 hours covered, and then 1/2 hour uncovered, but watch so that the sugar doesn't burn. Check as they cook, baste with sauce if they get too dry, and stir occasionally.

These should be cooked to a nice brown color. You might bake them on separate racks in two pans so they all get a chance to brown. Stir occasionally to brown all sides.

Ideally these should be served on a hot tray. But they can be served at room temperature if you keep them out only an hour or two.

Once a very dear friend (no names at a time like this) who was catering a large function didn't brown the wings enough and they stayed there in their purplish (marinade) hue uneaten...until Bill arrived and dug in. Then they disappeared as usual! We called them Drunken Chicken Wings, and they could have been a 15-pound chicken wing disaster!

Stuffed Cream Puffs

I know most of you out there think homemade cream puffs are hard to do. Wrong! Believe me, it's so easy. Looks so fancy and you get all those compliments.

1 cup water
1/2 cup butter
1 cup flour
4 large eggs

Heat the water with butter to a rolling boil in a saucepan.

Stir in the flour over low heat until mixture leaves the sides of the pan and forms a ball—about one minute.

Remove from heat and beat in the eggs—one at a time—and thoroughly. Beat until smooth and velvety.

Drop 1/8 cup or a golf ball size piece of puff mix from spoon onto an *ungreased* cookie sheet. I do the smaller ones - bite sized, but for a luncheon do them larger.

They puff up, of course, so leave a little distance apart.

Bake small ones at 400° for 25 minutes and large ones for 45 to 50 minutes. Check the cream puffs periodically so they don't get too brown. And since every oven is different, you might also want to test the puffs so they don't get too dry. (Just take care not to eat them all up in the testing process—because it's hard to stop with just one!)

Remove from oven and carefully remove from pan to wire rack to cool.

Cut off part of the top of each puff and save them to use as caps over the filling later on.. Scoop out any doughy part that may remain inside the shell.

You can serve cream puffs with a custard- flavored filling for desserts or with a savory filling such as chicken, crab, tuna, ham, or shrimp salad. Serve with fresh fruit cocktail in a lettuce cup for a meal, not a snack.

You can also add about 3/4 cup of Gruyere cheese to the cream puff batter and not stuff it unless you wish and serve as an hors d'oeuvre with wine, etc.

The world when seen through a little child's eyes,
greatly resembles Paradise.

Welsh Rarebit

🐾 *I just love this. When I was young, my first job was with the Bon Marché. In their lunch room they served this dish and made it just perfectly. I wanted to stay and just eat it, and not go back to work. Actually I was very hard to feed up to the time I became married–right, Uncle Doug? Like the time you took me to a "big dinner house" and wouldn't leave the restaurant until I ate all my food. There were canned peas, which – to this day – I still can't abide. And until you read this – assuming you read every little page, you never knew they mostly went on the floor, under the booth table! I don't know how you never stepped on some…I held my breath, I tell you! I have never, ever been back in there because I was afraid they would remember me – and the mess I left – but I wasn't about to be bullied. And you thought you got the last word! Bet your mom loves this story – there have been so many. Yes, there were and are some good times…*

2 Tbs. butter
3/4 cup flour
3/4 cup milk
1-1/2 cups grated sharp Cheddar cheese
Morton's to taste
2 drops of Tabasco
Dash of Worcestershire sauce (but I usually forget, and it tastes fine anyway).
1/2 lb. of lean bacon, fried crisp in quarters
2 large ripe tomatoes, chopped
Some recipes call for beer, but I don't like it (if using, add up to 1/2 cup)
1/2 loaf's worth of toasted, lightly crisp bread cubes (buttered a bit first if you like, and then
    kept warm

Melt the butter in large frying pan over medium heat.

Slowly mix in the flour, letting it cook for up to one minute. *Don't brown.*

Slowly add the milk, and it will form a roux-gravy likeness.

Add the cheese, Morton's, Tabasco, Worcestershire, mixing in well.

If using beer, add it in now. Let it simmer down so the sauce is thick, but slightly runny.

Pour over the bread cubes, top with bacon and chopped ripe tomatoes. *Yum!*

This is a one-dish meal. It tastes wonderful, and all you need is a glass of chilled wine or beer for those who like it.

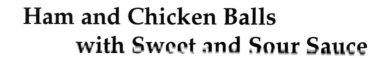

Ham and Chicken Balls
with Sweet and Sour Sauce

♥ *Meatballs*

1/4 cup chopped green onion
1 lb. cooked minced ham
2 minced chicken breasts, uncooked
1/2 cup *unseasoned* bread crumbs (remember there is a sauce!)
1/4 cup crushed sesame seed crackers
Morton's to taste
1/8 tsp. of ginger or freshly grated ginger, to your taste - carefully, it overpowers flavors.

Mix all these ingredients together in a large bowl. Butter your hands and shape parts of the mixture into balls a bit smaller than golf balls. Place the balls in a large, oiled baking dish.

Bake them, uncovered, in the oven at 350° for about 20 minutes—shaking the pan occasionally to brown the balls on all sides.

♥ *Sauce*

1/2 cup pure maple syrup
2 Tbs. cornstarch
1/2 cup milk
3/4 cup *unsweetened* pineapple juice from cubed pineapple

In a saucepan, combine all these ingredients, and cook over medium heat, stirring until thickened. Pour over the meatballs and bake another 20 minutes.

Keep hot and serve with toothpicks. Need I say *wooden* ones? You could sprinkle over chopped toasted almonds and/or chopped green onion over the top before serving for an additional touch.

These can be made the day before and reheated, covered, just before company arrives.

Mexican Platter - Debbie and Tom B.

 *When we invite this couple to a party, we tell them the password is their Mexican Bean Dip Platter. It's fabulous and so are they! Your friends may feel **very** sorry if they don't have a front row place near this dish. Our friends don't give up their spots until it's all gone!*

1 lb. lean ground beef
16-oz. can refried beans
16 oz. of sour cream
4-oz. can chopped green chile peppers
1 cup *each* grated medium Cheddar and Monterey Jack cheese
2-1/2 oz. can *each* chopped black and green olives
1 cup alfalfa sprouts
1 large tomato, chopped
Jalapenos to taste
Chopped red and green bell peppers (optional), to taste
Chopped onion (optional), to taste
Avocado, chopped and dipped in lime juice*

*Lime or lemon juice keeps avocado from turning brown—but it's best to chop the avocados at the last minute.

Brown the ground beef and pour off the grease.

Add the refried beans and heat through.

Spread the beef and bean mixture on a huge platter.

Spread the sour cream over the top of the hamburger/ beans.

Sprinkle or layer over all the remaining ingredients, topping with as many jalapenos as you wish, or leaving them out as a condiment on the side.

Serve warm or at room temperature with tortilla chips.

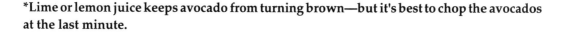

♥ ♥ ♥

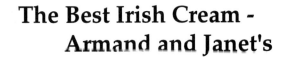

The Best Irish Cream - Armand and Janet's

Just try to leave this "little taste treat" alone, once it's made. We were so happy by the time it got around to dinner. In fact, did we eat? I know we sure taste-tested a bit... Alright—a lot—to make sure we had it just right. PURRRFECT is the word. Bill and Walter were not too pleased, as "life was just a party", and by the time they got there it was more than half gone! But, gee... there were two of us and we wanted to get the recipe right, didn't we? This makes a wonderful gift for friends in a fancy bottle.

1-1/2 to 2 cups Murphy's or Bushmills Irish Whiskey (use the best!)
1/4 cup Frangelico
1 pint whipping cream
14-oz. can sweetened condensed milk
2 Tbs. Hershey's chocolate syrup
1 Tbs. vanilla
1 Tbs. Kava crystals - my favorite coffee, even if it is instant
3 eggs, separately whisked

Mix all ingredients together in a large bowl. Then take parts and run through the blender. Do this no longer than 30 seconds, or you'll have Irish Cream *butter*, instead of liqueur! *Right, Dan Garcia? It took you two tries and a lot of wasted booze. Or, did you save it to put on your morning toast?*

Keep refrigerated, if you don't drink it all at once— like some people I know!

Easy Irish Cream

1 pint vodka
1 pint Half & Half
2 Tbs. Hershey's chocolate syrup
1 14-oz. can sweetened condensed milk

Mix well in blender and store in a sealed glass container in the refrigerator.

♥ ♥ ♥

Orange Liqueur - Lynn D.

Says Lynn: "This recipe came from my Mom, Mrs. Megorden. I use canning jars so I can simply turn the jar upside down every day. We have a friend who counts himself among the "Grand Marnier connoisseurs" of the world. I served him this brew "neat" and he said, "Now, this is what I call the drink of kings!" I didn't have the heart to tell him it was homemade! Especially, after he had finished his third glass!

1 cup sugar
1/2 cup water
3 cups (1 fifth) of *good* brandy of your choice.
2 tsp. orange extract

Bring the water to almost boiling and dissolve the sugar in it.

Place over low heat for three minutes, stirring constantly. Allow it to cool.

Add the brandy and orange extract. Stir in well.

Pour into tightly sealed *glass* containers.

Stir or shake every day for up to ten days to mix completely. Reseal tightly!

This becomes more "mellow" with age.

I like to make a double batch around Thanksgiving and then it is ready for the holidays. The best, however, is the batch I made up last year—if there's any left! Would I hide some?

Cuisine is another thing in whose name many crimes are committed.

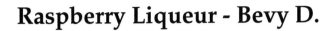

Raspberry Liqueur - Bevy D.

 This is absolutely wonderful! It makes great gifts for Christmas, Valentine's Day, a birthday treat—or for that matter, any special occasion. So little to do actually. Sip, or add it to some taste treat. What a deal! (I've used a lot of the different fruits and berries.) You can get empty, inexpensive bottles at beer and wine supply stores.

Raspberries or fruit/berries of your choice
Sugar cubes
Vodka

Fill a glass gallon jar, with lid, *half full* with raspberries or other fruit/berries.

Fill the other half with sugar cubes.

Pour vodka over the top of both, until the jar is full to the rings where the lid screws down.

Put wax paper over the top of the jar and squeeze the lid on tight.

Put the jar in a dark spot, turning back and forth to stir, every day, for two weeks. Then once a week for two months—total time. We usually only wait one month, it's so *irresistible*.

Strain through cheesecloth into bottles of your choice.

♥ ♥ ♥

New Year's Morning Fizz - Lynn D.

 Lynn says: "We have always had a full turkey dinner at midnight on New Year's Eve. I believe that the best way to start a New Year is by a full stomach and surrounded with your friends and family. So, I am very busy and up very late—early? As my treat, even when we have guests staying all night, my husband, David, makes this Fizz on New Year's morning. Then I get to watch football games all day."

3 oz. vodka
1 oz. Kahlua
2 large eggs
1/2 cup Half and Half
1/2 cup orange juice
2 tsp. sugar
8 regular-sized ice cubes
32 oz. Mr. & Mrs. T's Sweet & Sour mix or other of your choice

Place all the ingredients, *except* the sweet and sour mix, in the blender. Blend at highest speed until "frothy and icy."

Fill the rest of the blender with the sweet and sour mix and blend for about five seconds. Serve in champagne or other festive glassware and enjoy!

♥ ❤ ♥

Margaritas - Robin R.

4 cups tequila*
1-1/3 cup Triple Sec
2 cups water
1 12-oz. bottle Rose's lime juice

*It's a little more than a fifth, so get a gallon, and remember: *Better brand - better taste!*

Mix all of the ingredients in a gallon glass container. This recipe can be doubled.

Chill in refrigerator, covered until ready.

Pour as wanted/needed. So nice to have on hand! Get out the crushed ice, a squeeze of lime, and food: bean dip, salsa, nachos.

The Snatch - A Spiced Tea Pick-Me-Up

Lynn says: This is a fun drink that I developed with a friend while living in Guatemala. It has proved to be very versatile and a lot of fun! My mother, Mrs. Megorden, named it one afternoon as we were sipping a Hot Jamaican version and watching the International Weight Lifting competition. She watched a monster of a man "snatch" this huge weight off the floor and she said, "Wow! What a lift! Just like this drink ...It's a real pick-me-up! Ever since, we'll called this drink a "Snatch".

♥ Base

2 cups instant tea
3 cups sugar
1 27-oz. jar of Tang
1 tsp. ground cloves
2 tsp. ground cinnamon
2 tsp. dried ground lemon rind, optional

Mix all ingredients and store in an airtight glass jar.

To serve *hot*: Add two or more teaspoons per cup of hot water.

To serve *cold* - Add one tablespoon, or more, per glass of cold water or tonic, with a lime squeeze and serve in large tumbler over ice.

♥ Variations

Russian Snatch - add vodka
Southern Snatch - add Southern Comfort or bourbon and mint leaves
Northern Snatch - add a Canadian blend
Jamaican Snatch - add rum
Virgin Snatch - add nothing

These work for both hot and cold. Measure 1-1/2 oz.

Or get fancy, and add melon, Grand Marnier, or your own favorite "nip". Garnish as you wish.

♥ ♥ ♥

Yak Milk - Robin R.

 This is a recipe that Robin traditionally makes every Christmas with her friend Sue. From the old country? It's nice to go over and share their long-standing special time. It's even better when you get a taste treat to take home....

1/2 gal. whole milk
8 pkgs. Oetkers vanilla sugar
2 doz. large eggs, separated
6-3/4 cups sugar
1/2 gallon brandy of choice (better brand, better flavor!)

Boil the milk gently for ten minutes and let it cool.

Stir in the vanilla sugar.

Take all the *egg yolks* and beat well.   Add to the milk mixture.

Beat in the sugar.

Add the brandy.

Mix well and bottle in sterilized jar or bottles. Let it sit for a month in refrigerator. Shake once a week.

Keeps in refrigerator indefinitely. (Ha! Once you start drinking it *disappears*!)

Soups, Salads, and Sauces

To Everything there is a Season,
and a Time to Every Purpose under the Heaven...

Ecclesiastes 3:1

Cheese Soup

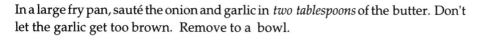

4 Tbs. butter
1 medium white onion, chopped
1 large clove garlic
2 medium carrots, grated
2 stalks celery, chopped
1/2 cup (or less, to taste) minced green bellpepper
Morton's to taste
1/8 cup flour
3 14-1/2 oz. cans or homemade chicken broth
   or 2 cans of broth and equivalent of 1 can whipping cream
1 cup grated sharp Cheddar cheese
Tabasco sauce to taste

In a large fry pan, sauté the onion and garlic in *two tablespoons* of the butter. Don't let the garlic get too brown. Remove to a bowl.

Add another two tablespoons of butter to the pan and sauté the carrots, celery, and green pepper. (I don't put in as much green pepper, because I think it takes over the flavor.) Season with Morton's to taste.

Sprinkle 1/8 cup flour over the vegetables, mixing well, and add the onion and garlic to this mixture.

Remove to a large pot. Pour the chicken broth (or chicken broth and whipping cream) over all. *Note*: I pour some broth into the frying pan first, to loosen all the crumbs in the pan and then put the vegetables into the pot. You can also sauté everything in the pot and not go back and forth.

Heat the vegetable/broth mixture through. To thicken it up, you might want to add some more flour. (When I do this I cook the flour first in a little butter with a dab of milk.)

Add the sharp Cheddar cheese and a few drops of Tabasco. Taste and adjust the seasoning as necessary.

Some restaurants add a little white wine to this ; I don't. Although a glass of wine on the side might be nice! Serve with a French roll or other good bread on the side.

♥ Variations

Throw in some leftover cooked or freshly steamed vegetables, crisp bacon or chopped ham.

Clam Chowder - Duke's 3-time Winner People's Choice of Seattle

Yields one quart

3 oz. diced lean bacon
1 medium diced white onion
3 stalks diced celery
3 oz. butter
1 pinch (or more, to taste) chopped fresh garlic
1 pinch (or more, to taste) white, black, and cayenne pepper
1/3 cup flour
1-1/2 cups chopped fresh or frozen clams (reserve juice, if any)
1-1/4 cup clam juice or nectar
1/4 lb. medium (not too big!) new potatoes, blanched and diced
White, black, and/or cayenne pepper, to taste
1/4 tsp. dill
1/2 tsp. thyme
1 tsp. *each* marjoram and Italian seasoning
2 bay leaves
2 tsp. fresh basil, chopped
1/8 cup chopped fresh parsley
1/2 cup Half and Half
4 cups heavy cream

In large soup pot: Sauté the bacon until it's transparent; then add the onion, celery, butter and garlic, sautéeing until al denté.

Add the flour to make a roux. Just sprinkle it over the vegetables and let it cook and thicken for a minute.

Add the reserved clam stock juice and nectar, and stir until smooth.

Add the diced potatoes and all the remaining spices. Let it simmer.

In a *separate* pan, heat the Half and Half and cream. Add it to the soup pot.

Add the clams *last* and heat the chowder until it's steaming hot, but *not boiling*. Don't overcook the clams or—like other shellfish—they will get chewy.

♥ *Helpful Hint*

Remember the adage: Soup boiled is soup spoiled; cook them gently and evenly.

Clam Chowder - Browny's

Browny's restaurant has since been sold, much to the loss of our north-end Seattle patrons. Michael Brown, its original owner, now has a Pizzeria in Kirkland that is going strong. This recipe was so good it made Sunset Magazine *one year.)*

6 slices lean bacon, chopped in quarters
2 thinly sliced peeled carrots
2 stalks of chopped celery
1 small white onion, finely chopped
1/2 small green bellpepper - destemmed, seeded and finely chopped
1 clove garlic, minced
1-1/2 lb. red potatoes, scrubbed and cut into 1/2" cubes
2 8-oz. bottles clam juice
8 6-1/2 oz. cans of chopped clams, reserving the liquid
1 bay leaf
1/2 tsp. Tabasco
1/4 tsp. black pepper
1 1/2 tsp. Worcestershire
3/4 tsp. dry thyme leaves
4 cups whipping cream
Salt to taste

Cook the bacon in a large heavy saucepan or soup pot over medium heat, stirring often, until crisp. Drain on paper towels.

Discard all but two tablespoons of the drippings.

Add the vegetables—carrots, celery, onion, bell pepper, and garlic—to the pan and sauté until slightly limp.

Add the potatoes and clam juice to the pot and bring the chowder to a boil. Reduce the heat, cover, and simmer until the potatoes are tender when pierced—about 15 minutes.

Stir in the clams and their liquid, the bay leaf, Tabasco, black pepper, Worcestershire, thyme, cream and the cooked bacon. Season to taste with salt.

Heat the chowder until it's steaming, but don't let it boil. Serve.

This recipe makes about four quarts—enough for eight to ten servings.

Cream of Broccoli or Asparagus Soup

3 14-1/2 oz. cans chicken broth (or use fresh)
  or the equivalent of 2 cans plus 1 can of evaporated milk or whipping
cream—my way
1/2 cup white onion chopped, sautéed slightly in butter
Dash of crushed dried thyme
Dash of garlic powder with parsley
3 Tbs. butter
1/4 cup flour
Morton's to taste
Fresh broccoli or asparagus spears
3/4 cup grated Jarlsberg or Cheddar cheese or 1/2 cup Gruyere
1 cup chopped leftover ham, crisp bacon bits, or cooked chicken (optional)

To a soup pot, add the chicken broth, the sautéed onion, and seasonings and simmer these ingredients for a least an hour to marry the flavors. I usually substitute a small carton of whipping cream for one can of chicken broth to achieve a richer flavor. Evaporated milk is much healthier, though. It's good too, and people can't even tell that's what you've used. Need I say, if using milk or cream add it just about 15 minutes before you're ready to serve— simmering it in the soup just long enough to blend in the flavors.

Make a roux by melting the butter, then slowly adding 1/4 cup flour and whisking the mixture until it's combined. Add the roux to the soup pot and whisk it in until smooth.

Season with Morton's to taste.

Wash the vegetable of your choice and break it into flowerets, or cut it into pieces. If using asparagus, cut off the rough ends first, and peel them if you wish. If you want a slightly thicker soup, you can purée the vegetables before adding to the pot. Otherwise just add the chopped broccoli or asparagus to the pot and let the soup simmer until the vegetables are just tender. *Or* precook the vegetable in a microwave or steamer, and then add it to the pot.

I always add at least 1 cup of leftover ham, chopped. Some leftover chicken is nice, too.

Now add the milk or cream (if used) and the grated cheese, and simmer the soup for a few more minutes or until the cheese is melted.

This is best served hot off the stove.

Tomato/Cheese Soup - Armand M.

4 small, 11-1/2 oz. cans or 1 large, 51-oz. can Campbell's tomato soup
2 cups grated sharp Cheddar cheese
2 lbs. bacon, cut in quarters
1-1/2 cups water
2 cups Creamora*

*If this isn't thick enough for you, add real cream, or evaporated milk *later*, but let everything else simmer for at least an hour first, to marry the flavors).

In a large soup pot or Crockpot, combine the tomato soup, water and cheese.

Fry the bacon until nice and crisp, unless you like it a bit soft, or bake it, or cook it in the microwave so you have less grease. Drain the bacon and add it to the pot.

Add the Creamora and simmer the soup for at least an hour to marry the flavors before serving.

Note: If you're using a Crockpot, add all the above ingredients, mixing well and let simmer away all day while you go and do something *fun*!

Serve with toasted cheese sandwiches, corn meal muffins with jalapenos, or good old saltines. Armand serves it with a salad and a lovely glass of wine.

♥ Helpful Hint

To prevent milk or cream from curdling when used in combination with tomato, add a bit of bicarbonate of soda to each before they are mixed. Also, add a pinch to milk or cream to prevent souring.

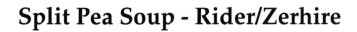

Split Pea Soup - Rider/Zerhire

8 oz. split peas
2 oz. or 1/4 lb. bacon, diced and fried crisp
2 carrots, chopped or sliced
2 medium yellow onions, chopped and sautéed in butter
4 pints water (I add a can of chicken broth and use less water.)
2 stalks of celery, diced
2 tsp. salt or less
1/2 tsp. pepper (I use Morton's instead of salt and pepper)
2 bay leaves (I use one large)
1/2 tsp. dried thyme (optional)
2 tsp. lemon juice
Ham bone - with meat on it, to chop up into soup later or browned ham hocks
Cream (optional)
2 tsp. butter (optional)

Rinse the peas and let them sit for an hour to soften.

Cook the bacon until brown and drain.

Sauté the onions in the butter. Add the celery and carrots, and stir them around a bit; they will finish cooking in the soup pot.

Rinse the softened peas *again*, and put them into a soup pot with *all the other ingredients*, including the water and/or chicken broth. (I would use a large can of chicken broth and the rest water just because it makes it a bit richer, but just water is fine.)

Let the soup stock simmer in your Crockpot all day, or start it in the evening, making sure you have lots of liquid, and simmer it all night .   (My mom just cooks on top of her stove at medium/low for one and half hours, stirring occasionally, and checking to see that the peas are cooked.)

I like to add a bit of cream, to make it creamy rich, toward the end.

Remove the bay leaves; they are not to be eaten.

I always add two teaspoons of butter to each bowl as I just love the taste of a rich creamy soup to warm my old bones.

♥ *Helpful Hint*
If soup has been over-salted, add a teaspoonful of sugar, or a few small pieces of raw turnip and simmer a little longer. It will neutralize the salt flavor. Or, grate in a raw potato. It will absorb the salt.

Carrot Salad - Mauny K.

4 large carrots, scrubbed clean
4 Tbs. white wine vinegar
1 Tbs. lemon juice
1 large clove garlic
Morton's to taste
1/4 tsp. Dijon hot mustard or regular, to taste

Set the carrots aside.

Blend the rest of the ingredients well in the Cuisinart with steel knife. Or in a bowl, using a whisk.

Grate or shred the carrots in the Cuisinart or with a grater.

Mix the carrots with the dressing well.

Cover and refrigerate at least one hour before serving, to marry the flavors.

Cucumbers - Granny Rider

2 large English cucumbers, rinsed and dried with a paper towel
1/2 cup apple cider vinegar
2 Tbs. sugar
Pinch of salt
2 tsp. soy sauce
Sesame seeds, toasted

Cut the cucumber into slices.

Mix together vinegar, sugar, salt , soy sauce and sesame seeds.

Pour this dressing over the cucumber slices and let it set for a few hours for tastes to blend.

Coleslaw - Bevy D.

♥ *Slaw*

4 cups shredded green cabbage (I use half green and half red)
2 large grated carrots
1 cup coarsely chopped cauliflower - left in kind of big—but not too big— pieces
1 cup coarsely chopped celery

(If you want to use more cauliflower or celery, go for it.)

Toss and cover, refrigerating all day or overnight.

♥ *Dressing and Topping*

1 cup sour cream
1 cup mayonnaise
1 Tbs. tarragon vinegar
1 tsp. salt
1 Tbs. sugar
1/4 cup chopped green onion
1/4 cup chopped green pepper (optional)
1/2 cup finely chopped English cucumber
2 Tbs. butter
For topping:
1 cup coarsely chopped, salted Spanish peanuts
1/4 cup grated Parmesan cheese

Mix together everything except the butter and peanuts.

Refrigerate the dressing, covered, until ready to serve.

Just before serving: Melt the butter and add the peanuts, toasting the nuts in a frying pan or in the oven until they're nice and brown.

Mix the salad together with the dressing. Sprinkle the Spanish peanuts with the Parmesan all over the top of the coleslaw.

Add more Parmesan and nuts to the salad *only* as you need it: this type of nut gets soggy.

This recipe makes a *very large* bowl for company, so pare it down if you have less than six. Keeps refrigerated in Tupperware for at least four days.

Layered Salad - Dennis L.

Wash and chop **one head of iceberg lettuce** and spread it on the bottom of a large glass bowl.

Layer on up with:

2 5-oz. cans water chestnuts, drained and chopped fine
10 oz. sack frozen peas, or more if you think necessary
2 cups chopped carrots
2 cups chopped celery
1 cup mayonnaise spread over the top (Here you might need a touch
      more.)
2 Tbs. Lawry's seasoning salt, sprinkled over the mayonnaise.
2 Tbs. sugar, sprinkled over the Lawry's
1 Tbs. garlic powder, sprinkled over the sugar and Lawry's
1/2 cup or more grated Parmesan cheese, sprinkled over all

Cover the bowl in plastic and let it sit overnight, or all day, in the refrigerator.

Just before serving:

Remove the salad bowl from the refrigerator and top with the following ingredients—best prepared ahead of time so you're ready to go!

2 small cans of chopped black olives
l cup (or more) of chopped English cucumber
2 cups cleaned, sliced mushrooms
2 large chopped tomatoes
1 cup crisp bacon bits
2 or 3 chopped boiled eggs (peeled of course!)

Top with alfalfa sprouts, or anything else—chopped green pepper, etc.— that you'd like to add!

♥ Variation

Add a layer of chopped chicken or ham to this salad.   Roast beef, or even some cooked hamburger seasoned with a touch of crumbled blue cheese is also good.

♥ Helpful Hint

To prevent a vegetable salad from becoming sodden when it has to stand for a few hours, place a saucer upside down on the bottom of the bowl before filling it with salad. The moisture will run underneath and the salad will remain fresh and crisp.

Greek-Style Green Salad - Kim B.

♥ *Salad*

1 large English cucumber, sliced and quartered
6 medium ripe red tomatoes (sliced in quarters or in large chunks)
1/4 lb. crumbled Feta cheese
1 small white onion, sliced in circles
3 -1/2 oz. can pitted black olives or equivalent amount of good
   Greek olives

Combine all of the above and chill.

♥ *Dressing*

Mix together the following in blender or mixer and refrigerate to marry the
flavors.

1/2 cup Extra Virgin olive oil
1/3 cup red wine vinegar
2 Tbs. fresh minced parsley
4 tsp. sugar
1/2 tsp. basil
1/4 tsp. salt
1/4 tsp. cracked pepper
1 tsp. lemon juice
(I keep a jar of Greek spices in the pantry. So, I add 1/2 tsp. of this as well.)

Put the salad in large glass bowl or serve individually.

Pour on as much dressing as you would like.

We serve this with hot garlic French bread or garlic pita bread with sprinkles of Parmesan and
shredded Cheddar, toasted.

Hearts of Palm Salad - Micha E.

14-oz. can hearts of palm, drained and washed
1/2 to 3/4 cup red wine vinegar
1 cup Extra Virgin olive oil
1 clove garlic, crushed or minced
Morton's to taste
Pinch of cayenne or red pepper flakes
Bib lettuce
Grated Parmesan cheese

Slice or chop the hearts of palm, or leave them whole. Put the palm meat in a bowl.

Whisk together the vinegar, oil, garlic and seasonings and pour the dressing over the palm.

Refrigerate, covered, to marry flavors.

Wash and drain the bib lettuce.

Arrange about 1/2 cup of the palm meat on the center of a bib lettuce leaf for individual plates and top with the grated Parmesan.

Variation

You can also combine some water-packed artichokes with the hearts of palm before marrying it in the dressing.

Macaroni Salad - Jeanie

Macaroni or other noodles of your choice
Chicken broth - canned or homemade - for boiling the noodles
3/4 cup Miracle Whip
1/4 cup mayonnaise
1 cup chopped ham
6-1/2 oz. can water-packed tuna or albacore, drained
1/2 cup chopped celery
10-oz. box frozen green peas, thawed
1/2 tsp. horseradish
1/2 tsp. regular French's mustard
1 cup grated *sharp* Cheddar cheese, grated or cut into small cubes
Morton's to taste
6 boiled eggs, sliced for garnish*
Paprika

*If you want some egg in the salad itself, boil and chop a few more.

Boil the noodles in the chicken broth and drain them.

Mix all the other ingredients except the boiled eggs (unless you want to add some egg to the salad) into the noodles.

Mix well and smooth down the top.

Put circles of boiled egg, sprinkled with paprika, on top. Cover.

Refrigerate for four hours to marry all the flavors.

♥ Helpful Hint

A drop of oil or a dab of butter keeps the pot from boiling over with noodles or rice. Or spray with or rub oil over insides of pan will keep starches from boiling over. An inch-wide strip of butter around the inside top rim allows boiling water to go to that point but not over.

Black-Eyed Peas - Billie Z.

This is great during the summertime as a side dish for chicken. Or, make it into a salad to take to a friend's house. Add the chopped up chicken and bring along some good bread, toasted flour tortillas with cheese, or pita bread with garlic butter.

2 15-oz. cans black-eyed peas, rinsed and drained.
3/4 cup chopped red onion
1/2 cup cubed Monterey Jack
1/2 cup cubed medium Cheddar cheese
1 tsp. lime juice
1 garlic cloves, minced
Morton's
1/2 cup of your favorite salsa! (We use Mark Cruz's or my sister Julie's)

Fold all the ingredients together.

Refrigerate for at least two hours so flavors have a chance to merge.

Pea Salad

1 large sack frozen green-peas, thawed
1/2 cup mayonnaise
1/2 cup sour cream
Morton's to taste
1/2 lb. bacon, diced, cooked crispy and drained
2 oz. cubed or grated sharp Cheddar cheese

Mix everything together and refrigerate to let flavors marry for two hours.

69

Pineapple Fluff - Auntie Jean W.

1 Tbs. unflavored gelatin
1/2 cup cold water
6 large egg yolks
1 cup white sugar
1 #2 large can crushed pineapple, drained
8 oz. miniature marshmallows - white, not colored
1 pint whipping cream
1 box of vanilla wafers

Mix together, or "soak", as Auntie Jean says, the gelatin and water.

Boil the egg yolks and sugar with the soaked gelatin, stirring constantly.

Add the crushed pineapple, marshmallows and whipping cream.

Crush the vanilla wafers in a large bowl.

Put half of the crushed wafers into the bottom of a 9" x 13" pan.

Pour in the fluff.

Top with rest of wafer crumbs.

Refrigerate for several hours.

Cut into squares to serve.

A plain cookie served on the side is nice, too.

Double Duty Fruit Salad Dish - Carol R.

I call this a double duty dish because it's almost like a dessert—but also great on a buffet table.

3-oz. pkg. orange-flavored Jell-O (no water)
16-oz. carton cottage cheese
1 #303 can pineapple chunks, reserving abut 1/4 cup of the juice
11-oz. can Mandarin oranges
8 oz. of Cool Whip

Pour the Jell-O right from box over the cottage cheese.

Mix in the pineapple and juice, Mandarin oranges, and Cool Whip.

Refrigerate for at least an hour for the flavors to marry.

This is also great on hot days or to just as a quick "something tasty" to whip up for the kids.

♥ Variation

Substitute fruit cocktail, drained, and strawberry- or raspberry-flavored Jell-O.

Fruit Dip Ida

3-oz. pkg. cream cheese, softened
7-oz. jar Marshmallow Creme
1 Tbs. cinnamon
1 Tbs. pineapple juice (or more, to taste)

Mix all of these ingredients well, and use it as a dip for apples, oranges, pineapples, pears.

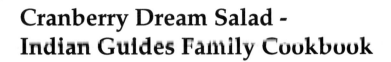

Cranberry Dream Salad - Indian Guides Family Cookbook

Bill and I put a cookbook together from recipes sent by each parent for Todd's third grade Indian Guide Group. This recipe was a hit. It's wonderful, and we've used it many times since.

1 cup heavy cream, whipped
1 cup crushed pineapple, drained
1 cup whole cranberry sauce, broken up
2 Tbs. mayonnaise.
2 Tbs. sugar
2 3-oz. pkgs. cream cheese, in chunks
3/4 cup walnuts, chopped fine

Fold the whipped cream and pineapple carefully in a large bowl.

Blend the cranberry sauce in a Cuisinart or mixer until smooth. Add the mayonnaise, sugar, cream cheese and blend well. Add the walnuts and chop to your preference.

Fold the cranberry mixture into the whipped cream and pineapple.

Pour into an oblong glass dish or small molds (sprayed with Pam), and freeze. (I make mine in little Jell-O molds that I collect. They make just the right serving. I set them on a tray to keep them together for easier handling.)

To serve, let sit at room temperature for 15 minutes. Cut into squares.

I like this dish best with turkey on a holiday table but it can be eaten as a dessert, too, says my Aunt Dorothy. This is especially good for those, like me, who really do not like cranberries. I find that it just takes the right things mixed together to make us realize most everything has its time and place, like spinach, eggplant, etc.

♥ ♥ ♥

Two Wedding Salads -
from Dolores's Wedding to Chet

#1

4 cups bread crumbs - white
1/4 cup minced white onion
7 oz. fresh crabmeat, broken into pieces (Use canned if fresh isn't available.)
7 oz. fresh shrimp, small size (Use canned if fresh isn't available.)
1-1/2 cup mayonnaise
Morton's to taste

Mix all together and chill. This is *so* plain, it's *wonderful.*

#2

2 cups slightly steamed broccoli flowerets
2 cups slightly steamed cauliflower flowerets
l cup shrimp
l cup mayonnaise
1/4 cup minced white onion
1/2 tsp. garlic powder
Morton's to taste

Mix together, although you may want a touch more mayonnaise.

I think a bit of toasted chopped almonds would be good in it, too.

♥ *Helpful Hint*
Cauliflower will keep its snowy white color if you add lemon juice, vinegar, or a little
bit of milk to the cooking water.

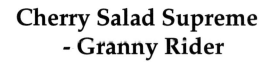

Cherry Salad Supreme
- Granny Rider

3-oz. pkg. raspberry-flavored Jell-O
21-oz. can cherry pie filling
3-oz. pkg. lemon-flavored Jell-O
1 cup tiny marshmallows
3-oz. pkg. cream cheese
1/3 cup mayonnaise
1 small can or 1 cup crushed pineapple, *undrained*
1/2 cup whipping cream

In a 7" x 11" oblong dish, dissolve the raspberry Jell-O in one cup of boiling water.

Mix in the cherry pie filling and chill until firm.

When the first layer is set, dissolve the lemon Jell-O in a bowl with one cup boiling water and add the tiny marshmallows. Stir until the marshmallows break down.

In blender, mix together the cream cheese, mayonnaise, pineapple and whipping cream.

Combine this with the lemon/marshmallow mixture.

Carefully pour over that mixture over the firm cherry/raspberry Jell-O layer.

Refrigerate until completely firm.

This can either be served as an accompaniment to the meal or as a dessert.

An old-fashioned wife is a woman who singles out a man,
doubles his joys, and triples his expenses.

Oriental Salad - Debra B.

One day before:

1 head green cabbage - washed and shredded
1 pkg. Top Ramen Chicken—*just* **the dry noodles,** *not* **the seasoning**
    packet that comes with it
4 to 6 chicken breasts, marinated—then cooked—in teriyaki sauce,*
    and chopped into pieces
3 green onions, chopped
1/2 cup sliced almonds, toasted

*Use Jim R's recipe for Teriyaki Sauce, which appears elsewhere in this section.

Mix together and make the dressing.

♥ *Dressing*

2 Tbs. sugar
6 tsp. rice vinegar
l tsp. pepper
2/3 cup Mazola oil
2 tsp. sesame oil

Mix together, taste and adjust.

Pour the dressing over salad the salad and refrigerate overnight or all day.

Just about the time you make ends meet,
someone moves the ends.

Spinach Waldorf Salad

2 Red Delicious apples with skin left on - washed, cored and cut in
    chunks
1 bunch fresh spinach - cleaned, destemmed, and chopped
1/4 lb. bacon, cut in quarters, fried crispy, drained and crumbled
1/3 cup orange juice
2/3 cup mayonnaise
Splash of Grand Marnier (optional)
Toasted chopped or sliced nuts of your choice for topping

Mix together the apple chunks, chopped spinach and crumbled bacon.

Whisk together the orange juice, mayonnaise and Grand Marnier, if used,
and toss it into the salad. (I would add some of my Morton's, too, but if you
do, *go easy*—as the bacon is also salty.)

Top with the nuts, and serve with rolls and butter.

♥ *Helpful Hint*

Perk up wilted vegetables by sprinkling with cool water, wrap in paper towel and refrigerate
for an hour or so. Perk up soggy spinach or lettuce by adding lemon juice to bowl of cold water
and soak for an hour in the refrigerator. Lettuce and celery keep longer if you store them in
paper bags instead of cellophane.

♥ ♥ ♥

Curried Spinach Salad - Frances F.

♥ *Salad*

2 red Delicious apples with skin left on - washed, cored and cut in chunks
1/2 cup raisins of choice, black or yellow, even currants - soak in dry
     sherry in a little boiling water, then drain
1/3 thinly sliced green onion
1 cup diced cooked chicken or turkey
2/3 cup Spanish peanuts

Mix together apples, raisins or currants and green onion.

♥ *Dressing*

1/2 cup white wine vinegar
2/3 cup salad oil of choice, lightest flavor
1 tsp. curry powder
dash of salt
1 tsp. dry mustard
1/4 tsp. of Tabasco

Blend all these ingredients together and pour it over the salad.

Add the chicken just before serving.

Sprinkle on the peanuts and serve immediately.

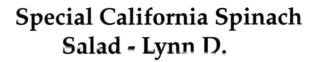

Special California Spinach Salad - Lynn D.

1 lb. lean bacon, cut in quarters
3 Tbs. bacon drippings
3 Tbs. each Wishbone Italian dressing, apple cider vinegar, sugar
    and water
1 bunch fresh spinach leaves - washed, destemmed and chopped
Mushrooms, cleaned and sliced
Almonds, toasted and slivered
Mozzarella, grated
Parmesan, grated
Red or white onion - chopped or in rings if you like
Bacon pieces.
Boiled eggs, chopped

**You can throw in some shredded red cabbage and carrots for some added color and texture, if you want to get real fancy or copy me!

Cook the bacon until it's *very crisp.* Set the bacon aside on paper towels to drain and reserve three tablespoons of the drippings for the dressing.

Combine the bacon drippings and equal amounts of Wishbone Italian dressing, apple cider vinegar, sugar and water in a small bowl. Whisk together well.

Pour the dressing into a saucepan and heat until bubbling and sugar is dissolved.

Arrange the spinach in a large salad bowl and spoon the warm dressing over it.

Add the mushrooms, almonds, cheeses and top with crumbled bacon bits and the chopped boiled eggs (Of course they are *peeled...*)

This dressing will keep in the refrigerator, but must be reheated before each use, of course.

A women never loafs: She shops, entertains, and visits.

Ed Howe

Tuna Salad Deluxe - JoAnne M.

6 -1/2 oz. can *solid white* tuna in oil, drained
1/2 cup green onion, chopped fine
1/2 cup celery, chopped fine
3 Tbs. green pepper, chopped fine
3 Tbs. chopped or sliced black olives, drained
1/2 cup mayonnaise
1 Tbs. cream
1 Tbs. garlic red wine vinegar
30-oz. pkg. dried Chinese noodles

Mix together all ingredients *except* the noodles. Let it sit overnight or at least four hours for flavors to marry.

Add the noodles just before serving and put either in large bowl for a self serving buffet or individual lettuce leaves on plates with smattering of noodles on top. Serve with some warm rolls, if you aren't counting those calories!

Or: Hollow out a french roll, toast it a bit with a light brushing of garlic butter, and fill with salad.

For garnish, you can add crumbles of boiled egg (put through a wire strainer) on top. Strips of green pepper, avocado slices or some chopped toasted almonds would be nice, too.

This is really a delightful dish that I've used over and over on *hot days*, as it's so refreshing when you need a little something to pick you back up.

Serve with a large pitcher of iced tea.

Be careful how you live -
You may be the only Bible some people read.

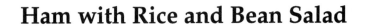

Ham with Rice and Bean Salad

3 cups cooked white rice (I use mix of white, brown, wild rice, too for
     more flavor)
15-1/2 oz. can kidney beans, drained and rinsed
1 cup celery, chopped fine
1/2 cup green onion, chopped fine
1 cup leftover ham, chopped in small chunks
4 oz. grated or cubed sharp or medium Cheddar cheese or 2 oz. of
     Cheddar and 2 oz. of Monterey Jack
Dash of Tabasco sauce
Optional: fresh chopped spinach and/or chopped tomatoes

Mix all together and add salad dressing of your choice.

I like Paul Newman's Oil and Vinegar, but you might also want to try a sweet
and sour dressing like honey/mustard, poppy seed dressing, or any good
vinaigrette dressing with a splash of cream or dry sherry.

Rice Salad - Granny Rider

1 cup long-grained white rice
2 cups fresh or canned chicken broth
1 cup celery, chopped fine
5-oz. can pineapple tidbits, drained
2 Red or Yellow Delicious apples, cut up fine, skin left on, but *washed*, right!?
3 cups chicken chunks, cooked *or* 1 6-oz. can albacore tuna
1/2 cup mayonnaise
1 Tbs. fresh squeezed lemon juice
Morton's to taste
Optional ingredients: toasted almonds, a touch of curry powder,
  and sliced green seedless grapes

Cook the rice in the chicken broth for about or 20 minutes or until done, *fluff it up,* and let it cool.

Mix the cooled rice together with all the remaining ingredients and refrigerate to marry flavors.

Rice Salad Deluxe

♥ *Salad*

1 cup celery, chopped
1/2 cup green onion, chopped
1/2 lb. bacon, quartered, fried crisp and drained
1 can water-packed artichokes, drained and chopped (always remove
    the fuzzy centers)
6-oz. box Uncle Ben's Wild and White Rice - cooked, following
    directions on the box and cooled
1/2 cup almonds, sliced and toasted
2-1/2 oz. can sliced black olive, drained
1/2 cup red onion, chopped fine and sautéed lightly in butter

Mix all these ingredients together in bowl and make the following dressing.

♥ *Dressing*

1/2 cup mayonnaise
1 Tbs. dry sherry
2 Tbs. Paul Newman's oil and vinegar dressing or a good vinaigrette
2 Tbs. Half and Half

Whisk all these ingredients together and toss it with the rice salad.

For best results, let the salad and dressing marry together for at least an hour before serving.

♥ *Helpful Hint*

Adding a few drops of lemon juice to simmering rice will keep the grains separate.

Chicken Salad - Sue F.

♥ *Salad*

4 cups cooked white and dark chicken meat, diced
6 green onions, chopped
2 stalks celery, diced
4 oz. walnuts, toasted
1 Tbs. fresh parsley, chopped
1/2 Tbs. tarragon
1 Red or Yellow Delicious apple, washed, cored and diced

Mix all these ingredients together in a large glass salad bowl and add the following dressing.

♥ *Dressing*

1-1/2 cups mayonnaise
1 cup plain yogurt
1 Tbs. red wine vinegar
1 tsp. hot Dijon mustard
1 tsp. salt
2 oz. chutney of your choice
1 tsp. tarragon
1-1/2 tsp. poppy seeds

Blend all these ingredients together and mix into the salad. Marry in refrigerator for at least an hour for flavor.

This makes *excellent* open-faced sandwiches. It is also good stuffed in pita bread with some alfalfa sprouts, a slice of avocado and tomato, or in a hollowed-out French roll for a lunch or light dinner.

♥ ♥ ♥

Chicken Salad - Granny's Favorite

1/2 cup mayonnaise
1/4 cup sour cream
2 Tbs. lemon juice
1/2 tsp. curry powder
2 cups cooked chicken (or turkey), diced
1/2 cup crushed pineapple
1/2 cup toasted almonds
1/2 cup yellow raisins, plumped in boiling water for better taste,
    then drained
1/4 cup minced water chestnuts
Morton's to taste

Mix all these ingredients together well and let marry in refrigerator for at least one hour.

Serve with a roll, in a lettuce leaf cup, a carved out french roll, heated in a flour tortilla, as a sandwich, or in a bowl.

♥ *Variation*

Use this salad in spiral roll: Remove crusts from the bread of your choice and roll the bread out just a tad. Spread it with salad and roll it up. Lay the roll seam side down on cookie sheets, covered until ready to slice and serve as a bite-sized appetizer.

A man shouldn't look for too much in a wife -
Just someone with whom to spend the rest of his life.

Green Salad - Granny Rider

1 head iceberg lettuce - washed, rinsed and chopped and placed in the
    bottom of a large glass bowl
1 bunch fresh spinach - washed, rinsed, destemmed, and chopped
1 to 2 carrots, shredded and grated or sliced in circles
1/4 head of purple cabbage, washed and shredded
l large ripe tomato, chopped
l large avocado, chopped and sprinkled with lemon juice so it doesn't
    turn brown
1/4 cup *each* salted sunflower seeds and toasted almonds
2 stalks chopped celery
1 cup sliced black olives
1 cup or more marinated three-bean salad, drained
1/2 lb. bacon, quartered and fried crisp
1/2 cup grated Cheddar - *or whatever is left in the refrigerator*
1/2 cup grated Swiss or Jarlsberg cheese
1/2 cup green onion, chopped
If I have leftover broccoli or cauliflower - steamed a bit first, they go in
    too
2 boiled eggs, peeled and chopped for the topping

Toss all together with the lettuce in the large bowl *except* the egg. Sprinkle that on top just before serving.

I make this salad in the morning, put damp paper towels over the top, and either cover it tightly with plastic or— if no company is coming—keep it in a large Tupperware container to stay fresh.

It will keep for days, refrigerated of course, if you redampen your towel.

Serve with garlic-buttered French bread.

A home is built of peace and love
And not of wood and stone
A place where understanding lives
and memories are sown.

Chinese Green Salad - Judy L.

♥ *Dressing*

Mix the following ingredients together and bring to a boil in a saucepan. Let the dressing cool for a bit.

4 Tbs. sugar
Morton's to taste
1 tsp. MSG (optional)
1/4 tsp. pepper
4 Tbs. rice wine vinegar
1/4 cup Wesson oil
Drop of sesame oil

♥ *Salad*

1 head of iceberg lettuce, chopped
1/2 cup almonds sliced toasted
Cooked crab or shrimp to taste (shredded chicken is nice, too)
1 pkg. rice noodles, quickly fried in dab of oil, until crunchy, and broken into pieces

Pour the dressing over the lettuce while the dressing is still warm. Reheat it if necessary. You can make the dressing ahead of time and then zap it in the microwave just before serving it you'd like.

Add the toasted almonds, cooked shellfish or chicken and the noodles, toss and serve.

There is no love more sincere than the love of food.

George Bernard Shaw

♥ *Helpful Hint*

To remove core from head of lettuce, hit the core end once against counter sharply. The core will loosen and pull out easily.

Blue Cheese Dressing - Jim R.

This dressing is so popular among my friends that we're offering the recipe in two sizes!

Party Size

1 gallon mayonnaise
2 lbs. blue cheese, crumbled
1 quart buttermilk
1 quart sour cream
1 Tbs. salt
2 tsp. white pepper
2 tsp. celery salt
2 Tbs. Worcestershire sauce
1 Tbs. Tabasco sauce
1 Tbs. granulated garlic

Family Size*

4 cups mayonnaise
1 cup blue cheese
1 cup buttermilk
1 cup sour cream
3/4 tsp. salt
1/2 tsp. white pepper
1/2 tsp. celery salt
1-1/2 tsp. Worcestershire
3/4 tsp. Tabasco
3/4 tsp. granulated garlic
*This makes about a quart

Blend all these ingredients well in a very large mixing bowl , leaving your blue cheese last so you still have lumps of cheese left. A Kitchen Aid works great. (Do in smaller batches and combine all in the end.)

Need I say put in the refrigerator in sealed containers?

Lots of bowls, kind of a pain. But as they say "No Pain, No Gain", and this recipe is sure worth it!

French Dressing - Uncle Freddy M.

*Now, my darling Uncle Freddy could play **anything** I wanted on the piano, if I would just sing the melody. Always full of fun and laughter, I thought he was wonderful! When he and my Aunt Marie moved to Portugal, he came back to visit his son Max, and stayed with us for a few days in Seattle before heading for California. He kept us entertained with his stories, and he made this dressing for our salad one night.*

1-1/2 oz. can Campbell's tomato soup
3/4 cup apple cider vinegar
1/2 tsp. paprika
1 Tbs. Worcestershire sauce
1/2 tsp. pepper
1/2 cup sugar
l tsp. minced yellow onion
1 tsp. dry mustard
1 cup Mazola oil
1/8 tsp. garlic powder or one fresh garlic clove, minced or crushed
3-oz. pkg. Roquefort cheese, crumbled

Mix all these ingredients in a large fruit jar, cover with the lid, and marry in refrigerator.

Shake well before each use. It gets better with time—*if* you can keep it around.

....And: until my Aunt Marie gets her copy of this cookbook, she may never have known that Freddie and I would sneak out and eat huge orders of French fries for lunch with a coke for me and coffee for him— as they weren't on his diet! But he was on vacation, wasn't he? What an absolute joy he was to be around! He just bubbled over with happiness and brought a glow of warmth into every room he entered.

Honey Mustard Dressing - Jim R.

Party Size

4 lbs. of mayonnaise
1-1/2 cups red wine vinegar
1/2 cup French's mustard
2 cups honey
1/4 cup chopped fresh parsley
2 tsp. salt
2 tsp. white pepper

*Family Size**

4 cups mayonnaise
3/4 cup wine vinegar
1/4 cup mustard
1 cup honey
1/8 cup chopped parsley
1 tsp. salt
1 tsp. white pepper

*Thanks to Robin for this conversion. It makes about a quart.

Mix all these ingredients well and put in airtight containers and store in refrigerator.

Now this dressing is outstanding on salad greens all by itself. But sometimes I toss a salad with a mixture of this *and* Jim's Blue Cheese dressing, along with about a tablespoon of fresh lemon juice. Some people prefer to serve a choice of salad dressings on the side.

And then, as anyone who has watched me will tell you, I also put crushed soda crackers all over my green salads—along with toasted almonds, black olives, cucumbers, tomatoes, grated Cheddar, Parmesan, Monterey, or whatever cheeses are available. Sometimes I add other vegetables, such as broccoli, cauliflower, pea pods, and crumbles of leftover meat, turkey, etc. I guess you might say I tend to approach salad-making as way of cleaning out the kitchen!

Now let's see: crisp bacon, shrimp....

Poppy Seed Dressing for Fruit

1 tsp. dry mustard
1 tsp. salt
1/2 cup sugar
1 Tbs. white onion, grated
5 Tbs. apple cider vinegar
1 cup Mazola oil
1 tsp. poppy seeds

Combine all these ingredients together, mixing well. Use a whisk—I use my Cuisinart.

Put this in a serving dish to use as a fruit dip, or pour over a handful of fruit placed in a lettuce leaf, or make a great big salad and keep it in Tupperware in the refrigerator, taking out a cup when you want some.

This dressing keeps at least four days over fruit. How long the fruit *itself* lasts will depend on the type of fruit you use, of course!

Barbecue Sauce - Jim R.

Like all of his recipes, this is a large batch—restaurant style, so you might want to break it down or give some of it away in gift jars.

In a large cooking pot, mix together well:

1-1/2 cups Worcestershire
1-1/2 cups soy sauce
1 cup cider vinegar
1 lb. of brown sugar
1/4 cup dry mustard
1/2 oz. chile powder
1 Tbs. salt
1 tsp. crushed red peppers
2 tsp. Tabasco
1 medium yellow onion, diced
1/4 cup minced fresh garlic
1/4 cup liquid smoke (optional)
2 tsp. dried tarragon *leaves*
1-1/2 quart tomato paste
1-1/2 quart - thin out with water to taste

Simmer for 2-1/2 hours. Store in refrigerator or freeze for later use.

Use it with beef ribs, pork ribs, other meat, and/or as an accompaniment to any dish that calls for finger lickin' barbecue sauce.

For its merit, I will knight it, and then it will be Sir-loin.

Charles II, to a fine cut of beef.

Salmon Marinade and Barbecue Sauce

This is a ten-star, *two -part recipe that I like to do in a Cuisinart.*

Marinade

In Cuisinart or blender, mix well:

1/2 cup Kikkoman BBQ Sauce
3/4 cup regular beer diluted with water (I use 1/2 cup beer to 1/4 cup water.)
3 large cloves garlic, mashed and chopped
2 Tbs. lemon juice
1/2 cup dark brown sugar
1/2 cup soy sauce

Marinate large salmon or similar fish of your choice in a large plastic bag. Turn occasionally. I usually do overnight or all day.

Drain off the sauce and save it in a jar.   The excess marinade will keep for up to one week in the refrigerator. You can use this marinade, by the way, on beef, pork, chicken, etc., but *do not* mix meats or poultry in the same sauce you've used on something else.

Barbecue Sauce

When nearly done grilling or baking your fish, brush this barbecue sauce on—but only in the last few minutes, and *watch closely* so it doesn't burn.

In a Cuisinart or blender, mix together:

1 stick (1/4 lb.) butter, softened
2 Tbs. A-1 Steak Sauce
1 Tbs. lemon juice
2 large cloves garlic, mashed and minced
1 Tbs. Worcestershire sauce
1/2 cup dark brown sugar
1/2 tsp. dry mustard
1/4 tsp. powdered ginger or use fresh ginger, about the size of a quarter - peeled and chopped

(This sauce is also good on steaks and other cuts of meat and poultry even if you don't marinate them first. So I keep it on hand—in a Tupperware container, refrigerated, for basting on a variety of things....It will soften at room temperature so you can brush it over the meat.)

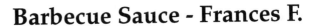

Barbecue Sauce - Frances F.

Combine in a saucepan:

1 cup Heinz or other catsup of your choice
2 Tbs. creamy or chunky Jiffy or other peanut butter of your choice
2 large cloves garlic, mashed and chopped
1/2 tsp. hot sauce (I use Tabasco.)
1/4 cup soy sauce
1/2 tsp. sesame seed oil

Heat over medium/ low until the sauce thickens. Cool.

Brush on food and let marry for one hour before grilling or broiling.

Reheat a bit to baste your meat while it's cooking.

Keep leftover sauce in Tupperware in refrigerator.

Pesto Sauce - Mr. McCutchan

3 oz. fresh, grated Parmesan cheese
2 large cloves garlic, minced
3 Tbs. toasted pine nuts
Morton's to taste
1/2 cup Extra Virgin olive oil
l cup firmly packed, destemmed, basil leaves, cleaned and rinsed well

In Cuisinart, blend all these ingredients thoroughly. Store in Tupperware. Refrigerate.

Serve over cooked pasta of your choice.

Pesto sauce keeps very well in the refrigerator in a sealed container, for other uses such as:

- ♥ a thin layer on sandwiches
- ♥ a dab for soups
- ♥ a touch in quiche

It also freezes well. It's a very concentrated sauce, so if you freeze it in an ice cube tray, you should have just the right amount you'll want to add to most of your recipes. Keep the tray in a plastic bag in the freezer until you're ready to go!

Our next-door neighbor, Bill McCutchan, always has a lot of basil blooming in his gardens—all summer, and well into fall. He uses it in various ways in the meals he dreams up while he otherwise directs the crews of his construction company, from his home. He's always in the kitchen, or trying a recipe he's cut from the paper. During the winter months when we stay in more – "Seattlites don't tan, they rust," – he will meander over with taste treats he has been experimenting on. He also passes along both the basil and his favorite recipes to his daughter Sondra to use at her Cabbage Patch Restaurant in Snohomish—along with home-style sausages from his and Mr. Mueller's Bestwurst Sausage Company. He's a peach. We really enjoy him and his wife, Jean.

Sweet and Sour Sauce - Frances F.

1/2 cup dark brown sugar
2 Tbs. cornstarch
1/2 cup apple cider vinegar
1-1/2 cup pineapple juice
2 Tbs. soy sauce

Whisk everything together in a saucepan over medium heat until the sauce thickens and becomes clear.

Keep the sauce in a sealed container in the refrigerator. Heat what you need.

Frances uses this for her pork dishes. It's also good for chicken, ham chunks, tempura prawns and tempura vegetables.

Serve with a side dish of sesame seeds.

Tartar Sauce Deluxe - Mrs. Scott

We find that this is so much better than store-bought tartar sauce— even when I have to resort to using onion powder in emergencies like the arrival of my son Jamey, who always makes a fuss when he detects onion pieces in his food....

1/2 cup grated white onion
1 cup mayonnaise
2-1/2 large diced dill pickles and a 1/2 tsp. of their juice
1/2 tsp. (or more, to taste) of horseradish (I use the creamy kind prepared by Beaver.)
Morton's to taste
1 tsp. lemon juice

Mix everything together in small bowl, by hand. Play with this until it reaches the consistency of your choice: thick, or a bit saucy—from the addition of the pickle juice.

This also keeps great in a sealed container, in your refrigerator, if you want to double the recipe, as I usually do!

Sauces

Mayonnaise from the Blender/ Cuisinart

1 large whole egg, room temperature
2 tsp. fresh lemon juice
3/4 tsp. salt
1/2 tsp. dry mustard
1/8 tsp. hot red pepper sauce - Tabasco
1-1/4 cup olive or vegetable oil (I use Mazola) of your choice

Place all the ingredients except the oil in a blender or Cuisinart.

Blend at low speed until the egg is pale and foamy, a few seconds.

With the machine running, add the oil in thin, steady stream and process for 30 seconds.

Sometimes it takes a few more seconds, but you be the judge....Sure you can!

Homemade mayonnaise does *not hold up* in warm or hot temperatures, so be careful to keep the sandwiches, salads and other food you prepare with mayonnaise *chilled*.

It also tastes a whole lot better!

White Sauces

This recipe makes a good sauce of medium thickness, to use on tuna and noodles, lasagna, moussaka, and other dishes that call for a basic white sauce. Some variations follow.

1-1/2 Tbs. butter	**1 small onion ring**
1-1/2 Tbs. flour	**1 small, whole bay leaf**
1 cup milk	**6 peppercorns**

In a small saucepan, heat the milk, along with the onion ring, bay leaf, and peppercorns. Let the seasoned milk sit for about five minutes so the flavors will marry.

Remove the onion, bay leaf and peppercorns.

On medium low, in a heavy sauté pan, melt the butter and add the flour, mixing together to form a paste. This also cooks the starchy flavor out of flour. Do *not* brown. Remember: You just want to take the raw flavor out of the flour. This also is why so many people's gravy or sauces never taste right. It just takes that little extra time and concentration to enjoy the glories of *good taste.*

Slowly add the cooled flavored milk and Morton's to taste. Using a whisk, stir the sauce constantly to avoid lumps. (You *did* remove the goodies from the milk first, right?)

Cook for *one* minute, but do not let the sauce get brown or too hot. The sauce will thicken up as it cooks.

Aurore Sauce

Make this sauce just as you would the basic white sauce, except that you:

♥   Substitute 1-1/4 cup chicken broth for the milk
♥   Add 2 tsp. tomato paste
♥   Whisk in 2 more Tbs. of butter after you remove the sauce from the heat

Pour Aurore Sauce over pork, fish, eggs, or veal, or be fancy and put it on the bottom of a plate with a serving of meat or fish of your choice on top.

Garnish with something pretty, like a tomato rose.

Mornay Sauce

To the before-mentioned, basic white sauce, add:

- ♥ 1/4 cup fresh grated Gruyere cheese
- ♥ 2 Tbs. fresh Parmesan cheese
- ♥ 1/4 tsp. Dijon mustard of choice

Stir in until cheese is completely melted.

This can used on scalloped or au gratin potatoes, vegetables, chicken, fish—a variety of things.

Bernaise Sauce from the Blender/ Cuisinart

1/4 cup dry white wine
2 Tbs. white wine vinegar
2 Tbs. minced shallots
1/2 tsp. dried tarragon
2 large egg *yolks*, room temperature
1 Tbs. *warm* water
1/2 cup or 1 stick *unsalted* butter (or use salted butter and omit the next ingredient!)
1/4 tsp. salt
Fresh ground pepper to taste

Simmer the wine, vinegar, shallots, and tarragon in saucepan on low heat until the liquid is almost completely evaporated. This will take about 15 minutes.

Put the reduced mixture into a blender or Cuisinart. Add the egg yolks and warm water.

Melt the butter in a saucepan until it's foaming.

With the blender/Cuisinart running on *low* speed, add the butter in a thin stream and blend in for 30 seconds.

Taste and reseason, if necessary, with salt and pepper.

Serve warm over foods of your choice: meats, vegetables—even fish.

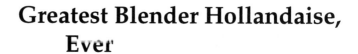

Greatest Blender Hollandaise, Ever

 This never fails, if you follow the recipe carefully! It's wonderful and fast.

3 large egg yolks
1 Tbs. lemon juice
Pinch of red pepper flakes
1/2 cup melted butter - hot, so it cooks the eggs

In your blender put the yolks, lemon juice and red pepper flakes. Cover and blend until smooth —in just a few seconds.

Crack open the blender lid and slowly pour in the hot melted butter while the machine is still running. *This only takes about 30 seconds.*

Use right away or keep the finished sauce in a bowl, over *warm* water, until you're ready to serve.

Pour over your Eggs Benedict, salmon, chicken, Dungeness crab, and on and on and on.

♥ ❤ ♥

Ten-Star Teriyaki Sauce - Jim R.

I cannot begin to tell you how truly fabulous this is.   No one makes a better one or one so easy. Jim is a chef who is a pleasure to work with. Always at an even keel, he's a calm and wonderful friend—he and his family.

Bring to a boil the following ingredients, *without* letting them boil over:

3 cups of Kikkoman soy sauce only!
3 cups of white sugar
1/4 cup of fresh chopped or sliced, peeled ginger
l Tbs. black pepper
l Tbs. of garlic powder*

*I use the one with parsley. Jim says, "Do not use garlic *salt!*" I must admit, I love garlic so I always add some minced up fresh, too.

When the sauce begins to boil, remove it from the heat and let it cool. Pour it into a glass jar and seal it. Refrigerate.

Take out what you would need to use per recipe: a couple of tablespoons for stir-fry, a 1/2 cup with a splash of water to marinate with, a dab added to hamburger for Teriyaki burgers—and don't forget to brown some pineapple slices in butter and a splash of this sauce.

This is a concentrate, so add a dash of water if you feel it's too strong for you.

Use it on chopped onions, sugar peas, green pepper and whatever else you might like to make a nice side dish of vegetables. I always add a dash of toasted sesame seeds.

This sauce can be used for one week marinating either *just* meat, or *just* chicken. Do *not* combine the sauce used on chicken with the sauce used on meat, because it causes bacteria that may make you very sick! If unused, you can leave it in the refrigerator indefinitely.

We also marinate fish—halibut, salmon, sole— in this sauce.

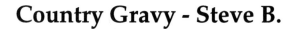

Country Gravy - Steve B.

1/2 lb. lean bacon - chopped in quarters
1 small white onion, chopped fine
2 Tbs. paprika (I use Hungarian sweet)
1/2 cup flour
1 quart milk or Half and Half

Fry the bacon, in a large pan until crisp. Drain on paper towel. *Save some of the grease and crumbs*
in the frying pan and reserve the rest for other recipes.

In the same frying pan, add the onion and sauté it lightly.

Sprinkle the paprika and flour over the onion.

Let cook for about 1/2 minute so flour loses its harsh taste.

Slowly add the milk and mix it in well.   (This is really tasty with Half and Half.)

Add Morton's to taste.

Simmer over medium/low heat, stirring, and it will thicken.

Serve over chicken, pork chops, chicken-fried steak, or other meats of your choice.

Put the bacon in the *baked potato* you're serving with the meal? Or save it for the scrambled eggs in the morning, or for pancake/waffle batter....

Main Courses and Side Dishes

Two are better than one...for if they fall, the one will lift up his fellow,
but woe to him who is alone when he falleth;
for he hath not another to help him up.

Again, if two lie together, then they have heat;
but how can one be warm alone?

Ecclesiastes 4:9-11

Joe's Special

2 Tbs. butter and 2 Tbs. Mazola oil
1 medium white onion, chopped
1 cup sliced cleaned fresh mushrooms
1/2 tsp. lemon juice
Morton's
1/2 lb. hamburger
2 Tbs. butter and 2 Tbs. Mazola oil
1 bunch of fresh spinach - washed/destemmed
Splash of cream or dry sherry (optional)
Fresh shredded Parmesan (I sprinkle some in with the eggs later on, too.)
4 large eggs, lightly beaten
Dash Morton's
Fresh grate Parmesan cheese

In a medium frying pan, sauté the onion and mushrooms in the first 2 Tbs. of butter and oil. Add the lemon juice and Morton's to taste. Remove from the pan.

Using the same pan, fry the hamburger until the pink is gone. Add another dash of Morton's. Drain and remove from the pan.

In the same pan add the other 2 Tbs. butter and Mazola with the spinach. When it begins to wilt, add the previously sautéed mushrooms and onions. Can put in splash of sherry and be fancy—stir it in.

Pour the beaten eggs over all, cooking until the eggs are just about set.

Remove to a plate and sprinkle with fresh grated Parmesan cheese.

Serve with hash browns or any fried potato of your choice, if you like.

I often serve mine with cottage cheese and toast, because I like it that way!

Galouskes (Austrian Cabbage Rolls) - Beverly D.

This is from a 150-year-old recipe that Beverly's in-laws used to make for Christmas Eve dinner. For years their children watched them make this with just a pinch of this, a dash of that—now it's nice to have it written down! The cabbage rolls can be made the day before, leaving the holiday free to be with your family. This is a wonderful recipe, but it's large, and if you don't have a lot of guests—like eight—wait to make it or freeze it ahead of time for when you have more company coming, so you can really enjoy their visit and not be in the kitchen the whole time.

3 lbs. lean ground beef
3 lbs. lean ground (but *not* heavily spiced, unless you really want it) sausage
    like the kind you form into sausage patties for breakfast
6 large eggs, beaten
2 large chopped white onions
1 cup long-grained rice, cooked and cooled
6 to 8 cloves of garlic, minced
Black pepper to taste
Morton's

Mix all together with *lots* of garlic and black pepper to taste. (I go easy on the pepper 'cause I don't care for a lot; I let my guests add it later.)

Take three large heads of green cabbage, separately, and place bottom down, cored, in a large pot of water and let it cook, until *just al denté*, so the leaves are pliable for rolling around the filling. Remove and drain well. Rinse in cold water to stop the cooking. Drain.

Pull the leaves off and form an assembly line for stuffing and rolling. I lay out about one head at a time. Divide the filling into three batches and put a tablespoon of filling on each leaf or more. I eyeball each one: some are smaller then other, so they use less. Roll up and place in a large, Pam-sprayed roasting pan, *in layers* as noted below.

Mix together:

16-oz. can tomatoes and bits
16-oz. can sauerkraut, squeezed and drained dry (I sometimes add more)
2 cubes of beef bouillon - boiled in 1 cup water
1 lb. bacon (I cook slightly, and save a few strips to place over the top layer)

Halve this mixture and put part on the bottom of the pan, then a layer of cabbage rolls, then part over the top of the cabbage rolls. (It looks like it may be too much, but once people start eating them, it's hard to stop!)

Lay strips of bacon over the top layer. (I line some on the bottom, too, before I start layering the sauce and rolls.)

Bake at 225° for 10 hours. Bevy always cooks them the night before, and then puts them back in the oven in the afternoon to reheat. Do in and electric roasting pan and then they don't interfere with other holiday cooking in the oven.

Freezes well. If you have some left! One night, one of our guests raided the pot and we awoke to no football treat. Oh well, at least they didn't go to waste—as the boys won't try them—let alone eat them. But someday they will—you'll see. A mother knows!

Waitresses all agree: Chaos is six women and one lunch check.

Tacos - Mom

1 lb. ground beef
1 pkg. Taco Seasoning
1 Tbs. butter
1 can kidney beans, drained
1 can refried beans
1/4 cup grated sharp Cheddar cheese
1/4 cup grated Monterey or Pepper Jack cheese
1/4 cup sour cream
Corn or flour tortillas

Brown the ground meat in large frying pan. Drain off the fat.

Add the dry taco seasoning with 1/2 cup water and let simmer 20 minutes. Push aside the mixture and add the butter to the pan, along with the drained kidney beans—mashing them, as they cook, into the butter.

Add the refried beans, Cheddar and Monterey, and sour cream and simmer for 15 minutes, to marry the flavors.

You can use either corn or flour tortillas. (If using the flour ones, I lightly butter them first so they will crisp up a bit as they cook.) I spread them with the taco filling, adding a sprinkle of grated Cheddar and the Jack cheeses, plus chopped onion for Bill, black olives if I've got them, and a dab of sour cream.

Fold the tortillas over like tacos and line them up in a bacon-greased oblong dish. Bake at 350° for 1/2 hour if using flour tortillas and for 15 minutes if using the corn tortillas, as they are precooked— unless you want to fry them up a bit yourself before shaping them.

For *condiments* with our tacos I always have salsa, slices of avocados, chopped tomatoes, chopped jalapenos for Bill, more grated cheeses and chopped red onion on the side.

♥ Variations

You can prepare tacos in the same way using cooked, chopped pork butt simmered in taco sauce or leftover steak (flank), roast beef pieces, or of course, chicken.

At one party a lady did beef brisket in salsa, baking it for three hours, chopping it up and serving the condiments for do- it- yourself tacos. It was great – and fast to put together, too.

You can shape your own bowl, to fill, by putting your flour tortilla/corn on top of hot oil in deep fryer and holding down with a tuna can or any larger can with wire handles so you don't get burned, cook a minute till brown. Do earlier in the day or night before and wrap in plastic. I know, you can buy them now. But sometimes you just can't find them, right? And a Taco Salad is so nice....

Enchiladas - Lynn W. Kocher

1 package flour (not corn) tortillas
2 cans of Enchilada sauce

For the filling:
1 lb. lean ground beef, uncooked
2 cloves minced garlic
1 stalk chopped celery
1/2 tsp. Morton's
1 tsp. cumin
1/2 tsp. baking powder
1 16-oz. can peeled new potatoes (they look like tiny balls)
1/4 cup salsa of your choice
1 cup grated sharp or medium Cheddar cheese
l cup grated Monterey Jack cheese

Optional condiments:
avocado slices or guacamole, onion rings, sour cream, black olives, hot salsa,
jalapenos, and more grated cheese

Pour enough of the enchilada sauce into a deep round dish or plate to dip the tortillas in one at a time before you fill them. Use half of the remaining sauce to cover the bottom of a 9" by 13" baking pan or dish. Save the rest of sauce for the baking.

Mix together in large bowl: the ground beef, garlic, celery, seasonings, salsa, baking powder and new potatoes.

Put 1/2 cup of this filling down the center of each sauce-coated tortilla. Fold shut.

Lay the enchiladas on top of the sauce in the baking dish seam-side down, so they won't unfold. Pour the remaining sauce over all. Be sure the enchiladas are completely covered with the sauce, so they won't dry out.

Bake, covered, at 350° for 20 minutes. Remove the cover, and sprinkle the grated cheese over the top. Bake covered for another 35 minutes and then uncovered for the last 10 minutes.

To serve, sprinkle on more cheese if you wish, sliced avocados or guacamole, onion rings, sour cream and black olives, hot salsa, jalapenos – or put these out in little dishes on the table for condiments on the side.

♥ ♥ ♥

Steak Bradford - Steve B.

4 beef tenderloins, cooked to your degree of doneness and seasoned*
1 bunch of fresh cleaned, destemmed spinach
Garlic butter
2 Tbs. Mazola oil and 2 Tbs. butter
1 cups cleaned/sliced mushrooms
1/4 cups chopped white onion
8 oz. of fresh Dungeness crab
Parsley
Hollandaise sauce (*see* "Greatest Blender Hollandaise Ever" and be thankful!)

*While the steaks are cooking, your *bakers*—baked potatoes—are done in the oven, right?

Sauté the spinach in garlic butter. Add Morton's and/or seasonings of your choice. Set aside.

Sauté the onions and mushrooms in the oil/butter. Add it to the spinach and mix it all together.

Put out four plates.

Put on a helping of spinach and mushroom/onion mix, lay your steak on top, and a helping of Dungeness crab on top of the steak. Top with the hollandaise and sprinkle with parsley.

Put a baked potato on the plate and let your company help themselves to the sour cream, bacon bits, and chopped green onions. Or empty the potato shells and mix it all together for "potato goop".

Add a French roll, a pat of butter, a nice glass of wine and *voila*: you have a party!

♥ Variations

Steve also uses the spinach/mushroom/onion mix as a base for fried sole with hollandaise and shrimp on top, or a baked chicken breast, with crab or shrimp, what ever is handy.

You also can add a bit of cream cheese with onion/mushroom and spinach mix plus some shrimp, and wrap it all up in the sole. Pour hollandaise on top. A few more shrimp on top is nice, too. Be sure to sprinkle a touch of fresh chopped parsley, toasted almond slices and chopped or sliced black olives on top.

Swallowing your pride is non-fattening!

Good Old Flank Steak - Mom

Pound out flank steak a little flatter than it already is! This will make it a bit more tender, too.

Don't forget that I always season the meat with a touch with Morton's because it has the garlic, celery, parsley, salt and pepper *all in one*.

Marinate (see Helpful Hint, below) the steak in BBQ sauce, teriyaki sauce, *or* a combination of garlic, dry sherry, fresh grated ginger, soy sauce, a dash of dark brown sugar and Morton's.

You *do* realize I gave you *three different ways*, don't you? (Oh dear, better come and cook with me for a while. I'll drive you nuts in person, but it would be so much faster than reading this cookbook!)

Grill the meat to whatever degree of doneness you like.

I serve flank steak with a variety of things. From fried potatoes, bakers, french fries, and rice to sautéed onions, green peppers, and vegetables of our choice.

♥ *Variations*

For Bill, I stuff the steak slices in flour tortillas with plenty of hot sauce—I forgot to add above that I *also* sometimes marinate the steaks in salsa or taco sauce, too!

I also stuff the steak itself with Stouffer's Spinach Soufflé, or with wild/white rice, which is nice, too. Add some blue cheese.

Since I have a Jenn-Air grill in the house and a *neat* gas grill outside, this is one great meal that is very easy to do! When I'm in a hurry, I bake it with the potatoes (for only the last half hour) Watch your own cooking time for doneness!

♥ *Helpful Hint*

In marinating, I always put meat in a Ziploc bag in the morning, for that night. Or do it in the evening and let it sit—turning occasionally—overnight, for the next day's dinner. And, yes, there are those times it's left in the marinade for a couple of days, with no harm done. By that time I have sometimes changed how I'm going to do the meal, though. From steak and potatoes, to stir fry, to....Oh, Ziploc! You've made our lives so easy.

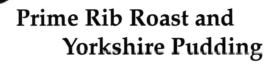

Prime Rib Roast and Yorkshire Pudding

♥ *Roast*

4 lb. beef rib roast - large end*
Morton's
1 garlic clove, minced

*I usually get four bones. And I love the end pieces. So does Todd. Ask your butcher to remove the bones and barbecue them later. (Of course you can leave them on, for a treat—right, boys?)

Rub the garlic lightly into the roast and sprinkle it with Morton's.

Put the roast in a large roasting pan with a rack in the bottom. Spray with Pam.

Bake uncovered at 350° for 1-1/2 to 2 hours. We do ours for three hours—to medium well. Reserve the roast drippings for the pudding.

♥ *Yorkshire Pudding*

1/4 cup roast drippings
4 large eggs (at room temperature)
2 cups flour
1 tsp. salt
2 cups milk

Put the drippings into a 9" x 13" pan, making sure the sides are oiled too.

Turn the oven up to 400°.

Beat the eggs on low speed for 1/2 minute.

Add the milk and beat for 15 seconds.

Add the flour and salt and beat until smooth.

Pour into the pan and bake for 30 minutes—until the pudding is puffy and browning.

Cut into squares and serve. Or cook in well-oiled muffin tins for 20 minutes. Serve with the rib roast or with a thick piece of prime rib *au jus*, with a baked potato and vegetable.

Rib meat is great for leftover sandwiches on garlic French bread the next day. Or: do like they do back East, and add some Cheddar cheese and tomatoes and heat through. I prefer mine plain with the juice or with a tasty bit of barbecue sauce on garlic French bread.

Everyday Roasts and Gravy

♥ **Sirloin Tip**. Bake for 1-1/2 hours at 350°, covered.

♥ **Brisket**. Bake for 2-1/2 hours at 350°, covered. This is so tender and makes the *best* gravy. This is the one they use in Texas. They roast the brisket in the oven first, then put it on the grill, smoke it a bit, and spread on the sauce. Grill just a bit to brown. Slice and serve.

♥ **Chuck/Rump pot roasts**. Bake for 1-1/2 hours at 350°, covered.

Now, I season *all* my roasts with Lawry's Seasoning Salt and/or Morton's and garlic powder—or, if I'm not in a rush, with minced garlic. It tastes better.

Put the roast in a Mazola-rubbed roasting pan with lid on and cook away. We like our meat well done, and we *always make gravy* (see below).

With chuck and rump roast I always add some carrots and onions during the last half hour. Sometimes I'm lazy or in a hurry and put the potatoes in with roast, too.

There are days when my Crockpot comes out, and in goes the roast, carrots, white onions, potatoes, and out the door I go, to come home—hours later—to a warm and wonderful meal. Be sure to put on the seasonings.

♥ *Variation*

Another way of doing roast in the Crockpot or oven is to spread a mixture of sour cream, a squeeze of lemon and a tablespoon of dry onion soup mix over the meat. Cover and roast. Serve with noodles.

♥ *Oh, You Can't Do Gravy?*

The trick to making gravy is to take the roasting pan and let it cool a bit. Remove most of the fatty grease.

Take *two to three tablespoons of flour* and mix it in with the remaining fat and bits and pieces— a bit at a time—in one corner of the pan, making a paste and then slowly mixing into the pan.

Put the pan on the burner, heat until it bubbles, and add *one cup of water*—or more, depending on how much gravy you want, and on whether you like it thick or runny. Mom always premixes her flour in a cup of water until most of the lumps are gone, and then pours it into the bits and pieces left simmering in the pan. (Or, instead of plain water, use Cream of Mushroom soup and 1/2 cup *each* water and milk. Whipping cream also makes very rich gravy, if you want to be fancy.)

Stir constantly. Season before serving. *This technique should make you the brownest, creamiest, gravy ever.* Use a whisk.

Meatloaf Supremo

Sara made this dish for company one night and the guys said, "Oh, meatloaf?"—Almost as if to say: How boring.... Then they took a bite and ended up scrambling for seconds! I take a meatloaf down down every summer when I visit my dear friend Doug and his friends from the San Jose Mercury News at his "Waldorf Wilkerson" at Lake Tullock, California. They devour this dish in no time out on that party boat—no matter if it is 110° degrees or more! Doug likes it on sandwiches with a spread of both the spinach dip and mayonnaise. Now, all his friends all eat it that way too! Anyway: eat, be happy, and share your life with others.

2 lbs. ground beef
2 Tbs. dried onion soup or 1/4 cup minced onion
2 Tbs. *dried* tomato soup or 1/4 cup of Campbell's Tomato Soup
1 large egg, beaten
1 tsp. garlic powder - or 1 small garlic clove, minced
l to 2 Tbs. Worcestershire sauce
Morton's to taste
1 Tbs. catsup
8 squares of crushed soda crackers
2 slices of small bread cubes
1/2 cup grated sharp Cheddar cheese
1 lb. of lean bacon
1 can Campbell's Cream of Mushroom soup plus 1 can of water

Mix all the ingredients—except the bacon and mushroom soup—together. Lay some of the bacon strips in the bottom of a bread pan and put the loaf mixture into the pan, then wrap more bacon pieces around the sides and over the top of the loaf.

Bake uncovered at 350° for an hour or until the bacon is brown. Pour off the fat.

Mix the mushroom soup with the can of water and pour it over the loaf, leaving some of the sauce on top. (You can use milk instead of the water, if you want it richer—I don't.)

Bake for another 1/2 hour, and it will make the *best* gravy. You *did* do potatoes in oven at the same time, didn't you?

This makes great cold sandwiches, and it also reheats well in a microwave.

The Best Stroganoff!

My mom and I have made this just for years, and years. She got it out of Sunset magazine. We added more sour cream and a little more Worcestershire, but it is just absolutely unbeatable. On a scale of 10 it's a 20! It freezes well, too—if there is ever any left over. That means, here I get piggish, and make way too much. But, this is a dish that calls to you in the middle of the night. Even when you thought you would never, ever, eat again when you left the table, because you just had to have one more bite. Enjoy!

1 large white onion, chopped
10-1/2 oz. can beef *consommé* with *no water*
1 8-oz. pkg. sour cream
2 cups cleaned and sliced mushrooms
2 large cloves garlic, minced
Morton's to taste
Mazola oil and butter
2-1/2 lbs. top or bottom round beef, cut in chunks (for company I use top sirloin or tenderloin)
2 Tbs. flour - sprinkled over all
2 Tbs. Worcestershire sauce
6-oz. can tomato paste

In a large roasting pan, sauté the onions, mushrooms and garlic in three tablespoons of butter and three tablespoons of Mazola. Remove to a dish.

Put another three tablespoons of butter and oil back into the pan and add the beef chunks. Sauté until brown. I sprinkle with Morton's.

Return the onions and mushrooms to the pan and sprinkle the flour over all. Add the Morton's Worcestershire, tomato paste, consommé and sour cream. Mix together well.

Bake at 350°, covered, for 1-1/2 to 2 hours. I cook mine up to two hours, until my meat just falls apart. Stir occasionally.

I serve this over rice, and Mr. McCutchan next door puts it over noodles. This can be reheated in the microwave, or even in a pan on the stove. I usually mix the leftover rice right in the sauce, making enough rice so that we have at least another meal out of it—even with the raids on the refrigerator.

Swiss Steak - Granny Rider

2-1/2 lbs. top or bottom round, pounded out and cut in serving sizes (6)
1-1/2 Tbs. dry mustard
1 tsp. Morton's or to taste
3/4 cup flour
2 Tbs. Mazola oil
2 Tbs. butter
16-oz. can peeled tomatoes and bits (I chop fine)
2 Tbs. dark brown sugar
2 Tbs. Worcestershire sauce
4 peeled large carrots, sliced or in tiny French cuts to your taste.
1 medium white onion, sliced (I do it in quarter chunks - so Jamey can pick it out!)

Shake the meat in a brown paper bag with the mustard, Morton's and flour. *Save the leftover flour to make gravy.*

Cover all of the meat well and pat in some leftover flour to coat any untouched places.

In an electric frying pan, brown both sides of the meat in the oil and butter.

Mix together the tomatoes, brown sugar and Worcestershire sauce.

Pour it over the meat, turning temperature to 300° —just a fast simmer.

Cook, covered, for 1 hour, then add the sautéed carrots and onion. Cook for 15 minutes more while making the potatoes.

Serve with mashed potatoes for all that great gravy this makes! Or, serve with baked potato halves or slices with butter, fresh chopped parsley, and Morton's to taste.

I *always* serve this with baking powder biscuits and grape jelly. I've done this since the boys were little. And, since I am a food mixer on some things and this is one, I put the steak on my buttered and jellied biscuit and dig in. Yep, Todd does too! With a little gravy, of course!

This dish freezes well and reheats well.

♥ *Variation*

You can put down a layer of the potatoes in a garlic-buttered pan for the next night, with the steaks, leftover vegetables and gravy. Cover and stick in the oven at 350° for 30 minutes. Yum!

Homemade Chile - Granny Rider

2 Tbs. Mazola oil and 2 Tbs. butter
1 cup chopped large white onion
1 large clove garlic, minced
1 lb. ground hamburger or chuck
1 Tbs. flour
16-oz. can tomatoes and bits - mashing up the tomatoes for Jamey/Todd
1 lb., 11-oz plus 15-oz. can of kidney beans, drained
l 6-oz. can tomato paste plus 1 can water
Morton's to taste
2 Tbs. of good *hot* chile powder
Sour cream and grated Cheddar cheese, for garnish

In a large pot, heat the Mazola/butter and sauté the onion and garlic.

Add the ground beef and cook until it looses its pink.

Sprinkle the flour over the mixture and add the tomatoes, kidney beans, tomato
paste with water, and seasonings. (I mash up the tomatoes first, for Jamey and Todd.)

Let simmer for two hours, stirring occasionally. Taste and add more seasoning as needed.

Bill always adds some Tabasco or other hot sauce, and/or whatever we have on hand that
sounds good. You also can add jalapenos, green chiles, or salsa.

Top with sour cream and Cheddar cheese to be fancy. Sprinkle with chopped green onions.
We always serve this with cornmeal muffins, but rolls, bread/butter, and crackers are fine.

Reheats/ freezes well.

Men can alter their lives by altering their attitudes.

William James

Hamburger Rice - Darlene M.

Darlene and I go back to the fifth grade. We use to stay at her Grandparents and go to all the social activities at the Lake Forest Park Church. We had so much fun square dancing at church suppers with Mike Hamilton and his parents, who taught it. It was an age of innocence. My mind flips through the pages of memories never to be forgotten with our group, which included Janice Pennington of The Price is Right. Years later I would take Todd and stay in L. A. with Dar-D and her three girls. This was a dinner the kids just loved.

2 Tbs. Mazola oil
2 Tbs. butter
1 lb. of lean hamburger, crumbled
8 soda crackers, crushed
1 medium white onion, chopped
1 garlic bud, minced
Morton's to taste
2 cups of Three-Minute Rice, raw
1/3 cup milk
1 can Campbell's Cream of Mushroom soup with 1/2 can milk

In a large pot, heat the Mazola/butter and add the hamburger, crushed crackers, onion, garlic and seasoning. Sauté this mixture until the hamburger loses its pink.

Add the rice, milk, and mushroom soup, and simmer over low heat. Stir occasionally.

If you feel it's too dry, add a bit more milk and let it cook in.

To be fancy, sauté some mushrooms in butter to add to it.

Serve with a veggie.

What did Dar-D serve with it for the kids? I honestly don't remember. We were so young and too busy trying to feed four active kids…

It is better to get Laugh Wrinkles than Worry Warts.

Tamale Pie – Granny Rider

1 lb. hamburger
1 large chopped onion
1 cup chopped celery
Morton's
1 pkg. dry taco sauce
1-1/2 Tbs. Worcestershire sauce
1 Tbs. chile powder
15-1/4 oz. can kidney beans, rinsed and drained
16-oz. can cream corn
8-oz. can tomato sauce
1/2 cup grated sharp Cheddar cheese
1 package corn tortillas
1 cup grated medium Cheddar cheese
1 cup grated Monterey Jack cheese

Brown the hamburger in a large sauté pan and drain. Add in and sauté the
onion and celery and season with Morton's to taste.

Add the taco sauce with 1/4 cup water and simmer until nearly all the water is gone—about
seven minutes.

Combine the beef mixture with the Worcestershire, chile powder, beans, corn, tomato sauce
and 1/2 cup of grated Cheddar.

Mix everything together well, and simmer it to marry the flavors for about 15 minutes.

In a round, bacon-greased casserole dish, put one tortilla, filling mix, the Cheddar and Jack
cheeses, then another tortilla, filling mix, cheeses, etc.—finishing with the filling sauce and a
sprinkling of more cheese.

Bake in a 350° oven for 30 minutes.

Cut into wedges and serve with a green salad.

Behind every Great Man stands an AMAZED Mother-in-Law.

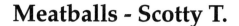

Meatballs - Scotty T.

This is one of those "special moment" meals we enjoyed at Lake Tullock—where, in 110° heat, Scotty stayed in the cabin and put together this fabulous meal of meatballs and the "Best Lasagna!" When we were getting ready to come home to Seattle, Bill asked him for this recipe, which he gladly gave us. It's written on the back of a paper plate. We should probably frame it! It's too bad we don't have him closer to cook for us and share a glass of wine, in which his taste is also excellent. He's such great company on party boats—and in general! Enjoy!

♥ *Meatballs*

2 lbs. of lean hamburger
1 lb. pork sausage - *not* hot
10-oz. box frozen spinach, thawed and squeezed dry
1/2 to 3/4 cup Parmesan or Parmano cheese (I put in more.)
Mazola, olive or other oil of choice

Mix all the ingredients except the oil together well. Roll into balls about the size of a golf ball, or smaller if you prefer. Brown the meatballs in a lightly oiled frying pan.

Remove to a lightly oiled, large casserole dish.

Reuse same frying pan for the next part. I don't wash it out. Just put in a little more oil and swish it around to get up the crumbs and go!

♥ *Tomato Sauce*

2 large yellow onions, chopped
2 Tbs. Extra Virgin olive oil
1/2 tsp. Italian Seasoning mixture, or to taste
1/8 tsp. oregano and sweet basil, or to taste
At least 4 cloves minced garlic, or to taste (We always like a bit more.)
16-oz. can of tomato bits and sauce - the kind that has pieces of Roma tomatoes in the sauce

Sauté the onion with the olive oil, seasonings and garlic. Cook the garlic only a minute and be sure it doesn't get brown.

Add the tomato sauce to the onion mixture and simmer for 20 minutes.

Pour the tomato sauce over the waiting meatballs, and cover with foil, and bake at 350° for 45-60 minutes.

Serve with cooked spaghetti, a dab of garlic butter, sprinkle of Morton's, Parmano, fresh pepper mill, handy, garlic French bread and a lovely red wine.

Hamburger Casserole - Granny Rider

2 Tbs. butter
1 tsp. salt
8-oz. pkg. flat egg noodles - same as with Tuna and Noodles
1/2 cup (or more) grated sharp Cheddar cheese
1-1/2 lbs. of hamburger
1/2 tsp. pepper
2 minced garlic cloves
5-oz. can tomato sauce
30-oz. pkg. cream cheese
16-oz. carton sour cream
6 green onions, chopped (She sometimes uses yellow ones chopped fine, too.)

Brown the meat. Drain off the fat.

Add the garlic, salt/pepper (I use my Morton's), and tomato sauce and cook for 20 minutes.

Cook the noodles al denté, drain, salt and butter lightly.

Add the chopped onion to the cream cheese and sour cream.

Garlic butter a soufflé dish.

Starting with the sauce on the bottom, intermix in layers: the noodles, cheese/sour cream, tomato/garlic sauce, noodles etc., ending with the sauce on top. Sprinkle on more Cheddar.

Bake at 350° for 30 to 35 minutes until it bubbles.

Serve with cornbread.

Chop Steak Hawaiian - Al S.

My good buddy in the kitchen moved to Florida with his wife Gloria, to be nearer their son, Rik, who is a baker. In the middle of all their packing, Al made sure he left me this recipe for you all, so we could enjoy it and think of him down there in the sun, palms, and Art Deco world of leisure…and all the new food tastes finally coming out.

Al uses his electric frying pan for this recipe.

1 pkg. of stew meat or top sirloin, cut in chunks
Mazola or other oil of choice
1 cup celery chopped medium
1 green pepper seeded and chopped medium or do in long strips
1 large yellow onion chopped in large chunks - smaller if you like
Garlic powder or fresh minced garlic - about 3 cloves
Salt and pepper (or Morton's) to taste
1/4 cup soy sauce
1/4 cup (approximately) water
1 cup of *bamboo shoots - not* bean sprouts!

In a large frying or sauté pan, brown the meat in a few drops of oil—Canola, Mazola, etc.

Add the celery, green pepper, and yellow onion and cook for two minutes. (I always think a dab of butter with the oil makes the vegetables taste better, although this is not necessary.)

Add the soy sauce and a little water, say 1/4 cup? (Hey: you're going to taste test, so don't panic! And you *do* watch your food a tad, don't you?)

Season with garlic and salt/pepper to taste (I use my Morton's.)

Let it simmer on low heat for an hour or so, until the meat just falls apart. *Watch* so it stays moist. You might have to add a touch more water. Shred and pull apart the beef with two forks.

Add the bamboo shoots and mix in well, retaste/reseason, and it's ready!

Serve over white rice.

This reheats well in a microwave or conventional oven—*if* there is any left over!

♥ ♥ ♥

Ham and Leek Casserole

2 cups chopped leftover ham or buy some at the Deli - I like Black Forest
6 large leeks, washed/cleaned and chopped-
    sauté for a few minutes in butter
1/4 cup grated Gruyere cheese
1-1/2 cup Bechamel sauce (*see* Soups, Salads and Sauces)
Fresh grated Parmesan cheese for topping

Garlic butter the sides and bottom of a 7" x 12" casserole dish or favorite baking dish.

Mix the ham and leeks. Add the cheese and Bechamel sauce.

Sprinkle the top with fresh grated Parmesan cheese.

Bake at 400°, uncovered, for 12 to 15 minutes until hot, brown and bubbly.

Serve with a roll or garlic French bread and a glass of wine.

Baked Ham - Mom

Todd loves ham done this way better than honey baked, which costs quite a bit more! Me – I like to spoil myself sometimes and get the store bought treat. I love the taste! But, in case:

Cure 81 ham
Whole cloves
Dark brown sugar
1/4 to 1/2 cup honey

Take the ham and put the whole buds of cloves all over the top, leaving a bit of space in between. Pat on some brown sugar and pour over the honey. The amounts to use depends on how big your piece of ham is.

Bake at 350° for one hour, covered.

Now, my friend Maggie puts on some *mustard* first. Either way, it's great.

I pour some of the leftover juices over the ham slices to sugar coat it.

Have the butcher slice/tie the ham up for you, for faster, easier serving.

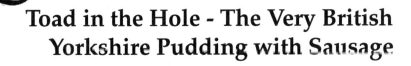

Toad in the Hole - The Very British Yorkshire Pudding with Sausage

2 large eggs, beaten
3/4 cup milk
1/4 cup water
1 cup flour
1/4 tsp. salt
1 lb. *link-style* sausage of your choice - mild or hot

Combine the eggs, milk, flour and salt. Refrigerate for 1 hour.

Preheat the oven to 375°

Pierce each sausage and cut into smaller pieces. Fry over medium heat until brown—about 8 to 10 minutes. Remove and drain. *Reserve the drippings.* (I always add a bit of water when cooking sausage to make sure it's cooked, and doesn't shrink as much.)

Butter a 9" square pan or 10" quiche dish and heat it in the oven until the butter melts. Add a tablespoon of the reserved drippings—just a tad, and the drained sausage. Pour the batter over the sausage.

Bake until puffy and browning—30 to 35 minutes. Cut into squares or wedges.

♥ *Variations*

Now *this* recipe I would play with! It can be served for breakfast/brunch, or for dinner with a salad.

Add some chopped green onion to the batter and garlic butter the pan. Instead of sausage, put in some chunks of ham/pineapple or shrimp and a smattering of cheese of your choice.

You might even try some cooked hamburger, sautéed spinach/mushrooms, a touch of oregano, and sprinkle in a touch of Feta. Oh boy, there are lots of little "things" we could do. Change the sausage, too!

Or stop at the mushrooms, and have a puffy Joe's Special, huh? Or Mexican, or... isn't this *fun*?

♥ ♥ ♥

Ham Hocks and Baby Lima Beans
- Al S.

Bill and I would never, ever eat this—until Al served it to us one night. We both took only a bite and ended up going back for **thirds***! Add that Tabasco, serve it with corn bread and sweet potato pie, and you are "down South"—right, Carolyn and Ron? Boy, those people down there sure know how to eat! At Lake Tullock we get a bowl of beans from Carolyn next door, and some mornings the smell of biscuits and gravy over there makes you drool. Luckily, she shares that with Todd, as it's his favorite breakfast, lunch or snack.*

1 16-oz. bag or box of baby lima beans
3 cups of fresh water (I always substitute 1 small can of chicken broth for
    1 cup water)
2 stalks of chopped celery
2 large carrots, chopped or sliced
1 tsp. of garlic powder with parsley
1 tsp., at least of Morton's can reseason later as ham might be salty
1 medium white onion, chopped and sautéed in butter* first for
    better flavor
Tabasco sauce
2 large ham hocks and some leftover ham (2 cups), if you have any

*Throw in the other vegetables, too, for a moment - although it isn't necessary if you're in a hurry!)

Rinse the lima beans well, and let soak in water all night. Or: boil them, let them sit for an hour and rinse well.

Put the soaked, re-rinsed beans and three cups of *fresh* water (or 2 cups water and 1 can chicken broth) in a Crockpot.

Add all the remaining ingredients, let simmer away all day while you work, and come home to warmth and comfort food. If you're home, stir it once in a while. Just make sure there is plenty of liquid, if you're going to be gone all day. But this should be enough.

Al always serves this with green salad, garlic French bread and a glass of wine.

Pork Chops, Bratwurst and Sauerkraut - Jeannie

🐾 *This is great for football game day, or in front of fire in the fireplace when few friends drop by. It's one of those yummy dishes that your husband might not be inclined to try at home, but would clean off the plate if he were offered it while he was eating out. (Except for Bill, who would eat it anytime!)*

1/2 lb. bacon
1 medium white onion, chopped
6 to 8 pork chops
4 to 6 links bratwurst
1/2 cup (plus a splash) of white wine (I use Reisling)
3/4 cup applesauce
1 lb. of sauerkraut, rinsed well and squeezed dry
Mazola oil
1/2 cup butter, melted
1/2 cup apple juice

In a large, heavy frying or sauté pan, sauté the bacon until slightly crisp. Remove to drain. In the same pan:

Sauté the chopped onion until limp. Remove to a bowl, and in the same pan:

Brown the pork chops, and lightly brown the Bratwurst—either cut up in 2" pieces or whole— in a dab of Mazola and a dab of butter. Remove the pork chops to drain and scrape up the goodies with *a small splash* of the white wine. Simmering it for a minute it will help rinse the scrapings free. After simmering, put the pork chops into a large oblong pan and reserve 1/2 cup of the white and goodies for later.*

Garlic butter the pork chops. Layer the pork chops, applesauce, sauerkraut, Bratwurst, bacon and onions. (I like to mix the applesauce, sauerkraut, bacon, and onions together and then do in layers.) Repeat the layers.

Melt the 1/2 cup butter and pour it over all.

Mix the apple juice and a 1/2 cup *white wine and goodies and pour over top.

Cook covered at 450° for 1/2 hour. Then lower the temperature to 220° and bake covered for four to six hours. For the last 20 minutes or so, remove the cover.

I've also done this dish in a Crockpot and cooked it the next day until meal time.

Pork Chops and Gravy - Bill's Favorite

8 pork chops
2 Tbs. *each* Mazola oil and butter
Morton's to taste
Garlic powder or fresh minced garlic, to taste
3/4 cup water and a splash of champagne (optional)
1 medium white onion, sliced *or* onion powder to taste
1 can Cream of Mushroom soup plus a can of water

In an electric frying pan, sauté the pork chops in the oil and butter.

Sprinkle with the Morton's and garlic. Sauté until it starts to brown.

Add the water and (if you want, some champagne*), cover, and simmer for 20 minutes or so.

(Now, if Jamey didn't throw such a fit over onions, I would brown the white onion in the Mazola and butter, leaving them in with the pork chops while they cook. With him, I have to hide them—using onion powder, and serve the fried ones to Bill on the sly.)

When the water has nearly evaporated and the chops are brown, remove the cover. Add the Cream of Mushroom soup with 1 can of water and let it boil down a bit.

Simmer the pork chops in this sauce for a while, to brown it up a bit, along with the scrapings off the bottom of the pan.

We serve this with rice or mashed potatoes and salad.

This reheats great in the microwave, and it is the *best* gravy with *no trouble*.

* My friend Nancy would pour in some champagne straight from the bottle they were sharing. But Jamey doesn't like it that way. So only once in a while do I get fancy with this. It's really so good as it is that you don't have to!

♥ *Side Dish*

You know, green beans are nice with this, and since I haven't mentioned them anywhere else, I think I'll mention them here. Cook some *bacon*. Add *1/2 cup chopped onion* and sauté a bit. Add cleaned *green beans* with *1/4 cup water* and steam a bit, covered. Add a touch of *butter,* and a bit of *Morton's*, then throw in some *toasted almonds* for a treat just before serving. Tasty!

Pork Chop and Rhubarb Casserole

Oh, I know… it just sounds awful. I can't stand rhubarb either, but this is one meal I'll eat. Must be the brown sugar, but as the food gurus would say today in the 90's, "It's in the breakdown of the chemistry." Yeah, right? Whatever, it's great!

6 meaty pork chops – not those thin little wastes of breath
Morton's to taste
1 Tbs. butter and 1 Tbs. Mazola
2 cups bread cubes
1/2 stick butter
1 clove mashed garlic
1/4 tsp. salt
1/2 cup dark brown sugar
1/2 cup white sugar
3 Tbs. flour
1/2 tsp. cinnamon
6 cups peeled and diced rhubarb

Melt the butter with the mashed garlic and pour it over the bread cubes. (Make the bread cubes kind of small). Toast for about 10 minutes at 350°. Watch.

Brown the chops in a tablespoon each of Mazola and butter.

While they're cooking, combine the toasted bread cubes in a medium bowl with all the remaining ingredients to make a dressing.

In well garlic-buttered casserole dish, layer the pork chops, dressing, pork chops and end with the dressing last.

Bake at 325° for 60 minutes, covered, until the chops are tender – maybe a bit longer. Test with a fork; they should pull apart. Then uncover and cook for 15 minutes more.

This can be prepared the night before, refrigerated and put in the oven just before company is coming, or when you get home from work and need that hour to calm down and become human again.

Doesn't everyone have a freezer full of rhubarb? It grows like a weed!

♥ ♥ ♥

Roast Leg of Lamb

3-lb. leg of lamb
Head of fresh garlic
Mazola oil
Morton's

Make a lot of little slits in the lamb and stuff with a *mass* of garlic cloves, peeled and sliced in half.

Rub all over with Mazola oil and sprinkle to taste with Morton's.

Brown in a large roasting pan at 350°, uncovered, for 20 minutes, then covered for at least 1-1/2 hours. We like it well done—but not dry. So you might want to check for your own doneness level.

We serve ours with *mint jelly*. Make your own: It's easy and fun. Some people like lamb with mustard sauce, but we think mint jelly is yummier.

♥ *Gravy*

This makes the best gravy. Just let the juices cool a bit, remove most the fat.

Put **3 Tbs. of flour** in a half a cup of water, mixing well, and slowly pour it in the roasting pan, whisking it into the juices. Add more water to this "roux" to make the gravy. (You can also add a can of Cream of Mushroom soup and water to make a richer gravy.) Turn the heat to medium/high and let it boil up. Thicken as needed with more flour and water.

Season once again, with Morton's if needed and more minced garlic if you want: the garlic is what makes this dish so *yummy*.

We have mashed or peeled potatoes, boiled a bit and put in the roasting pan the last hour, making wonderful browned potatoes.

♥ *Variation*

This is also good done with a boneless leg of lamb laid out flat with a layer of Stouffer's Spinach Soufflé, thawed, put down the center with crumbled Feta cheese, a touch of oregano, Morton's and garlic, then rolled up and tied to roast.

Rub the roast with Mazola or Extra Virgin olive oil, mixed with a bit more minced garlic and Morton's. Bake, covered until the last 20 minutes.

Serve with Armenian bread, French bread, and a salad of cucumber, tomatoes, red onions, oil/vinegar dressing with a bit more crumbled Feta and a dash of seasoning.

Lamb Marinade
- Duke's Restaurant

This is just the best marinade for roasted or grilled lamb! At Duke's they serve it with a mustard sauce. Everyone thinks is great, but Todd knows how his Momma and Granny Rider "love" their mint jelly and they have that available, too. To be perfectly honest, everything at Duke's is the top of the line!

In a saucepan, combine:

1-1/2 cup apple juice
1 cup soy sauce
1 Tbs. lemon juice
1/2 Tbs. fresh garlic, minced
Juice of 1 large orange (I use 2 Tbs. of *concentrate* plus 1 Tbs. water, mixed.)

Bring the marinade to a boil and remove it from the heat. Let it cool.

This makes about three cups.

You can use this on rack of lamb, leg of lamb or 1/2" thick lamb chops. Prime New Zealand lamb is highly recommended!

Marinate the lamb for at least 48 hours. Turn occasionally. (I used to put it in Ziploc bags and flip it back and forth. Then, Joanie gave me a wonderful, covered marinating container, from Tupperware, that works just great.)

Drain and cook as desired.

This marinade can be reused two more times, if kept in a sealed jar in the refrigerator—but for no longer than a week. Do *not* mix meats, poultry, etc! If the marinade becomes cloudy, throw it away.

Blessed are they who help clean up.

Baked Chicken - Todd's Favorite

This is so easy and simple, yet tastes so good. It can be used for other things if you don't eat it first this way. I always try to cook three to four extra breasts so we can use them for chicken salad, fettuccini, cold chicken sandwiches, clubs, etc.

8 chicken breasts (I use breasts with bone from Sam's or Costco)
Garlic butter (I make my own and keep a tub handy in the refrigerator)
Lawry's Seasoning Salt - regular with orange cap and label

Garlic butter a 9" x 13" oblong baking pan on the sides and bottom.

Put the chicken in the pan uncovered and sprinkle it with the seasoning salt.

Bake at 350° for 30 minutes, brushing butter over the top of the chicken as it cooks. I usually turn the chicken over a couple of times, so that it browns in the garlic butter. Check for doneness.

I've also cooked frozen chicken, uncovered—just keeping my eye on it so it doesn't dry out. It takes about 45 minutes or so to cook, and in the meantime I go do something else.

To go with this, I put on Three-Minute rice and a vegetable in the microwave, or have a green salad ready to go in the refrigerator under wet paper towels. Or I make one of those fancy new rices with vegetables in a cheese or some other kind of sauce. I add a little more rice if there are more than three people over for dinner, though...Well, we run out!

Cornish Game Hens - Pinky

 Pinky is a nurse. She works odd hours sometimes, so that old Crockpot really comes in handy for her, as it should for you, when you're tired and you open the door to this wonderful smell filling your home and only have to put on some rice, get out the salad and relax.

2 Cornish game hens—or just 1, split down the middle and cut in half.*
Oil and vinegar dressing of your choice

*This is easier to handle unless you're stuffing them. But cook on lower heat.

Rinse the hen(s) and pat them dry.

Place the hens in a bowl with the oil and vinegar dressing and rub the dressing all over. Remove them and place them in the a Pam-sprayed Crockpot on high setting.

In the eight hours or more in which you've been slaving away at your day job, the hens will have been cooking—and you'll have a nice hot dinner when you come home too tired to do it.

Put on some rice and a veggy in the microwave, grab a glass of wine and before you've sipped too much—or gone to sleep, your dinner is ready to serve!

♥ Variation

When company's coming, Pinky also puts *apricot preserves* mixed with a bit of water over the hens in a buttered/oiled Crockpot, but you have to make sure you don't burn the sugar in the preserves, so add just a *little* water. Later, add a splash of *Grand Marnier* to the preserves, if you want to get fancy.

♥ ♥ ♥

♥ Helpful Hint

If stuffing them, lay a large piece of cheesecloth in the cavity of the hen, folding over outside the bird so you can reach in with stuffing, then seal. Easy to remove and none is left clinging to the bones. It's easier to dish up and does not effect the taste either. Try this tip when stuffing chicken and turkey, too.

Stuffed Chicken Breasts - Mom

6 boneless chicken breasts
Box Stouffer's Spinach Soufflé, thawed
Morton's to taste
6 slices Jarlsberg cheese, cut to fit in chicken breast on filling
6 strips of raw bacon
Splash of white wine, champagne, or peach wine (optional)

Pound the chicken breasts out between wax paper—carefully, so you don't tear them. Sprinkle with Morton's to taste.

Put at least 2 Tbs. of the spinach soufflé on one half of each breast.

Place one slice of cheese on top of that and roll up the breast like a bundle.

Wrap a strip of bacon around the bundle, holding it with toothpicks you have soaked in water for 20 minutes—so they don't burn. Repeat until all are stuffed.

Place in a garlic-buttered baking dish. Add a splash of wine if you want.

Bake at 350° for about 30 minutes, covered, and then for 7 minutes, uncovered, so they can brown. Check for doneness. *Serve with some sautéed, garlic-buttered mushrooms over the top and rice.*

♥ *Variation*

Or: Take a box of fresh, sliced mushrooms, and lightly sauté them in garlic butter. Add a splash of champagne, if you have it—for a treat with this meal— or white wine. (Peach wine is great too.) Add a sprinkle of Morton's. Combine all with a can of Campbell's Cream of Mushroom soup mixed with Half and Half. Pour it over chicken after 30 minute, as follows:

Bake the original recipe for 30 minutes, covered, *add the sauce and bake for another 10 minutes, covered, and then for 15 minutes, uncovered—or until the sauce bubbles up and browns a bit.

A sprinkle of toasted almonds on top just before serving with wild and white rice, vegetables, and your glass of champagne makes a real *party* !

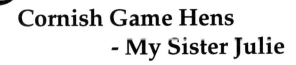

Cornish Game Hens
- My Sister Julie

This is for two hens.

2 Tbs. Dijon mustard-we use *hot* Dijon when we can find it.
3 Tbs. Beaver Stone Ground Mustard
1/2 cup mayonnaise
1/2 cup maple syrup (I use Mrs. Butterworth's.)
Morton's to taste

Mix everything together. You want the consistency to be kind of between a paste and thick/creamy.

Rinse the hens and pat them dry.

Spread the sauce all over the hens and even in the cavity.

Put them on a rack in a covered pan or baking dish.

Baste with the drippings, if you want— once or twice if you have time.

Bake* at 350° for 45 minutes, covered, then for 10 minutes uncovered to bring out color.

Serve with baked potatoes and a vegetable. Pour leftover sauce on bakers.

*You can also cook this is a Crockpot, for about eight hours.

Take time for all things.

Benjamin Franklin

Chicken Casserole - Shay H.

4 cups lightly steamed broccoli flowerets (crunchy)
3 cups cooked, cubed chicken
1 Tbs. butter
Morton's
2 cans Campbell's Cream of Chicken soup
l cup mayonnaise (Best Foods is a good brand that doesn't break down when cooking)
1 Tbs. lemon juice
1/2 tsp. curry powder
2 cups bread crumbs
1 cup toasted cashews, chopped

Garlic butter a 9" x 13" oblong dish.

Spread the broccoli flowerets over the bottom.

Place the cubed chicken over the top of the flowerets. I add in *at least* one tablespoon of butter, broken into pieces, for taste.

Sprinkle with Morton's to taste.

Mix and heat together the chicken soup, mayonnaise, lemon juice and curry powder:

Pour this sauce over the chicken and broccoli.

Top with the bread crumbs mixed with the toasted cashews.

Bake at 325° for 35 minutes.

Serve with rolls of your choice.

Fancy Chicken - Lynn D.

Says Lynn: "We don't eat much red meat at our house, and I do a lot of dinner entertaining, so I need to have a variety of "easy to fix" chicken recipes that also look pretty when served. This has turned out to be my favorite way of doing things. I usually use the oven method, and I also like to add fruit-flavored brandy to the chicken just before serving. Most people think I have slaved away for hours. And until now…I never told them any differently!"

The following recipes are for approximately four large chicken breasts or four halves of Cornish game hen. For chicken parts I prefer thighs and breasts – enough to serve as many as needed.

♥ *Chicken Jubilee*

1 or more 16-oz. cans Cherry Pie filling

Brown the chicken in a little oil in a heavy frying pan. Add the canned cherries. Cover and cook over medium heat until tender. Serve on a bed of rice pilaf.

♥ *Hawaiian Nut Chicken*

15-oz. can crushed pineapple
1 heaping Tbs. cornstarch
1 cup water
1/4 cup shredded coconut
1/4 chopped cashews

Brown the chicken in a little oil in a heavy frying pan. Place the pineapple in a small saucepan and heat. In a bowl, add the cornstarch to the water, and mix until it dissolves. Slowly stir the cornstarch mixture into the pineapple. Stir until the pineapple juice is clear and then pour the sauce over the chicken. Cover the chicken and cook it over medium heat until tender. Serve over rice pilaf and garnish with coconut and cashews.

♥ *Lemon Chicken*

3-oz. pkg. Lemon Pudding mix
1 thinly sliced lemon
Sprigs of parsley

Brown the chicken in a little oil in a heavy frying pan. Prepare the pudding as directed. Add the lemon slices and pour over the chicken. Cover the chicken and cook it over medium heat until tender. *Serve with rice pilaf.*

♥ *Apricot Chicken*

16-oz. can apricot halves - you can also use apricot nectar
1/2 to 3/4 cup apricot preserve

Brown the chicken in a little oil in a heavy frying pan. Remove the juice from the apricots and mix thoroughly with preserve. Add the apricots to juice mixture and pour it over the chicken. Cover the chicken and cook it over medium heat until tender. ***Serve over rice pilaf.***

Sweet and Sour Chicken - Sally C.

2 Tbs. Mazola oil
1 tsp. Morton's
1 small can frozen pineapple concentrate - thawed
1/2 cup water
1 large clove minced garlic
1/3 cup dark brown sugar
1/2 cup red wine vinegar
1 tsp. soy sauce
8 boneless chicken breasts - actually can use either, but I prefer the boneless
1 can of fruit cocktail, drained (optional)

Mix all the ingredients—*except* the chicken and (optional*) fruit cocktail—in your Cuisinart, blender or mixer.

To be fancy: Add the drained *fruit cocktail, *after* mixing, if you're going to have company. Makes it pretty and decorative. Let the sauce marry with the chicken for *at least* an hour—or all day or overnight—in a Ziploc bag .

Pour the chicken and sauce into a garlic-buttered 9" x 13" pan.

Cook at 350° for 45 minutes, covered, and for 15 minutes, uncovered, to give the chicken some color.

I serve with rice and a vegetable—cauliflower or broccoli with cheese and toasted almonds, or Brussels sprouts (although they would be wasted on my kids, as they gag!). *The possibilities are endless...*

Do try it. It reheats really well , and though we've never had enough left to freeze, I'm sure it would. It also makes wonderful leftover chicken salad sandwiches—using the chicken only, unless you want to use a few pieces of the fruit, drained, so it isn't runny.

Beauty is in the eye of the beholder.

Stuffing for Turkey - Micha E.

I never, ever, ate stuffing until Micha, Jamey's Godmother, made this one holiday for us. It was so wonderful! Now, I make it and tell people, "Try it, you'll love it!"

♥ Dressing

This recipe doesn't call for any sage or poultry seasoning. But if you want, add it to yours. I usually cook at least a 23- to 25-lb. hen turkey.

1 pkg. dried bread crumbs, unseasoned (I sometimes mix in some cooked
      wild rice w/white)
1 pkg. dried cornmeal bread crumbs
6 slices of bread of your choice, chopped into medium cubes*
1 large yellow onion, chopped (although I have used white or red)
3 stalks of chopped celery
2 cups cleaned sliced fresh mushrooms
3/4 cup walnuts and/or pecans, toasted in butter
1 tsp. of garlic powder (I think that fresh is overpowering.)
2 small cans chicken broth

*I use leftovers: Croissants, French bread and Broadmoor bread is a must with all its goodies.
Sesame, poppy seed and/or 9-grain bread also add so much to the flavor.

Mix the bread and bread crumbs together in a large bowl.

Sauté the onion in the butter and oil and mix it into the bread mixture with the celery, mushrooms and nuts.

Add the chicken broth and Morton's to taste. Let sit for one hour, then stuff it lightly in your bird. Any leftover stuffing can be cooked in an oiled baking dish.

♥ Helpful Hint

I baste my turkey with butter while it's cooking, so it doesn't dry out, but stays nice and moist. I have found that cooking my turkey *upside down* keeps the breast meat very moist. Turn it over for the last 1/2 hour to brown, or put it under the broiler for a few minutes. (You must have a rack or on a foil strip you lay over the bottom and over the sides of the pan for handles to lift out with.

Pecan Chicken-Stuffed Tomatoes

4 chicken breasts
15-oz. can chicken broth
1 stalk celery
1/2 small white chopped onion
1 cup pecan halves
1-2 Tbs. butter
1 stalk *sliced* celery
1/2 small white onion, minced
2 cups mayonnaise
6 large ripe red tomatoes

Poach the chicken in the broth with the celery stalk, the first 1/2 cup chopped onion and (if you want) a bay leaf.

Remove the chicken and chop it up. (Keep the broth for soup.)

Sauté the pecans in butter until crisp and brown. Watch so they don't burn. Cool and chop coarsely.

Slightly sauté the remaining celery and onion in butter/oil and combine it with the mayonnaise, chopped chicken, and chopped pecans (about 3/4 cup). Reseason to taste with Morton's.

Make tomato into the shape of a hat by just slicing off the top, leaving some of the stem. After removing the lids—or "hats", hollow out the tomatoes.

Stuff the chicken/pecan filling in the tomatoes and top with the tomato top/lids, add a celery leaf decoration, and/or lemon piece, held on with a toothpick to give it a jaunty air!

Or: cut a basket with a handle; use a zigzag cutter to crimp the edges. There are lots of little things to do with vegetables.

Add a roll of your choice, a pat of butter, and have some friends in to share this tasty treat.

Bill eats *two* tomatoes—yes he does! So keep that in mind, when feeding a man. Well, not *all* the tomatoes are really large all the time, huh Honey?

I always find, too, that when you're making a filling for vegetables or a sandwich, it's better if you let it sit and marry at least an hour, to bring out the flavors.

Fancy Seafood Rolls

2 Tbs. butter and 2 Tbs. Mazola oil
1 Tbs. dry sherry
1 cup fresh chopped/destemmed spinach, rinsed and patted dry
1/2 lb. scallops
1/2 lb. cooked lobster
1/2 lb. shrimp
1/4 lb. salmon
1/2 cup whipping cream
Whites of 3 large eggs, beaten until stiff
Morton's to taste

Sauté the spinach in the butter and oil with the sherry until limp. Let it cool.

In a Cuisinart bowl, chop up the seafood to *chunky consistency with the spinach.

Add the whipping cream. Blend *only* to the degree that you still have some seafood in chunks.

Pour the mixture into a bowl and fold in the beaten egg whites.

Set up squares of 4" x 4" foil in an assembly line and spray them with Pam. Put about 1/2 cup of filling onto each square. Roll up and seal, shut tight.

When all of mixture is used up, drop the foil packets into a pot of boiling water three at a time—not crowding them—for about four to five minutes. Check for doneness. Keep them *warm* in the oven—set at 150°. Serve as soon as possible.

A side dish of cooked rice, with chopped artichoke bottoms sautéed in garlic butter—mixed—is nice. (Or on a hot day, serve chilled, with hot garlic French rolls and a glass of wine).

As a sauce for the seafood rolls, use blender hollandaise (*see* Soups, Salads and Sauces), or try this:

♥ *Cucumber-Dill Sauce*

Fresh dill
1 Tbs. yogurt and 1 Tbs. cucumber
1 tsp. minced white onion
2 oz. cream cheese, softened
1 Tbs. whipping cream

Mix all these ingredients together to a dip or cold sauce consistency.

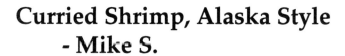

Curried Shrimp, Alaska Style - Mike S.

2 cups fresh medium shrimps, shelled and deveined, of course!
1 cup fresh mushrooms, cleaned and sliced
1 medium green pepper, seeded and chopped fine
1 medium white onion, chopped fine
1 can Campbell's Cream of Mushroom soup plus 1/2 to 1 can water (you want it kind of thick) and/or some Half and Half*
4 to 6 hard boiled large eggs, chopped
1 Tbs. curry or more to your taste
Morton's to taste

*I'd add some Half and Half with the water to the mushroom soup. But I am not a heavy curry person, and this might take away from the hotness of the curry. However, since it *would* make the sauce richer, you could go ahead and use it—and add a dab more curry.

Cook the shrimp until they're *just pink,* either by steaming them, putting them in microwave, or lightly sautéeing them in butter and oil.

Mix all the remaining ingredients together, and cook over medium/low heat for 1-1/2 hours to marry flavors, in a large sauce pan. Stir occasionally. Taste and adjust the seasoning.

You could also simmer this in a Crockpot all day on low. Stir occasionally. But add the cooked shrimp near the end, so they don't get tough from over cooking.

Pour over rice and serve with broccoli, rolls, and a glass of wine.

Baked Halibut - Steve's Way

2 Tbs. butter, melted
1/8 cups white wine - Chablis is fine or a Sauterne
1 Tbs. lemon juice
Morton's to taste
1/4 tsp. garlic powder or small clove garlic, minced
4 3-oz. halibut steaks or fillets (boneless is easier to eat and to place in
the dishes)

Mix together the butter, wine, lemon juice and seasoning.

Arrange the halibut in four oval, single-serving baking dishes, sprayed with
Pam and buttered.

Pour this dressing over the fish and bake at 400° for about five minutes.

Remove the dishes from the oven.

♥ *Sauce*

1/2 cup sour cream
1/2 cup mayonnaise
1/2 cup sharp Cheddar
1/4 cup Parmesan cheese
1/2 cup chopped white onion sautéed in butter/oil (always optional for us when Jamey's
around)

Mix all these ingredients together and spread it over the baked halibut. Put the dishes back in
the oven for another five or six minutes until done—bubbly and startling to brown.

Serve with rice and a vegetable of your choice.

♥ *Helpful Hint*

Thaw fish in milk. Gives it that fresh-caught flavor.

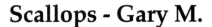

Scallops - Gary M.

1/2 lb. bacon, lightly cooked - cut in half slices just before browning
1 lb. scallops - larger size to wrap bacon around
2 Tbs. butter, melted
1 Tbs. white wine - Chablis
Morton's

Wrap 1/2 slice bacon around each scallop.

Mix the butter, wine and Morton's and pour over the scallops in an oblong dish.

Let the flavors marry for at least one hour in refrigerator.

Bake at 350° for 8 minutes. Stir once. You can also cook it in the microwave for 4 minutes, but *test*! Don't over cook, or the scallops will become stringy.

I find that by turning on the broiler for a minute in the beginning, the bacon cooks up a bit. But *don't over bake*, unless you like rubbery scallops.

♥ Sauce

Sun-dried tomatoes
White onion, sliced
Splash of white wine
1 Tbs. lemon juice
1/4 cup whipping cream

To serve individually in boats, or shells, add the tomatoes, onion—sautéed lightly in butter/oil, the white wine, and a squeeze of fresh lemon. Then add the whipping cream and cook it down to make a "lite" (ha ha!) sauce. Pour the sauce over the scallops and gently stir in into their juices.

♥ Helpful Hint

Dip bacon in cold water before frying for no curling. To keep from sticking in wrapping, roll in tube shape and hold with rubber band. For a large order of bacon, lay in four-sided cooking sheet and bake at 350° for 10 to 15 minutes. Watch carefully as some ovens are hotter than others. That's how the restaurants do it!

Partytime Salmon - Gerard's

This is a fabulous company dish from Gerard's Restaurant in Bothell. He taught a cooking class at the Washington Athletic Club, where I was taken as a guest by Nancy Van der Wel, one of my classmates at Magnolia Kitchen's cooking school. You meet the nicest people at those lessons, and you learn so much more than just the class itinerary. Well, I did!

4 lbs. salmon fillets (I remove the skin)
1 lb. sole fillets
Morton's, 1/2 tsp. or to taste
l tsp. lemon juice
l large egg white (save the yolk to seal the pastry)
2 to 3 cups of cream
1 cup fresh chopped spinach, washed and destemmed
1 pkg. frozen Puff Pastry dough, thawed

Mix the sole in a Cuisinart with the Morton's lemon juice , egg white and cream until it is the consistency of mayonnaise and *not runny.*

Add the spinach and blend in well. You do not want this to be too thick *or* too runny—just held together. *This is to be spread on the top of the salmon fillets.*

Take the thawed puff pastry and cut the dough into pieces large enough to enclose a salmon fillet, with the sole/spinach mix on top, and another piece of salmon, so it's like a sandwich. Either fold it over or do ravioli style.   Seal with egg yolk and fork prongs. (You can make designs out of leftover pastry and seal on with egg.)

Place the stuffed pastry on ungreased cookie sheet, cover with plastic, refrigerate and bake when your company gets there.   Bake at 400° for 30 minutes.

♥ *Mustard Mayonnaise*

3 large egg yolks
1 Tbs. Dijon mustard
Pinch of Morton's
2 Tbs. red wine vinegar
2 cups Mazola oil
1 Tbs. brandy
1 tsp. Worcestershire sauce

In a Cuisinart, blend together the egg yolks, Dijon mustard, Morton's, and wine vinegar.

Slowly add the Mazola, brandy, and Worcestershire sauce. It's *heavenly*, and it keeps well. It also goes well with other fish dishes.

Good Old Tuna Casserole

Don't tell me you didn't expect this in here. A creature comfort food!

1 can *oil-packed* solid white (Bumble Bee*) tuna
2 Tbs. butter
2 Tbs. flour
1 cup milk
Morton's
Butter for the noodles
1 pkg. broad egg noodles

*I like the taste, and what size can depends on how much you want to make. I use the smaller, 6-1/2 oz. size, usually, for just us.

Melt the butter in a large frying pan, add the flour and mix together.

Add the milk, slowly mixing in, and let thicken. (We've used 2% milk for years.)

Sprinkle in Morton's to taste and the tuna and let heat through.

Cook your noodles, al denté. Drain and put them back in the pot.

Mix in a tablespoon of butter, Morton's, and pour the sauce over the noodles. Mix in and retaste for seasoning.

Serve with broccoli or peas. I serve it with corn, because that's Jamey's favorite.

Sometimes I get lazy, and since one less saucepan to clean up is great, I pour a box of frozen peas in with the sauce when I add the tuna. Just let it simmer along while the tuna gets a tad warm and the peas heat up.

And talking of hot, Bill likes Tabasco on his. Lots of pepper too. He does his own. Since the boys have grown, they like it that way too. Not me!

♥ Variations

This is a *party dish* if you want to add toasted almonds to it—*yum*—with some sliced black olives, and chopped green onions (not if Jamey's home, though!)

This casserole also could be done with leftover *cooked chicken or turkey*. Pour the sauce over baking powder biscuits, or cornmeal muffins. Toasted cubed garlic bread is wonderful, too!

Sole - My Way

6 nice pieces of sole fillets, washed, left damp
1/2 cup flour
1/4 tsp. Morton's* - use more if you wish on all the seasonings
1/4 tsp. garlic powder
1/4 tsp. ground ginger - can use fresh if you have - minced
1/3 cup finely chopped almonds
2 Tbs. Mazola oil
2 Tbs. butter

Put the damp fish pieces in a small brown paper/plastic bag. Add the flour, seasonings and nuts, and shake to coat the fish completely. I always throw in the left over crumbs and pat into the fish.

Fry in a large sauté pan with the Mazola and butter, until crispy. *Don't over cook* or the fish dries out.

Serve with Mrs. Scott's Tartar Sauce (*see* Soups, Salads and Sauces), a steamed vegetable or green salad, and rice.

Some people like lemon wedges to squeeze over sole, so have some handy.

♥ *Cream Sauce*

1 Tbs. butter
1/2 cup whipping cream
Morton's
Sherry or liqueur of choice

You can also make a nice cream sauce for this dish, *with the leftover crumbs in the pan*, by just adding the butter and cream, Morton's to taste, a splash of either cream or dry sherry, Amaretto, or Frangelico and letting it simmer down for a bit. To be honest, most of the time I don't bother with the sauce, as I like this dish just as it is...but it may make a nice touch on that one evening you want to show off.

The detective story is the normal recreation of noble minds.

Philip Guidalia

Pasta Swirls

 *The best thing about a meal like this is the friends there to share it! Or, when your kids are home and sharing some of their precious time with you.*

2 *sheets* of fresh pasta - either homemade or bought from the Deli
16-oz. carton of Ricotta cheese
10-oz. box thawed, drained, chopped frozen spinach or Stouffer's Spinach
    Soufflé
Morton's to taste
1/2 tsp. *each* of oregano and basil (I don't use but a pinch, as I'm allergic)
1/4 cup grated Parmesan and (I add) 1/4 cup grated sharp Cheddar cheese
1/2 medium white onion, chopped and lightly sautéed

Combine all the filling ingredients and spread it down one side of each pasta sheet.

Roll up the pasta and wrap it in plastic—*sealing well*, and then wrap it in cotton cloth, *tying up the ends*. Drop the rolls into boiling water and let them cook for five to six minutes.

Drain, let cool and put in the refrigerator until an hour before dinner. Then remove the wrappers and cut the rolls into green and white circles.

Take three cups of meat sauce with tomato bits (you of course make your own spaghetti sauce— your grandma's recipe from the old country, right?) and pour 1 cup into a 9" x 13" oblong pan. Lay the pasta swirls on top. Add the rest of the sauce on top of that.

Sprinkle with more Parmesan cheese, and heat through, uncovered, at 350° for 30 minutes.

Add more Parmesan on top when you serve it— if you're like me!

Plate: red sauce with green and white swirls—*Italy's colors*, you know!

Serve with garlic French bread and Burgundy or Cabernet. A guest's gift of wine will do too!

Chicken Fettucini

Fettucini
Boneless chicken breasts
Extra Virgin olive oil, lemon juice and Morton's to taste

Cook the noodles al denté and lightly coat in Extra Virgin olive oil. Reheat by dunking in boiling water for a minute. Or cook when the sauce is completed.

Sauté the chicken or bake it in the oven at 350° with lemon juice and Morton's to taste. Cut the meat into pieces and remove to a bowl. Use the same pan to make the sauce.

♥ Sauce

2 Tbs. butter and 2 Tbs. Extra Virgin Olive oil
2 large minced garlic cloves - I use more on occasion - do your own thing!
    Don't let get too brown and taste bitter.
1 medium zucchini, sliced or 1" sticks of asparagus say at least 1/2 a bunch
1/2 cup sour cream
l cup whipped cream
Morton's to taste
1/4 cup Parmesan grated (I use Parmano for better taste.)

Sauté the garlic and zucchini in the butter and olive oil.

Add the sour cream, whipping cream, Morton's and cheese.

Return the chicken to the pan and reheat it in the sauce. (You can reheat the noodles in the sauce pan if it's large enough.)

Pour the chicken and sauce over the cooked noodles and serve with more fresh grated Parmesan cheese on top.

♥ Variations

I also use this basic recipe and add ham and peas to the sauce. Or, if I have any left over smoked salmon, I just throw it in. Add a touch of lemon juice, maybe a touch of dry sherry or chablis, a drop of Tabasco. Throw in any leftover sautéed vegetables if you have any. Get out the hot French bread, smothered in garlic!

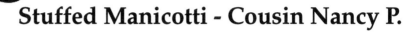

Stuffed Manicotti - Cousin Nancy P.

1 lb. lean hamburger
Mazola oil
1/2 cup chopped white onion
1 large minced garlic clove - I use more
2 6-oz. cans tomato paste plus two cans water
2 Tbs. chopped fresh parsley
1 Tbs. dried basil crushed - I use half, as I'm allergic
Morton's to taste
3 cups fresh Ricotta or (if you want) cream style cottage cheese
2/3 cup grated Romano/Parmesan - sold as *Parmano* in some stores
2 slightly beaten large eggs
1/4 cup chopped parsley
8 Manicotti shells
1/2 cup grated Parmano

In a large sauce pan brown the meat, draining off the fat. Remove to a dish.

In the same pan, sauté the onion and brown the garlic in the Mazola. Add the tomato paste and water, some parsley, basil, and Morton's to taste. Put the meat back in.

Simmer on medium/low, uncovered, at least 30 minutes for the flavors to marry—longer if possible. Stir occasionally.

Meanwhile, combine the Ricotta, Parmano, eggs, remaining parsley, basil and Morton's.

Cook the manicotti shells in boiling water until al denté. Rinse in cold water, drain and stuff with cheese mixture. Use a small spoon to stuff. Nancy cuts one side down a bit, but if you're careful, it can be done whole. They cook more as they bake.

Pour half the tomato meat/sauce in a 9" x 13" garlic- buttered dish, arranging the manicotti on top. Then cover with the remaining sauce and top it off with more Parmano.

Bake at 350° for 30 to 35 minutes. Serve with green salad and garlic bread.

Some women will go anywhere for dinner, except the kitchen!

Spinach-Stuffed Shells

Make *lots* of your favorite spaghetti sauce. Double the recipe and freeze what you don't use here for later.

1 pkg. or box large pasta shells of your choice
1 small white onion, chopped
1 clove (or more) minced garlic (I use at least three)
1 Tbs. butter
10-oz. pkg. frozen chopped spinach, thawed and squeezed dry
2 large eggs, beaten
2 cups Ricotta cheese
1 cup sharp Cheddar
1/4 cup Parmano
1 Tbs. fresh parsley
1/8 tsp. oregano - can use more
Morton's to taste

Cook the pasta shells in salted and olive-oiled water until the are just *partially cooked* so they will hold their shape. Drain. With stuffing, they'll finish cooking.

Sauté together the onion, garlic and spinach, and let cool.

Add the beaten eggs, cheeses and seasoning.

Mix everything well together in a medium bowl.

Fill the shells with three tablespoons of the filling, laying them face up in oblong dish *with an inch of the spaghetti sauce* on the bottom. You can either put more spaghetti sauce around the shells or just keep the extra sauce warm to pour over the top. *Leave some of the sauce extra* for lining on the plate you're going to serve them on—like a puddle. Or keep the extra sauce to freeze for spaghetti. We make enough to pour over the top, plus have leftovers.

Bake at 350° for 40 minutes and uncovered for 10. Top with more Parmano and a sprinkle of fresh parsley to serve. Get out the hot French bread and wine, right?

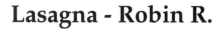

Lasagna - Robin R.

Mazola oil
2 large cloves minced garlic
1 large stalk of celery diced
*I add 1 chopped, medium yellow onion, too.
6-oz. can tomato paste plus 1 can water
16-oz. can tomato sauce and bits
1/2 tsp. Morton's, basil, oregano or to taste
1/2 pound ground beef
1/2 pound sausage - *not* spicy, unless you prefer it that way!
16 oz. Ricotta cheese
2 cups grated Mozzarella cheese
1 cup (or more) grated Parmesan cheese
1 box lasagna noodles

Sauté the garlic, celery and onion in the oil.

Add the tomato paste and sauce, water and seasonings. Let simmer for one hour to marry the flavors.

Brown the ground beef and sausage. Drain the meat and set it aside.

Cook the lasagna noodles al denté, and drain.

Layer all in a Pam-sprayed oblong, 9" x 13" baking dish in the order shown:

Sauce, noodles, meats, Ricotta, Mozzarella, grated Parmesan, and sauce—repeating and ending up with the sauce *last*.

Top with more Parmesan.

Bake at 375° for 45 minutes.

Serve with garlic bread, a green salad and a glass of Burgundy.

♥ ♥ ♥

The Best Spaghetti Sauce - Frances F.

I think that this is the first thing I learned to cook. My mom is a wonderful cook and I just never had to go into the kitchen for anything, except to find my little eating place in the kitchen nook. So one day, after watching Frances Fodor make this dish for her family, I waited until Mom and Dad did their Saturday morning shopping and cooked it for them! Boy, was I proud of myself. And although I really didn't cook much at home—even after that, I always remembered a few of the recipes from the Fodor residence, which I thought served the best food around. Of course, once I married Bill, I found I loved to put a meal on the table and it just kind of unfolded into this book many years later. So, anyway...you almost lost me to memories...

1 lb. or more hamburger
2 Tbs. Mazola oil
1 Tbs. of butter
1 large yellow onion, chopped
1 to 2 large garlic cloves (or more), minced
6-oz. can tomato paste plus a can of water
8-oz. can tomato sauce plus a can of water
Morton's to taste

Brown the hamburger in a frying or sauté pan. Drain and remove it.

In the same pan, sauté the onion until limp, then add the minced garlic. Sauté lightly—*do not brown* or the garlic will taste bitter.

Combine the meat, onions/garlic in a large pot. Add the tomato paste and sauce with the water and mix well. Simmer at low heat for a few hours. Add more seasoning to taste, after it's simmered a bit. (You can also put it in a Crockpot and cook it all day or for a few hours.)

Pour over, and mix into cooked spaghetti or pasta of your choice.

Of course, you'll need fresh grated Parmesan cheese, a nice green salad, a large loaf of garlic French bread and a glass of Burgundy.

If you cannot get rid of the family skeleton,
you may as well make it dance.

George Bernard Shaw

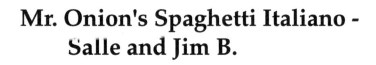

Mr. Onion's Spaghetti Italiano - Salle and Jim B.

2 cups cleaned and sliced mushrooms
1 *very* large red onion, sliced
3 6-1/2 oz. jars marinated artichoke hearts, keeping oil - I defuzz-chop
4 large cloves minced garlic
1/2 cup Extra Virgin olive oil
1/2 cup fresh chopped parsley
2-1/2 oz. can sliced black olives or use more if you wish.
Morton's to taste
1/2 cup grated Parmesan cheese
1 lb. spaghetti

Jim uses a touch of oregano, dill sometimes too, or basil (but you know I can't have any, and it still tastes wonderful without it, so.... do your own thing, folks)

Jim also adds zucchini, broccoli, green peppers—to change the base—once in a while.

Sauté the mushrooms and red onion in oil from the artichokes and olive oil.

Add the minced garlic and chopped up artichokes. If you are adding in the green pepper, zucchini, etc., do it here. Even some fresh, chopped ripe tomatoes.

Steam a bit of the broccoli, and add at last minute to the sauté , so it gets some of the flavors, but isn't so hard that your mother couldn't eat it—right, Granny?

Cook the spaghetti until just *al denté*. (I also add salt and a bit of oil to the cooking water for pasta.)

To the cooked and *drained* spaghetti, add the sautéed vegetables, black olives and parsley, mixing in well. Sprinkle in the Parmesan cheese. Season and serve. (I also add a bit of Morton's while sautéeing the vegetables.)

This is a dish that can be served hot or at room temperature.

We always sprinkle on *lots* of fresh grated Parmesan cheese and serve *tons* of garlic French bread, and a glass of Burgundy. Great company dish!

Clam Linguini - My Sister Joy

6 Tbs. butter
6 large cloves garlic, minced
2 cups fresh cleaned and sliced mushrooms
1 tsp. lemon juice
2 6-oz. cans chopped clams, drained but reserving the nectar*
2 6-oz. cans minced clams, drained but reserving the nectar
2 Tbs. butter
1 large whipping cream (In an emergency I use Half and Half, but it's not as
    rich.)
Morton's to taste
1/4 tsp. dried thyme leaves - crushed between your fingers, to bring out the
    flavor
1/4 tsp. nutmeg (optional; I omit)
2 to 3 drops of Tabasco
2 Tbs. dry sherry - *not* cooking sherry, which has salt
5 oz. fresh grated Parmesan cheese
1 beaten large egg yolk

*Or one large can from Costco or Sam's, saving the nectar

In a large frying pan, sauté the mushrooms in the *6 Tbs.* butter until partially cooked, adding the garlic last so it doesn't burn.

Add the lemon juice. Cook for a few seconds, then remove to a bowl. Add the reserved nectar only, not the clams--it makes them too tough.

In the same pan, melt the remaining, *2 Tbs.* butter and add the whipping cream, seasonings and sherry.

Cook on medium heat for five minutes to reduce the liquid down, and add *half* of the reserved clam nectar. Simmer for a few minutes, taste and season. Let simmer to reduce down for five more minutes. Then *slowly* add the Parmesan and eggs, to thicken the sauce.

Return the mushrooms and garlic and add clams to the pan just long enough to heat through*. Reseason, if, you think it needs it.

Serve over noodles of your choice: fettucini, angel hair, tortellini, etc., and with a large green salad, garlic French bread, a lovely glass of wine.

**Clams are very touchy, so just heat through, or you'll get chewy clams, ruining your dish.

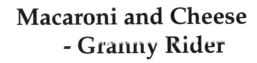

Macaroni and Cheese
- Granny Rider

 *This is the best next to **Kraft**, right, Todd? I know: Joy thinks so too! (I love it also, kids.)*

8 oz. macaroni, cooked, rinsed and drained
1-1/2 cup grated sharp Cheddar cheese
3 large eggs, beaten
1-1/2 cup milk or Half and Half to be really rich
1 tsp. Morton's
1/2 tsp. Accent
1 tsp. Worcestershire sauce
2 shakes Tabasco sauce - or more, if you like a touch of *hot*
1 Tbs. (approximately) butter*

Mix all the ingredients together well and pour into a butter baking dish.

Place in a shallow pan of water and bake at 350° for 40 to 45 minutes.

*Now, I always add a touch of butter. I just think it tastes better. I add it after I've rinsed the macaroni and mix it in well.

♥ ♥ ♥

Hungarian Turos Juisa - Oscar F.

Could any dish be easier for a Mom, faster and taste so good? To me, as an only child, the Fodor house was a haven of creature comforts: lots of kids—busy, noisy, talented, and a father who loved to cook. Being Hungarian, he made a lot of dishes that I considered the most wonderful dishes in the world! Even their peanut butter sandwiches tasted better. They always served this dish with tomato soup first and a green salad on the side. They always had dessert, too, and though I didn't and still don't care whether I eat it or not, there it was a must! I don't eat soup— or for that matter a lot of dishes—now, without recalling how I tried to wangle as many meals as I could at the Fodor house.

1 lb. plus lean bacon, cut in quarters, fried crisp, and drained
l pkg. jiffy corkscrew noodles
2 Tbs. butter
2 Tbs. reserved bacon grease
1 large carton large curd cottage cheese
Morton's to taste

Cook the noodles in a large pot of salted water with a drop of oil, so they don't stick, until al denté.

Drain and return the pasta to the pot. Add the butter and reserved bacon grease to the pot over the drained noodles.

Sprinkle with Morton's and add the cottage cheese, mixing everything together well.

Throw in the bacon*, mix in and serve *immediately*.

This reheats in a microwave or in the oven at 350° for 20 minutes. You can add more cottage cheese, and/or more bacon, if you have mostly noodles in leftovers.

Frances puts her leftovers on a cookie sheet the next day and makes the noodles crunchy for her grandkids. We're lucky if we have *any* left over— right, Mark!? And you're always welcome here....

*Jamey usually picks out most or all of the bacon, if I don't watch him closely, so I add more.

Green Tomato Pie - Joy M.

Make a 2-crust pie shell.

6 large green tomatoes
Butter
1/4 cup white sugar to 1/8 cup cinnamon
Dash of pumpkin spice or fresh grated nutmeg
Dark brown sugar - about 1/4 cup

Wash and dry the tomatoes and slice them about 1/4" thick—need we say *without* the cores?

Layer them in the bottom shell on up to rim and dot with butter.

Sprinkle the white sugar/cinnamon mixture over the top. Can add a dash of pumpkin spice or fresh grated nutmeg, and some dark brown sugar, as I do.

Put on the top crust, seal, and make design.

Bake at 375° for 35 minutes.

Serve with grated Cheddar cheese on top when it comes out of oven, if you wish. It melts faster than a slice.

You honestly cannot tell it is tomatoes. It *tastes* just like apple. And *yes*, it's good!

Baked Beans - Mrs. G., Peter's Mom

🐾 *I put everything in our big Crockpot early in the morning, on low, stirring occasionally, and let it go all day. I also taste-test during the day to see if I need more seasoning...and of course, it's smelling so good, and surely "a sample" won't be missed?*

6 slices bacon chopped in quarters (I use 3/4 lb, as Jamey picks it out for
    himself, and we would like some, too!
1 cup chopped white onion
1 large clove minced garlic
16-oz. can butter beans, drained
16-oz. can baby lima beans, drained
16-oz. can pork and beans in tomato sauce
16-oz. can garbanzo beans, drained
16-oz. can green beans, drained
3/4 cup Heinz (or other) catsup
1/2 cup light molasses (I use dark.)
1/4 cup dark brown sugar
1 Tbs. Worcestershire sauce
1 Tbs. French's regular mustard
Morton's to taste

Fry the bacon until crisp....Heck, do it your way!

Save the grease.

In a large pot, sauté the onions in about 3 tablespoons of bacon grease. Add the garlic. Don't let it get too brown, or it will turn bitter.

Add all the rest of ingredients, mixing together well.

Mrs. G. cooks this in her large electric frying pan, covered, stirring occasionally.

Bake at 375° for one hour, covered. Uncover for the last 15 minutes or so.

Good Old Baked Beans Deluxe

To a 16-oz. can of S &W baked beans add:

1 small chopped onion, sautéed in butter until limp
1 cup leftover ham*
1/2 cup chopped leftover cooked bacon, or real bacon bits - 1/4 cup
1/2 cup Heinz catsup
1 Tbs. French's mustard
1/3 cup dark brown sugar

* Sometimes I add 1 Tbs. of dark molasses, too

Simmer over medium/low for at least 1/2 hour or more. Your crockpot works fine for doing these early in the day.

Goulash Beans - Granny Rider

1 lb. lean ground beef
1 large yellow onion, chopped
14-oz. can tomato pieces with sauce
2 15-oz. cans pinto beans with jalapenos
6 slices (or more) of lean bacon, diced and fried crisp
1/2 cup dark brown sugar

In a medium pot that can go from the stove to the oven, brown the hamburger, then add the onions. Sauté together until onions are practically cooked.

Season with Morton's.

Mix in the remaining ingredients and bake at 350° for two hours.

Stir occasionally.

A woman's "last word" never is.

158

Sweet and Sour Bean Casserole - Granny Rider

3 strips to a 1/2 lb. lean bacon, chopped in quarters
1 lb. hamburger
1 large white onion, chopped
Morton's to taste
28-oz. can tomatoes/bits with sauce
2 15-1/2 oz. cans red beans—not kidney beans, drained
1/2 cup dark brown sugar

In a large pot, fry the bacon until crisp. Remove to a side dish. Drain out most of the bacon grease.

Add and brown the hamburger and onion together. Drain, and season with Morton's. Put the bacon back in.

Add the tomatoes, beans and brown sugar. Mix well.

Bake, stirring occasionally at 350° for 1 hour, covered.

Potatoes Romanoff

2 cups small curd cottage cheese
1 cup sour cream
1/4 cup green onions, minced
1 small clove garlic, minced
2 tsp. salt
5 cups potatoes, peeled and cut in small cubes
1/2 cup grated Jarlsberg cheese, Gruyere, Swiss or cheese of your choice

Preheat the oven to 350°.

Mix all the ingredients together and put in a garlic-buttered, 7" x 11" oblong dish.

Top with dots of butter.

Bake for 40 minutes, covered and ten minutes, uncovered—if you like it a bit brown . Test the potatoes for doneness, as sometimes they take longer to cook then others.

Corn Soufflé

Pinch of red pepper flakes
1/4 cup butter
1/4 cup Jarlsberg cheese, grated
1/4 lb. bacon, cut in quarters and fried crisp
10-oz. box frozen corn, thawed/drained
7-oz. can creamed corn
2 Tbs. flour
Morton's to taste
l cup Half and Half or whipping cream, for richer taste
3 slightly beaten large eggs - whites beaten separately and folded in last to give volume

Mix all the ingredients together, folding in the egg whites last.

Pour into a well-buttered soufflé dish.

Bake at 325° in a shallow pan with water for 1 hour and 15 minutes.

♥ *Variation*

I also crush some soda crackers, mix it with melted butter, and put it over the top as it bakes. (I use two tablespoons of butter to eight crackers). Cover for the first hour and then uncover for the last 15 minutes. Don't let get too brown.

♥ ♥ ♥

Chili - "Melly Belly's" Way

Now, "Melly Belly" is another one of those men who are dreams in the kitchen. Mel just loves to cook, and whenever we just happen to drop in for some of his warm and excellent hospitality, he is usually found whipping up one of his "specialities." I know some of the folks at Boeing are sure glad they work near him, 'cause he brings in little taste treats.

Mazola oil
1 large chopped white onion
3 cloves minced garlic
1 large green pepper, destemmed and seeded, chopped medium (chunky)
Hot chili peppers and jalapenos to taste
Morton's to taste
2 15-oz. cans pinto beans
2 15-oz. cans kidney beans
2 15-oz. cans Campbell's Tomato Soup
2 16-oz. cans peeled tomatoes

In a large pot, sauté the onion, garlic, green pepper and chili peppers lightly in the oil.

Season with a touch of Morton's.

Add the rest of the ingredients and let simmer for 1-1/2 hours, stirring occasionally.

Taste and reseason to your suit your palate. Bill and Mel love it hot!

(Yes, I'm sure you could add some chorizo, hot sausage or ground beef, lightly fried.)

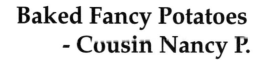

Baked Fancy Potatoes
- Cousin Nancy P.

This is just the best! And you'll be so grateful for the free time it gives you...

8 large peeled russet potatoes
8 oz. carton sour cream
8 oz. pkg. cream cheese, softened
Morton's to taste
1/4 cup butter - or a tad more if you like
Paprika, to sprinkle over the top

Boil the potatoes and mash them with all the other ingredients except the paprika.

In an oblong baking dish, garlic butter the sides and bottom. Or use just plain butter.

Spread the potato mixture in the dish and dot the top with butter.

Sprinkle with paprika.

Bake at 300 ° for 1/2 hour.

This can also be done the day before, then baked the next day. We use it for the holidays—it gives us more time with family and friends!

♥ Variation

Bev sometimes puts chives in hers, and tops it with canned French onions. You could also add 1/2 cup of grated Cheddar.

♥ ♥ ♥

Hash Brown Casserole

🐾 *This is a fast and easy dish for a Sunday Brunch. You can also prepare it the night or morning before and pop it into the oven the last hour while your meat is cooking. I sometimes substitute it for the mashed potatoes w/sour cream and cream cheese, which I also like to serve for my potato-loving family, when I am doing a large ham or salmon, no gravy item.*

32 oz. shredded potatoes, tater tots or frozen and thawed hash browns
1 cup butter, melted and separated into 1/2 cups
1 can Campbell's Cream of Chicken soup
1 cup grated, sharp Cheddar cheese
8 oz. sour cream
1 tsp. Morton's
1/2 small white onion, chopped
2 cups cornflakes

Garlic butter bottom and sides of a large (9" x 13") glass dish.

Put in the potatoes.

Pour 1/2 cup melted butter over the top.

Combine the cream of chicken soup, cheese, sour cream and Morton's and pour the mixture over the buttered potatoes.

Mix the cornflakes with the remaining 1/2 cup butter and top the potatoes with this mixture.

Bake at 350° for 40 minutes, *uncovered.*

Reheats great—*if* there is any left!

Scalloped Potatoes - Mom

4 large potatoes of your choice (I use white potatoes, not red)
Butter
1 cup chopped leftover ham
1 cup (or more) grated sharp Cheddar cheese
1/4 cup Gruyere (if available) or Jarlsburg cheese
1/4 cup+ Parmano cheese
Morton's to taste
2 cups whipping cream or Half and Half (Milk is fine, but it isn't as nice
**   and rich)**

Garlic butter a large 9" x 13" baking dish.

Scrub the potatoes. Cut in thin slices. Put a layer down.

Dot with butter and sprinkle part of ham and cheese, and *some of the cream* and seasoning over the top.

Add another row of potato slices with dots of butter and repeat the layers.

Pour the *remaining cream* over the top.

Bake at 325° for 1 hour or until done to your liking. I like a touch of brown.

♥ *Variations*

Sometimes we get fancy and use Cougar Gold Cheese from WSU College. It's the *best*. You can call the College and they will mail it; some local stores—QFC— carry it .

We also like, along with the Cheddar, crumbles of blue cheese and toasted hazelnuts on top, like they did for the '84 IACP Convention Dinner held Seattle. Fancy, fancy!

Or—*if Jamey isn't around*—some chopped onion is great. Sauté the onion—in a bit of butter first for better flavor, 1/2 cup water, and 1 Tbs. sugar—until all the liquid is gone.

Yams - Micha E.

4 large yams (or sweet potatoes —*right*, Joan?)
1/4 lb. (1 cube) butter
1 cup dark brown sugar
Toasted pecans (optional*)

Cook the yams with their skins in boiling, salted water until tender (a fork goes in easily). Drain and let cool.

Peel and cut the yams in long slices, or in circles.

In a large frying pan, melt the butter.

Add the brown sugar. Mix in well. (If I'm in a hurry, I melt the sugar and butter together).

Place the yam slices in the pan. Spoon the butter/brown sugar sauce over the top.

Cook on medium-low for one to one and a half hours. Turn occasionally so the sauce will coat all the pieces.

Or butter a glass dish and put half the sauce on bottom, add the yams, then the other half of butter/sugar on top.

*I also add toasted pecans to my layers of sliced yams. I pour the sauce over the top of pecans for a caramel effect. *Watch so sugar doesn't burn.*

Bake, covered, at 325° for one hour and uncovered for a half hour. Again—watch so the sugar doesn't burn.

Reheats in microwave.

So good with ham, turkey, pork roast and lamb!

Baked Onions

8 medium sized yellow onions, sliced in rings 1/4" thick
1 Tbs. *each* butter and Mazola oil
1/2 cup Jarlsberg cheese
1/4 cup grated Parmesan or Parmano cheese
1/2 cup whipping cream
1/4 cup dry sherry
Morton's to taste

Sauté the onions in the butter and oil until limp. Add 1/4 cup of water to partly steam them done. This takes out the harshness of the onions' bite. Throw in a dash of sugar.

Combine the cheese with the cream, sherry and Morton's.

Butter a 7" x 11" baking dish. (I use a fancy baking dish; it makes the food look and taste better!)

Pour the cream and cheese mixture over the onions. Mix and pour into buttered dish.

Bake *uncovered* at 375° for 15 to 20 minutes until top gets bubbly and brown.

♥ *Variation*

You could play with this one and hollow out larger onions and stuff with the cheeses and chopped out centers. Maybe add some toasted nuts? A different cheese?

Fried Tomatoes - My Dad, Carl Rider

Bobba always loved this dish. I thought everyone got them for breakfast with bacon and eggs! I remember so well how he would sit at the dining room table—alone at the head of the table, with his music playing—enjoying this dish. He didn't like to be bothered with small children, but would sometimes let me dip a piece of his toast— cut in finger strips—in the center of his eggs, which were cooked sunny side up. Popping the egg-dripping toast into my mouth I would stand there like a little lady, quietly, beside him —for two seconds! I would later hear how hard I was to feed. A bit of bacon was always added in, as I ran off to play—not to disturb his meal.

Big red, almost ripe tomatoes, cut in 1/4" slice
1/4 to 1/2 cup flour
Morton's to taste
1 Tbs. butter
1 Tbs. Mazola oil

Carefully dust both sides of the tomato slices in a plate of flour —seasoned with Morton's to taste.

Fry the tomatoes in the butter and oil until they begin to brown.

Serve on the side with bacon and eggs, hash browns and toast.

This is *very, very English*, but so was he.

*In much later years, I would find, he was always there when the chips were down... And he would place them right side up again! How very much he was cheated out of watching his grandsons grow up. He would have enjoyed their energy. Oh, **life**: you questionable, unanswerable thing!*

French Green Bean Casserole

16-oz. can French-cut green beans, drained
5-oz. can water chestnuts, drained, rinsed and chopped fine
1 cup celery, chopped fine
1 cup white onion, chopped fine
11-1/2 oz. can Campbell's Cream of Mushroom soup
1 cup grated sharp Cheddar cheese (optional)
French-fried onion rings

Mix together the beans, water chestnuts, chopped celery and onion.

Spread in well-buttered casserole dish—I use my garlic butter if I have some on hand.

Pour over the mushroom soup with 1/2 cup water mixed in. I usually add the grated Cheddar, too.

Top with the onion rings.

Bake for 45 minutes to an hour at 350°, covered. Bake, uncovered, for the last ten minutes. Watch that the French-fried onions don't get too brown.

Broccoli Casserole - Cousin Nancy P.

We've done this recipe with frozen vegetable mix, cauliflower, and other specialities via the frozen food section.

16-oz. pkg. frozen broccoli, chopped (If you want to use fresh, cook this dish
    longer.)
1 can Campbell's Cream of Mushroom soup
3/4 cup grated *sharp* Cheddar cheese
1 egg, beaten
1/4 cup milk
1/2 cup mayonnaise
2 Tbs. melted butter (or just drop softened pieces in and mix)
Morton's to taste

Mix all the ingredients together in large bowl.

Transfer to a well-buttered casserole dish. (Once again, I would get out my garlic butter!)

♥ *Topping*

Saltine crackers
Walnuts or almonds
Butter

Top with eight broken up saltine crackers you have browned in butter, lightly. I also add some walnuts or almonds—browned in butter—to the crackers if I have some on hand (unless *Benji*'s coming – he's allergic to nuts. …I always check.)

Bake at 350° for 40 minutes, uncovered. Watch the top, so it doesn't get too brown.

Eggplant Parmesan - Robin R.

2 *medium* eggplants - not big ones, as they are tough
2 large eggs (might need more, so keep some handy)
1/2 cup flour
Peanut oil
Olive oil
2 large cloves garlic, minced
1-6 oz. can tomato paste
1 16-oz. can tomatoes and bits
1 stalk of celery, chopped fine
Morton's to taste
16 oz. Mozzarella cheese, sliced
Fresh grated Parmesan cheese

Peel and slice the eggplants into 1/4" pieces. Lay the slices on a paper towel, and let them drain for about 30 minutes, *weighted down* a plate or pan.

Whip the eggs in a shallow bowl.

Put the flour in another large shallow bowl.

Dip the drained and patted dry eggplant slices first in the flour, then in the egg and back in the flour.

Have a frying pan ready with a little peanut oil, heated medium/high. Fry the coated eggplant until they're brownish on both sides. Put them on paper towels and season with Morton's.

Now make a *meatless spaghetti sauce*:

Brown the garlic in the olive oil and add all the other ingredients *except* the cheese. Simmer for a 1/2 hour and *add a bit more liquid* if you think it's too thick since you don't want this to dry up.

Garlic butter the bottom and sides of a 9" x 13" oblong dish. Layer first the sauce, then the eggplant, slices of Mozzarella cheese, then sauce, eggplant, cheese and more sauce over the top sprinkled with fresh grated Parmesan cheese. (Now I sprinkle the Parmesan over *each* layer of eggplant, because I like the taste.

Cover and bake at 400° for 1/2 hour and 10 minutes, uncovered. Serve alone, with garlic French bread, or as a side dish with roasted chicken breast, lamb, or meat you like.

Spinach Casserole - Frances F.

3 10-oz. pkgs. frozen chopped spinach - thawed and drained.
10-oz. can water-packed artichoke bottoms, rinsed, drained and cut into
    quarters.
1 tsp. lemon juice
1 Tbs. dry sherry
6-oz. pkg. whipped cream cheese
2 Tbs. mayonnaise
6 Tbs. Half and Half

(I add 1 cup sautéed, sliced mushrooms (1/2 lb. fresh) and crisp bacon, cut
    in quarters)

Mix all the ingredients together and put in garlic-buttered dish.

Bake at 375° for 20 minutes.

Leeks Argentine Style - Micha E.

3 large leeks, well cleaned
Extra Virgin olive oil
White wine vinegar
Salt and pepper to taste

Split the leeks down the center and wash them *well*. They get dirt between layers.

Sauté in Extra Virgin olive oil. Add a touch of white wine vinegar and salt/pepper. Maybe a touch more olive oil—*you* decide, but you don't want them *oily*. Let cool.

A slice of Black Forest ham, and one of these leeks on unsalted, buttered French bread would be wonderful!

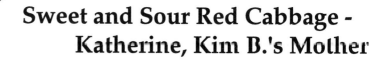

Sweet and Sour Red Cabbage - Katherine, Kim B.'s Mother

1 medium head red cabbage, cored, shredded and washed well (1-1/2 lb.)
2 Tbs. vinegar or lemon juice
4 slices diced bacon
1/4 cup dark brown sugar, packed
1/2 cup water
1/4 cup red wine vinegar
1 tsp. salt
1/8 tsp. pepper
2 Tbs. flour
1 small white onion, sliced and sautéed in butter

In a large pot, cook the shredded cabbage in salt water for about ten minutes. Add the vinegar or lemon juice to keep color. Drain. Put the cabbage back in the pot.

Fry the bacon crisp. Remove, drain, and pour all except about one tablespoon of bacon grease from the skillet.

Add the water, wine vinegar, dark sugar, salt/pepper (I use a few shakes of Morton's instead) and onion. Cook, stirring frequently, sprinkling in the flour, for about five minutes or until the mixture thickens.

Add the bacon and sauce to the large pot with the cabbage. Stir together gently on medium/low to heat through.

Serve with roast pork, pork chops, ribs, etc.

A good woman inspires a man,
A brilliant woman interests him,
A beautiful woman fascinates him,
But a sympathetic woman gets him.

Helen Rowland

Infallible Rice - Granny Rider

1 small white onion, minced
2 Tbs. butter
1 cup long-grained rice
2 cups heated canned or homemade chicken broth

In a medium-size pan that can go into the oven, sauté the onion in the butter until it's transparent.

Add the rice and broth. Bring to a boil and put on the lid.

Put in it in the oven at 325° for 20 minutes.

It's quick and easy and you don't have to watch it. It does it all itself.

Zucchini Bake

4 medium zucchini, scrubbed, trimmed and sliced
1/2 tsp. Morton's
1/2 cup white onion, chopped fine
3 Tbs. butter
Mornay sauce (*see* Soups, Salads and Sauces)
1/2 cup melted butter
2 cups cornflakes

Drain the zucchini slices in a colander, *sprinkled with salt* to remove the water, about 30 minutes.

Sauté the onion and then the zucchini lightly in butter. Layer in a garlic-buttered baking dish.

Pour over the Mornay sauce.

Top with the cornflakes which have been tossed in the melted butter.

Bake at 400° for 20 minutes until browning and bubbly.

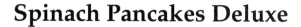

Spinach Pancakes Deluxe

2 10-oz. pkgs. frozen, chopped spinach - thawed, or 2 bunches fresh,
    cleaned, rinsed
1/2 cup heavy cream
Pinch of Morton's
1 cup sliced mushrooms
1 Tbs. *each* butter and Mazola oil
Splash of white wine or champagne and a squeeze of lemon
1/2 lb. bacon, cut in quarters and fried crispy
2 Tbs. Mazola or other oil of your choice
1/2 small white onion chopped fine - 1/4 cup
3 Tbs. flour
2 large eggs, slightly beaten
Morton's
1/2 cup peanut oil

Mix the spinach with the cream and Morton's.

Sauté the mushrooms in the butter and Mazola oil with the wine or champagne and lemon.

Fry the bacon until crispy and drain.

Heat the *peanut* oil in a large frying pan.

Mix the spinach, sautéed mushrooms, bacon and the rest of the ingredients together and pour the batter into the pan to make little dollar-sized pancakes or larger ones. Watch them carefully so they don't get too overdone. Turn *once*.

♥ Serving Variations

Serve with hollandaise sauce over the top with breast of chicken, pork chops, lamb, etc.

Throw in some crumbles of Feta cheese and a squeeze of lemon, if accompanying the lamb.

A Cheddar cheese sauce, drizzled over the top (you don't want too much) is nice, with some toasted almonds and chopped black olives. Let the family or guests pour more sauce if they wish.

Corn Casserole
- Everyone's Favorite

1 small box Jiffy Cornmeal Muffin mix
1/3 cup milk
1 large egg, beaten
17-oz. can creamed corn

Combine all these ingredients, mixing well. Pour into a garlic-buttered 9" x 13" oblong dish.

♥ *Topping Variations*

Now there are two or three different ways to do the topping/filling:

♥ Carefully drop, in clumps, *two 15-oz. cans of Stagg chile with green chiles* all over the top of the above mixture.

♥ Sauté *one pound of hamburger*. Drain, add in and simmer one package of *taco sauce* with 1/4 cup water. Add one 15-oz. can of drained, *kidney beans* in the corner of the pan, with one tablespoon of *butter*—mashing it into the beans. Mix everything together, cooking for 10 minutes. Drop in clumps over the above mixture.

♥ Add *cooked chopped chicken breasts* to *taco sauce*. Simmer for 10 minutes. Throw in some *minced green pepper, chopped onion, jalapeno or salsa*, if you like.

On top of the filling, carefully spread a mixture of:

8-oz. carton sour cream
1 cup sharp Cheddar cheese, grated
1/2 cup Monterey Jack cheese, grated.

Bake at 425° for 30 minutes until it's bubbling up the sides, browning the edges.

This is great for parties, and reheats wonderfully. I've never frozen it, as there is *never* any left.

I had an 80th birthday party for my mom, Edith, and with all the other food I put out, this was gone in the flash of an eye. Which variation did I cook? The one with the canned chile—her favorite. I was rushed for time. This can be done ahead.

Quiche Zerhire

♥ *Pastry Shell*

1-1/4 cups flour
1/4 tsp. salt
2 Tbs. Crisco
4 Tbs. *butter*
1/4 cup cold water

In a Cuisinart, mix all the ingredients together until they just start to hold together. Remove to a plastic wrap and refrigerate for 30 minutes, while you make the filling.

♥ *Filling*

1 bunch fresh spinach - cleaned and destemmed
2 Tbs. butter
2 Tbs. Mazola oil
1/4 cup or 1 small white onion, chopped fine
1 cup mushrooms, cleaned and chopped
1 Tbs. brandy or cream sherry
Squeeze of lemon
Morton's
1 cup *Black Forest* or *honey baked* ham
1/2 lb. lean bacon, cut in quarters and fried crisp
4 eggs
1 cup whipping cream
1/4 cup *each* Gruyere, sharp Cheddar, and Parmesan cheese
Grated Parmesan cheese to sprinkle on top

Sauté the spinach in the butter and Mazola with the onion and mushrooms, brandy or cream sherry with a squeeze of lemon, and sprinkle to taste with Morton's. I usually have some leftover Black Forest or honey baked ham to add in with some crisp bacon, when the vegetables are done.

Whisk together the eggs, whipping cream, and Morton's to taste, then mix in all the cheeses. I combine this with the other ingredients and let the filling sit while I partially bake the crust.

Remove the chilled dough from the refrigerator. Roll it out on a marble slab or between wax paper. Fit it into a quiche dish and put an oiled foil square over the crust with a layer of dried beans.

Bake at 400° for 10 minutes. Take it out and remove the beans and foil. Prick the dough with a fork on the bottom and sides. Put it back into the oven at 375° for 10 minutes.

Remove and pour the filling into the crust. It will nearly overflow. I sprinkle a tad bit more Parmesan on top and bake for 30 minutes and/or until the top begins to brown.

Let the quiche sit for five minutes—*ten if you can*— to firm up a bit. Cut and *enjoy*!

This can be served hot or at room temperature. It reheats well in the microwave and freezes well if you want to save it for weekend company.

Can be served for dinner with a glass of wine and a salad, too.

There just won't be anything left—right, Todd and Kevin? Bill likes to take the quiche to work (Who said that "Real men don't eat quiche")?

(Jamey thinks it's OK—but then he doesn't like leftovers. Oh, does that man have a lot to learn!)

Jamey has since moved on his own...Now, my refrigerator looks real good! Thank heavens for refrigerators, Moms who love to cook, and kids who are always hungry! Do you need any apple pie to take down to work? Grandma's a little bored...Oh, you'd rather have cinnamon rolls? Well, she'll be right on it—for nine thirty or so delivery in the morning. We love that baby!

♥ ♥ ♥

Red Beans and Rice - Kimmie F.

This really isn't anything my kids would try, but it is very good—and with cornbread and a green vegetable it's a great meal! And of course my husband Bill eats it! What a guy!

1/4 cup Mazola oil, plus I add at least 1 Tbs. butter
l medium white onion, chopped
3 medium garlic cloves, minced
1/2 (or more) chopped green pepper (I use only about a 1/4 cup)
2 cups leftover ham, pork, pork butt, or ham hocks already cooked
1/2 tsp. or more, to taste, crushed dried red pepper flakes
1 cup water
1 can chicken broth
16-oz. can of kidney beans, drained
Tabasco sauce
3 cups of white rice

In a large pot:

Sauté the onion, green pepper and then garlic in the Mazola/butter.

Add the meat pieces* and sauté them lightly. Make sure the garlic doesn't get brown and turn bitter. Add the red pepper flakes and Morton's to taste.

Put the cup of water and chicken stock, along with the kidney beans, into the pot. You might need a bit more liquid. Throw in a dash or two of Tabasco. Cook for at least 1-1/2 hours on medium/low to marry the flavors. Keep checking the liquid; you don't want it to dry out. (I put mine in the Crockpot and let it just simmer away.)

*If using ham hocks or ham bone, remove the meat from the stock just before finishing. Take the meat off the bone, chop it up and return the pieces to the pot. (Leave out the bones, right?!)

Taste and reseason with Tabasco or hot sauce of your choice before serving. This dish also reheats and freezes well.

Now, Kim just serves her red beans over the rice, but I cook up my rice and add it to the pot—with the boned meat, and with just a touch more liquid if necessary–and heat through.

♥ ❤ ♥

Zucchini Fritters

1 lb. zucchini, unpeeled and grated
1 tsp. of finely chopped onions, sautéed in butter
1 tsp. of finely chopped parsley
1 cup buttermilk pancake mix of your choice
Morton's to taste
1 egg, beaten
1/2 cup Mazola oil

Combine everything but the oil.

Heat oil to 375° and drop batter by tablespoons into the oil.

Turn once. Cook until golden.

Drain on paper towel and serve.

Scalloped Pineapple

 This is excellent with ham and for the holidays!

3/4 stick butter, softened
2 large eggs
2 cups sugar
1 large can of pineapple chunks, drained and juice reserved
8 slices of cubed day-old bread

Cream butter, eggs and sugar. Add pineapple chunks, reserved juice and bread. Mix all ingredients.

Bake in a greased casserole pan at 350° for half an hour.

Excerpts From:

The Empty Book

Filled with the Treasures of My Life

For Janet
From Daddy

He was very ill in the hospital... Angry, frightened, bored, and bedridden: A man who was always in control, now, no longer at the helm of his boat, facing his own mortality. So, I gave him this blank-paged book and said, "Write me the Treasures of your Life. Your Shakespeare, poems, the laws you've lived by and the things you would have me and mine **Intole.***"*

This was his Gift...which I hope will help you, as it has helped those of us who have been fortunate to wander through its many pages over the years. May they bring you peacefulness in good or trying times. God bless.

Daddy 1901–1970

A big, strong man
A hand to hold,
A voice that
Eased my fears.

A dog so big,
A guard so safe,
We shared this man,
did we!

A room filled with
Music, wisdom and faith.
Where problems were settled
and peace entered in.

And quietly, together…
We would face the world
yet unknown.

…Janet

From Daddy with love

Bobba with his Airedale, "Gizmo"

From the moment they saw each other, Gizmo was a fixture at Bobba's side, as if an extension of himself, and you always felt as if she understood everything he said and everything that was going on. She followed him everywhere, too; eventually, to their greener pastures, vast flower gardens, bluer skies and I hope a little more peace and quiet, with music—beautiful, beautiful music—because she was his faithful companion to the end, and belonged at his side only.

The following pages hold comments and truths of
GREAT IMPORTANCE
in the Art of Living...

Read Slowly, Chew and Digest...

From Daddy with love

Last night as I lay sleeping
A dream came fluttering down,
Its cobweb clothes in keeping
With far-off slumber town.

The little dream was shivering
With cold but not with fear;
It climbed beneath my bedding
And whispered in my ear.

It told me how the dreamlets
Play by day and night,
And bathe in silver streamlets
And pools of shining light.

It sang to me of flowers
Blooming so bright and gay
And birds that sing for hours
And never fly away.

We both of us were sleepy
The dream could not remain
So it climbed upon a moonbeam
That whisked it home again.

Carl H. Rider

Sometimes it was very hard for me to get to sleep. At those times my Daddy would sit up and tell me stories or sing to me. This poem always made me sleep better.

*There is always music
among the trees in the garden,
But our hearts must be very quiet
to hear it.*

Minnie Aumonier

Doesn't this remind you of your favorite hymn? "I come to the garden alone, while the dew is still on the roses, and the voice I hear, falling on my ear, the Voice of God discloses...."

Bobba could always be found sitting in his garden, watching the birds and bees feed. He always had a verse or thought, which would flow from his lips, being read from the pages, in the memories of his mind. And you too, would be caught up in it...Then, somehow, the spell would be broken and you would return once more to this world.

From Daddy with love

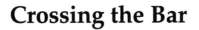

Crossing the Bar

Sunset and evening star,
and one clear call for me!
And may there be no moaning of the bar,
when I put out to sea.

But such a tide as morning seems asleep,
too full for sound and foam
When that which draw from out the boundless deep,
turns again home.

Twilight and evening bell,
and after that the dark!
And may there be no sadness of farewell
when I embark;

For 'tho from out our bourne of time and space
the flood may bear me far,
I hope to see my Pilot, Face to Face,
when I have to cross the bar.

Alfred Lord Tennyson

Bobba was an orderly man who made a daily list of things to do. I see in the passage of time that both I and my children, have acquired this trait. It makes one's days a little more easy when referred to. "Crossing the Bar" was written on the manila folder he left to spell out for us how to run the house with him no longer there to guide us, take care of us, or do for us.

We cannot change the direction of the wind...
But we can adjust our sails.

The Voyager

The wind came blustering out of the East
To push sailboats out of the way.
The Voyager turned, not dismayed in the least
And decided to stay.

We slackened the sheet to ease her sail
For the strain was a danger sore;
But she pointed her prow to the teeth of the gale
And challenged the wind for more.

Dainty, capricious and full of zest
Is my Mistress of the Seas:
And sweet as the curve of a maiden's breast
Is the swell of her jib in the breeze.

Carl H. Rider

Mom could see Dad's beautiful sailboat, The Voyager, from our front yard. With her binoculars, she used to watch him tack back and forth across Lake Washington with all the motor boats and skiers zooming around him as he went along merrily—sails billowing, stretched tight by the wind. Their whiteness so stark against the blue/green of water, land and sky… an easy path to follow but—for Mom— only from the safety of the house, for she could not swim and that fear kept her body landside while her heart went sailing with him.

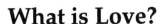 *From Daddy with love*

What is Love?

Love is, above all, the Gift of Oneself... and
Love is a Strange Thing

It is a flower so delicate
that a touch will bruise it,
And so strong
that nothing will stop its growth.

How often we miss love —
By a wrong gesture
By an unspoken word
By not keeping silent at the right time.

How easily we lose love,
By interference of others
By lack of money
By a quarrel over nothing.

Yet we cannot live without love.

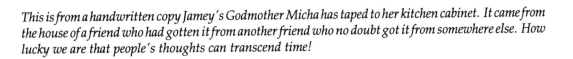

This is from a handwritten copy Jamey's Godmother Micha has taped to her kitchen cabinet. It came from the house of a friend who had gotten it from another friend who no doubt got it from somewhere else. How lucky we are that people's thoughts can transcend time!

Love...

A Love Poem

If all the girls in all the land
were standing in a line,
And you were at the farthest end,
O dearest one of mine—
And they told me I might choose
but one or always live alone;
And only once might scan that line
to choose one for mine own—
Unhesitating I would stride,
although the end grew near,
And never could be satisfied
'til I found you, my dear.

If you were offered as a slave
Then I would sell my land;
All I could borrow, steal and save
would meet the price demand.
Then I would lead you by the chain
And far away we'd go;
But I would set you free again
Because I love you so.

The beauty that was yours, it seemed
Was mine from year to year;
'Til You had gone, I never dreamed
How much I'd miss you, dear.
For Heaven once an Angel sent
And gave her all to me;
I thought He gave; He only lent;
You're just a memory.
There are other girls, both young and free,
And other men, it's true
But there was only one of me,
And only one of you.

Carl Rider

Love...

O Mistress Mine

O Mistress Mine, where are you roaming?
O stay and hear; your true love's coming,
That can sing both high and low;
Trip no further, pretty sweeting,
Journeys end in lovers meeting,
Every wise man's son doth know.

What is Love? 'Tis not hereafter;
Present mirth hath present laughter;
What's to come is still unsure;
In delay there lies no plenty;
So come kiss me, sweet and twenty,
Youth's a stuff will not endure.

Twelfth Night, William Shakespeare

♥

Madrigal

Take, O take those lips away
that so sweetly were forsworn,
and those eyes, the break of day.
Light that do mislead the morn
and my kisses bring again—
Measure for measure,
Seals of love, but sealed in vain.

William Shakespeare

Love...

A slumber did my spirit seal:
I had no human fears:
She seemed a thing that could not feel
The touch of earthly years.

No motion has she now, no force;
She neither hears nor sees;
Rolled round in earth's diurnal course,
With rocks, and stones, and trees.

William Wordsworth

♥

My Wife

Trusty, dusky, vivid, true,
With eyes of gold and bramble-dew
Steel-true and blade straight
the Great Artificer made my mate.

Honor, anger, valor, fire,
A love that life could never tire,
Death quench nor evil stir,
The mighty Master gave to her.

Teacher, tender, comrade, wife,
A fellow-farer true through life.
Heart whole and soul free
the August Father gave to me.

Robert Louis Stevenson

From Daddy with love

Love...

You have known happiness;
The Prince's arms were round you,
Cinderella, his kisses on your lips;
The Gods themselves cannot take that from you.

Jerome K. Jerome

♥

Winter must be Cold for those with no Warm Memories.

♥

When I thought of my Beloved
My body seemed Weightless,
As if I walked on Air.

♥

She was so Beautiful, so Wondrous Beautiful;
It was as if an Angel had entered the room,
And all else became Plain and Earthly.

♥

Her faults add spice to her virtues,
For it is the many facets of the diamond that gives it its sparkle.

Love...

To Ophelia...

Doubt thou the stars are fire;
Doubt that sun doth move,
Doubt truth to be a liar;
But never doubt I love.

O Dear Ophelia, I am ill at these
numbers; I have not the art to
reckon my groans; but that I love
thee best, O most best, believe it. Adieu.

Thine evermore, most dear lady,
Whilst this machine is to him, Hamlet.

Hamlet, Act II, William Shakespeare

♥

When I am dying...

When I am dying, lean over me
tenderly, softly.

Stoop, as the yellow roses droop;
In the wind from the South.

So may I, when I wake,
If there be an awakening,

Feel that which lulled me to sleep:
The touch of your lips on my mouth.

From "Til I Wake", Indian Love Lyrics

Love...

A Woman's Last Word

Let's contend no more, Love.
Strive nor weep:
All be as before, Love
—Only sleep.

Be a god, and hold me
with a charm!
Be a man, and fold me
with thine arm.

Teach me, only teach, Love!
As I ought.
I will speak thy speech, Love,
Think thy thought.

Must a little weep, Love,
(Foolish me)
And so fall asleep, Love
Loved by thee.

Robert Browning

Children...

We remain forever Children:
We are always running after New Toys.

Anatole France

♥

As I look back, I have only Partly Lived.

♥

It is well we cannot foresee the future:
There are few boys of Fourteen
Who would not be ashamed of themselves at Forty.

♥

Youth is Wasted on the Young.

Mark Twain

Health...

To have good health,
A rich man should eat like a poor man, and
Consume no food or drink except
That which will benefit him.
He should avoid excess.

♥

Better is the poor man being sound of body
Than the rich man who is afflicted.

Ecclesiastes

♥

Your dog will turn his nose away from
tobacco smoke, alcohol, and spiced foods.
He is interested in foods that are good for him.

♥

In personal hygiene,
most animals are more particular
than the average man.

Worry...

Obsessed by worry?
Need a real problem to worry about?
Put a rock in your shoe.

♥

Mark Twain once said,
"In my Life I had many worries,
most of which never happened."

♥

Write down the worry of today on a piece of paper.
Read it tomorrow and it will seem trivial.

♥

Life is ruled by fear of things that never happen.

♥

Problems seem worse at night.
In the daylight of tomorrow, They are often less serious.

♥

It does no good to worry.
The neurotic person worries himself to despair,
which accomplishes nothing.
He spins his wheels.
As problems arise, consider what to do, and take action.
If you can't figure what to do,
Turn to a more experienced person for discussion and advise.

Knowledge...

The Knowledge that one is correctly attired
gives us a sense of well-being
that Religion is powerless to bestow.

Jerome K. Jerome

♥

Cast no dirt into the well that gives you water.

♥

Our joke is generally another's pain.
The man who sits on a tack rarely joins in the laugh.

♥

It is not what men think of you.
It is what you are that counts.

♥

What doeth it profit a Man, if he loses his immortal soul?

♥

We have a way of living through everything—
Triumph, adversity, poverty, illness, an unhappy marriage.
Nothing is impossible to Pains and Patience.

♥

We are forever wanting what we have not,
only to find, when we have it, that it is not what we wanted.

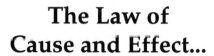

The Law of
Cause and Effect...

Results follow actions.
If you jump out the window, you will drop.
If you want wheat to come up, you must plant wheat.
It is impossible for any other result to take place.

♥

Therefore, if you desire a certain result,
Do the things that will make it possible, even inevitable.

♥

Though most of Man's problems are of his own making,
He often blames them on Providence.

♥

Let George do it. But remember:
George will bill you later.

♥

A Problem Well Stated is Half Solved.

♥

When two men exchange dollars, they are even:
When they exchange ideas, each doubles his holdings.

♥

If men must learn wisdom by violence today,
Then who can expect that there will be a tomorrow?

♥

Good Fences make Good Neighbors.

From Daddy with love

Great Truths...

The greatest Truth of all time is called
the Golden Rule:

Do unto others
as you would have them do unto you.

This is stated in the Christian Creed ,
and with slightly varied wording
in ALL the major religions.

♥

Polonius' Advice to His Son:

Those friends thou hast, and their adotition tried,
grapple them to thy soul with hoofs of steel;
But do not dull thy palm with entertainment
of each new-hatched unfledged comrade.
Costly thy habit as thy purse can buy,
But not expressed in fancy: rich not gaudy;
For the apparel oft proclaims the man.
Neither a borrower nor a lender be;
For loan of loses both itself and friend,
And borrowing dulls the edge of husbandry.
This above all: **To Thine Own Self Be True**
And it must follow, as the night the day,
Thou canst not then be false to any man.

William Shakespeare
Hamlet, Act I

Thoughts...

Caliban, a crude monster,
is explaining a beautiful dream...

And then in dream, the clouds methought would open
And show riches ready to drop upon me.
That, when I wakened, I cried—to dream again.

From the Tempest, William Shakespeare

♥

I suppose we have all had such a dream,
where we were reluctant to wake up...
I tried to hold on to the dream 'till it just melted away...

Carl H. Rider

♥

Details change constantly
Materials things decay,
But Principles are Eternal.
Might it not be, that it is the Material Things,
Deceiving us as being All-Important,
Which are really only a Dream?

Carl H. Rider

♥

A little philosophy inclineth a man's mind to Atheism,
But a depth in philosophy brings a man's mind to Religion.
I had rather believe all the Fables in the Legend
Than that this Universal Frame is without a Mind.

Francis Bacon

From Daddy with love

Death...

He leapt to arms unbidden.
Unneeded, over-bold;
His face by earth is hidden,
His heart in earth is cold.

Curse on the reckless daring
that could not wait the call,
the proud fantastic bearing
that would be first to fall!

O tears of human passion
Blur not the image true,
This was not folly's fashion,
This was the Man We Knew.

Sir Henry (John) Newbolt

♥

Grow old along with me
The last is yet to be
The last of life, for which the first was made
Our times are in His hand
Who saith a whole I planned?
Youth sees but part
Trust God, see all, nor be afraid.

Rabbi Ezra Benezra

♥

I strove with none, for none was worth my strife;
Nature I loved, and next to nature, art;
I warmed both hands before the fire of life;
It sinks, and I am ready to depart.

Walter Savage Landor

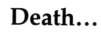

Death...

The Celestial Surgeon

If I have faltered more or less
in my great task of happiness;
If I have moved among my race
and shown no glorious morning face;
If beams from happy human eyes
have moved me not;
If morning skies, books, and my food, and summer rain
knocked on my sullen heart in vain;
Lord, thy most pointed pleasure take
and stab my spirit broad awake;
Or Lord, if too obdurate I, choose
thou before that Spirit die,
A piercing pain, a killing sin,
And to my dead heart run them in!

Robert Louis Stevenson

♥

Cowards die many times before their time:
The Valiant only taste of death but once.

Julius Caesar, William Shakespeare

♥

It seems most strange that men should fear Death,
seeing that Death, a necessary end, will come when it will come.

Julius Caesar, William Shakespeare

♥

Yea, though I walk through the Valley of the Shadow of Death
I will fear no evil, for Thou art with me.

From the Twenty-Third Psalm

Miscellaneous Passages...

Of the Spoken Word, I am the Slave;
of the Unspoken Word, the Master.

♥

Had I but served my God
with half the zeal I served my king,
He would not in mine age
Have left me naked to mine enemies.

Cardinal Wolsey,
in Shakespeare's King Henry VIII

♥

Sticks and Stones may break my Bones
But Names will never hurt me.

G.F. Northall

♥

Marriage can be the Grave of Love, if we take each other for granted. Why shave on
Sunday? There is no one there but his wife. The secret of keeping Romance alive is
to treat her as you did during Courtship.

♥

We love those with human interest, and human failing—not the faultless.

♥

I wept because I had no shoes, until I saw a man who had no feet.

Old Persian Proverb

♥

Avoid using Generalities—including this one.

♥

Statistics can be used unjustly, to prove various conclusions.

Miscellaneous Passages...

Man who does not have a smiling face,
should not open a shop.

An Old Chinese Proverb

♥

What you see in another's Eyes
Is usually more truthful than his Words.

♥

He who overlooks a fault, invites the commission of another.

♥

There is nothing Stronger in the world than Gentleness.

♥

Do not betray, even to your friends,
too much of your real purposes and thoughts:
Ask questions rather than express opinions.
Offer data and information rather than judgements and beliefs.

Francis Bacon

♥

Never brag:
It is better that others should mention your accomplishments.

♥

A Man of Intelligence would often be at a Loss,
were it not for the Company of Fools.

From Daddy with love

On Winston Churchill...

"He marshalled the English language,
and took it into Battle,
at a time when they had Nothing Else."

Edward R. Murrow

♥

Winston Churchill was invited to
address the students an English
equivalent of high school. All the
students were assembled and waiting.
His fiery words snapped pencils in their
hands. His address consisted of six words only:

Never give up. Never! Never! Never!

♥

The Prime Minister was also famous for this short command:

"Having gained your point, quit talking!"

Bobba loved Winston Churchill, and these are passages he would repeat to me as I grew up. Remember...
I was very hard to get to sleep, so I would tax his mind, with all his vast store of quotes he had memorized
in his lifetime to talk me to sleep. When my friends would stay over, we would sit listening to his stereo
playing quietly in the background and that wondrous voice telling us tale after tale. He had great scary
stories, and we would make a fire in the fireplace, and we would listen raptly while he read or recited "The
Monkey's Paw," which today, still brings shivers. I'd be so scared, but I knew we were safe. He was
there with us...my Daddy. So imposing—who would ever challenge him?

Time...

When all the world is young, lad,
and all the trees are green;
and every goose a swan, lad
and every lass a queen:

Then boy for boot and horse, lad,
and round the world away;
Young blood must have its course, lad,
and Every Dog His Day.

When all the world is old, lad,
and all the trees are brown;
when all the sport is stale, lad,
and ale the wheels run down;

Creep home and take your place there,
the spent and maimed among;
God grant you find one face there,
You loved when all was young.

Kingsley

From Daddy with love

Youth...

When I Was a Boy at School

I often think of the days gone by,
when I was a boy about four feet high,
No happier was there a boy than I,
when I was a boy at school.

My exercises were not always correct
Often due to carelessness, often neglect;
and I sometimes got what I didn't expect
when I was a boy at school.

I fell in love with a sweet young thing,
And I bought her a gilt engagement ring,
and I swore to her through life I'd cling,
when I was a boy at school.

But what do you think, in a month or two
I got fed up, as most fellows do,
But that didn't matter, she had cooled down too,
when I was a boy at school.

And now as I sit in my lonely den,
and thinking of memories, lay down my pen,
and I sigh for the days to come again,
when I was a boy at school.

Herbert Asquith

In Closing...

I am only one, but I am one.
I can't do everything, but I can do something.
What I can do, I ought to do,
and what I ought to do,
by the grace of God I will do.

Motto spoken and lived
by Edward Everett Hale

♥

Don't Quit

When things go wrong, as they sometimes will,
When the road you're trudging seems all uphill,
When the funds are low and the debts are high,
And you want to smile, but you have to sigh,
When care is pressing you down a bit—
Rest if you must, but don't you quit.

Life is queer with its twists and turns,
As every one of us sometimes learns,
And many a person turns about
When they might have won had they stuck it out.
Don't give up though the pace seems slow—
You may succeed with another blow.

Often the struggler has given up
When he might have captured the victor's cup;
And he learned too late when the night came down,
How close he was to the golden crown.

Success is failure turned inside out—
So stick to the fight when you're hardest hit,
It's when things seem worst that you mustn't quit.

The Bread and
Breakfast Sampler

And Jesus said unto them,
I am the Bread of Life:
He that cometh to me shall never hunger;
and he that believeth in me
shall never thirst.

St. John 6:35

Avocado Bread

2 cups flour
3/4 cup sugar
3 sun-dried tomatoes (not dripping in oil but still a bit damp), chopped
1 tsp. baking soda
1/2 tsp. baking powder
1/4 tsp. cinnamon
1/4 tsp. salt
1-2 large avocados peeled, mashed equal to 1 cup*
1 large egg
1/2 cup buttermilk
1 tsp. lemon juice
1/2 cup chopped walnuts, toasted almonds or pistachios
*or try premixed guacamole dip from the refrigerator section of your
supermarket

Mix together flour, sugar, baking soda, baking powder, cinnamon, salt in Cuisinart.

Add egg, buttermilk, lemon juice, avocado.

Add the nuts and sun-dried tomatoes last so they don't get chopped up too much.

Fold into two 9" x 5" loaf pans.

Bake at 350° for 50 to 60 minutes. Test centers for doneness.

Remove from oven and cool ten minutes, then remove from pans to cake racks.

Good served with chile. I like to pour chile over these bread slices after toasting them. Butter bread and top with sharp Cheddar cheese.

It's also a good snack bread toasted crisp—and with a touch of cream cheese mixed with a dab of salsa, too.

The best time to make friends is before you need them.

Blueberry Bread

2 cups flour
1 tsp. baking soda
1 tsp. salt
3/4 cup sugar
1/2 cup Mazola oil
2 large eggs
3 Tbs. butter, softened
3/4 cup buttermilk
2 cups fresh blueberries or 1 can blueberries, drained (retaining juice)
1/2 cup shredded coconut or 3/4 cup chopped nuts (optional)

Preheat the oven to 350°.

Sift together the flour, baking soda and salt.

Add the sugar and oil.

Beat in the eggs, butter and buttermilk, and (if used) the coconut and nuts. If the mixture is too stiff, add some reserved berry juice or a little bit of water.

Fold in the blueberries.

Pour the batter into a loaf pan sprayed with Baker's Joy.

Bake for one hour and ten minutes. Test. Remove the cake from the oven and let it cool for five minutes.

Remove it from the pan to a cake rack and sprinkle with powdered sugar.

I got this recipe from a lady in a bar, while Bill drowned his sorrows after losing his job with Bethlehem Steel twenty-seven working days before his twenty-year anniversary and with no pension until he was sixty-five. I think it—the BLUEberry bread—fit the occasion. He works for Boeing now....

♥ ♥ ♥

Blue Cheese Bread

2 oz. regular—*not* fast-acting—yeast
1-1/2 cups *warm* water
2 Tbs. sugar
1-1/ 2 cups unbleached white flour (plus an extra dab for kneading)
1 cup milk
2 Tbs. milk
2 Tbs. sugar
1 Tbs. salt
3 Tbs. butter
2 Tbs. dried onion or 1/4 to 1/2 cup chopped fresh onion—sautéed in
    butter first
1 to 2 large eggs, beaten
1 tsp. Worcestershire
5 to 6 cups flour
2-3 oz. coarsely crumbled *good* blue cheese (I prefer more for stronger
    taste.)
1 Tbs. chopped garlic chives

Dissolve yeast in the warm water. Stir in sugar and flour until smooth. Let sit 20 minutes until it bubbles.

Scald the milk and pour it over the sugar, salt, butter and onion.

When the milk mixture becomes lukewarm, stir it into the yeast mixture. Add the eggs and Worcestershire.

Stir in the flour, blue cheese and garlic chives.

Empty the dough onto a floured surface, and knead until smooth —for about ten minutes.

Put it into large greased bowl and lightly oil the top.

Cover in plastic wrap and let rise for one hour in warm spot. Or, in an oven that's been turned on, preheated to 200° and then turned off and left with the door open when the bread goes in.

Punch down and form into three loaves. Or, make into rolls. Let rise 45 minutes, covered. About ten minutes before baking, score the tops. Brush with milk.

Bake the bread at 400° for ten minutes, then for 35 minutes at 325°. Bake rolls at 375° for 25 minutes. Watch and don't let it get too brown. Sounds hollow when you tap it.

Hawaiian Nut Bread

3-1/2 cups flour
4 tsp. baking powder
1/2 tsp. soda
1/2 tsp. salt
1 cup chopped macadamia nuts, plain or Kona (chocolate) covered
6 Tbs. butter
1-1/2 cups dark brown sugar
2 large eggs
1 16-oz. can crushed pineapple

Preheat oven to 350°.

In Cuisinart or mixer, combine dry ingredients and nuts.

In a separate bowl, cream the sugar and butter. (If using a Cuisinart, remove the mixture to another bowl, and use the same bowl for this step.)

Add the eggs one at a time.

If using a mixer, add the dry ingredients to the creamed mixture in three parts, alternating with the crushed pineapple. If using a Cuisinart, mix in the dry ingredients and pineapple and use the on/off switch to keep the pineapples chunky.

Divide the batter into two sprayed loaf/bread pans.

Bake for 50 to 60 minutes. Test.

Remove the cake from the oven, dust the top with powdered sugar and let it stand for five minutes.

Remove from pans to wire racks, and dust the cake with powdered sugar again.

This is very good drizzled with melted chocolate, too, for company.

A friend is a person who runs interference for you
in your pursuit of happiness.

Lemon Almond Bread

1 large egg, beaten
8 oz. plain yogurt
1 small (one-layer sized) box of yellow cake mix
2 tsp. finely shredded lemon peel
1/2 cup chopped almonds
Powdered sugar for dusting the top

Preheat the oven to 350°.

In a bowl combine the egg and yogurt, then the cake mix and lemon peel.

Add the nuts last.

Pour into a sprayed 8" x 4" x 2" loaf pan.

Bake for 35 to 40 minutes until done. Test. Remove from oven.

Dust the top with powdered sugar and cool for ten minutes.

Remove from pan to cake rack and dust with powdered sugar again.

♥ *Variations*

For topping you can also mix a little lemon juice in with the powdered sugar to make a glaze. Throw in a bit of the lemon peel in this, too for extra zip.

Or spread the top with cream cheese and enough fresh-squeezed lemon juice to make it creamy.

You can use this same recipe with oranges instead.

*To **find** a friend, one must close one eye—to **keep** him, two.*
Norman Douglas

Old-Fashioned Peach Bread

3 cups fresh peaches, or use frozen slices - removing most of the juice
6 Tbs. sugar
2 cups flour
1 tsp. baking powder
1 tsp. baking soda
Pinch of salt
1 tsp. cinnamon
1/2 tsp. pumpkin pie spice
1-1/2 cups sugar
1/2 cup Crisco
2 large eggs
1 cup chopped toasted walnuts, almonds, or pecans
1 tsp. vanilla
Peach-flavored liqueur, optional*

*I sometimes throw in a splash of peach-flavored liqueur in this recipe, and different liqueurs for other fruit recipes. See Bevy's *Raspberry Liqueur* elsewhere in this cookbook.

Put fresh peaches in boiling water for 30 seconds or, a bit more, then in cold water. Skins just slip off in a flash. (This works on tomatoes, too, you know.) Slice up, get rid of the pit.

Purée in Cuisinart or mixer.

Blend in the sugar.

In a separate bowl, combine the baking powder, soda, salt, cinnamon and pumpkin pie spice.

In Cuisinart or mixer, cream the sugar and the shortening. Add the eggs, one at a time.

Add the puréed peaches and the vanilla to the creamed mixture.

Add the dry ingredients and the nuts last, so they don't over-chop if you're using the Cuisinart.

Fold into two Baker's Joy-sprayed bread pans.

Bake at 325° for one hour. Test. Remove to counter and dust with powdered sugar.

Let cool in pans, then turn out on wire racks, and dust with more powdered sugar.

Pineapple-Carrot Bread

3 large beaten eggs
2 cups sugar
1-1/4 cups Mazola oil
2 cups grated carrots
20-oz. can crushed pineapple
Vanilla, optional*
3 cups flour
1 tsp. baking soda
1 tsp. salt
1-1/2 tsp. cinnamon

*My mom thought this didn't have enough flavor, so we added 2 tea-
    spoons of vanilla.

Combine and mix the egg, sugar, oil, grated carrots, pineapple and vanilla (if
used) in large bowl.

Sift together remaining ingredients and stir into above until mixed.

Pour the batter into a 9" x 5", sprayed loaf pan.

Bake at 350° for one hour. Test. Take out of oven to cool.

Remove carefully after five minutes to cake rack. Dust with powdered sugar.

I also think that cream cheese icing with a touch of rum/raisins and some chopped nuts is
sooooo....*nice*.

Money may not buy you more friends,
but it does attract a better class of enemies.

Rhubarb Bread - Sara T.

1 cup dark brown sugar
1 large egg
1 cup sour milk (1 Tbs. cider vinegar or lemon juice in 1 cup milk)
2/3 cup Mazola oil
2-1/2 cups flour
1 tsp. vanilla
1 tsp. soda
1/2 tsp. salt
1-1/2 cups cleaned, peeled rhubarb
1/2 cup chopped walnuts
1/2 cup dark brown sugar and 1 Tbs. butter for topping
Powdered sugar for dusting (optional)

Preheat the oven to 325°.

Put all the ingredients except the rhubarb and walnuts into the Cuisinart and blend.

Add the rhubarb and nuts. If using a Cuisinart, turn the off/on switch a few times just to mix in, leaving them a bit chunky.

Pour the bread batter into two 5" x 9" loaf pans sprayed with Baker's Joy.

Top with 1/2 cup dark brown sugar and one tablespoon of butter mixed together.

Bake for one hour.

Test center for doneness.

Cool for five minutes and remove to cake racks. Dust with powdered sugar.

Serve with butter.

Freezes well.

God should not be judged on the basis of this world—
it is just one of his rough sketches.

Vincent Van Gogh

Strawberry Bread

2 sticks butter
1-1/2 cups sugar
1 tsp. vanilla
1-1/2 tsp. lemon extract
4 large eggs
3 cups sifted flour
1 tsp. salt
1 tsp. cream of tartar
3/4 tsp. baking powder
1/2 tsp. baking soda
1-1/4 cups strawberry preserves
1/2 cup strawberry jam
1/2 cup sour cream
1 cup chopped walnuts

Preheat oven to 350°.

In Cuisinart or mixing bowl, blend the butter, sugar, vanilla and lemon extract until fluffy.

Add the eggs one at a time, beating in well.

In a larger bowl, sift together flour, salt, cream of tartar, baking powder and baking soda. When sifted, combine with the strawberry jam, preserves, and sour cream.

Gradually add the butter mixture. When blended, add the nuts. If using a Cuisinart, just turn the off/on switch a couple of times after adding the nuts, so they will remain chunky.

Divide the bread batter between two loaf pans sprayed with Baker's Joy.

Bake for 55 minutes, testing. Cool for five minutes and then remove from pans onto cake racks to cool through.

Dust with powder sugar.

You might want to spread on butter or cream cheese.

A friend is a present that you give yourself.

Robert Louis Stevenson

Zucchini Bread - Jim R.

You may never, ever, go back to your old recipe after trying this one! This is the best— bar none! We just love it, and among our family of friends it's one thing that disappears fast whenever it's put out. So I would suggest you make two recipes, freezing one batch so you always have some on hand.

3 large eggs
1 cup Mazola oil
1-1/2 cups sugar
3 cups grated zucchini, drained
3 cups all-purpose flour
1 Tbs. cinnamon
1 Tbs. pure vanilla extract (NOT imitation)
1 tsp. salt
1 Tbs. baking soda
1 Tbs. baking powder
1 cup chopped walnuts
2 Tbs. toasted sesame seeds per loaf top

Preheat the oven to 350°.

In large bowl, combine the eggs, oil and sugar. Cream for two minutes.

Add the zucchini. Mix in the flour, cinnamon, vanilla, salt, baking soda, baking powder and nuts. (*Or*, do like I do: Blend everything *except* the zucchini and the walnuts in a Cuisinart. *Then* add the zucchini and the nuts, and turn the off/on switch a few times so the batter remains chunky.)

Pour the bread batter into two 5" x 9" bread pans, sprayed with Baker's Joy.

Sprinkle the sesame seeds on top.

Bake for 1-1/4 hours, testing center for doneness.

Cool for five minutes, and then turn the bread out on cake racks to cool through.

We all put butter on this bread.

Dipping slices of it in an egg/milk mixture and pan frying it like French toast is also a nice treat!

My Mom's Yummy Croissants

🐾 *This recipe may sound kind of confusing with its separate steps, but just follow the directions as given and it will come together for you. It is worth it for the taste!*

1 cup flour
2 Tbs. regular or fast-acting yeast
1/4 cup sugar
2 tsp. salt
1 cup water
3/4 cup canned evaporated milk
1/4 cup butter
1 large egg, beaten
4 cups flour
1 cup (two sticks) sliced butter

Mix together the flour, yeast, sugar and salt.

Heat together the water, milk and butter until warm.

Add the yeast mixture and the beaten egg to the heated ingredients, blend it all together for three minutes and set aside.

Cut the sliced butter into the four cups of flour until the butter pieces are the size of a pea.

Pour the yeast mixture over the flour and mix lightly.

Cover for at least two hours or overnight in refrigerator.

Knead about six times, in a folding over motion.

Divide into four parts. Make a 14" circle and cut into eight wedges.

Roll and twist from tip up. Let rise about one hour on greased cookie sheets.

Brush with one large egg beaten with one tablespoon of water.

Preheat the oven to 350° and bake for 18 to 20 minutes until light brown.

Serve with butter and jam of your choice.

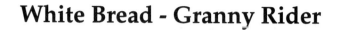

White Bread - Granny Rider

This is something Granny likes to make when it snows out and she's feeling b-o-r-e-d! You just have to give her things to do, or down the hill she'll go! I mean this literally! For really, she'll be ninety-two, going on sixteen, her next birthday. And when it snows, we all hold our breath so that she won't get too adventurous on her trips down the drive to the mailbox, or to knock snow from the cars, plants and trees, and suddenly decide that, yes, she **can** *drive—the road is not* **that** *bad. Ha! 10 inches. So, we give her projects—and this is a delicious one!*

1 Tbs. regular or fast-acting yeast
1 tsp. sugar
1/4 cup *warm* water
6 cups flour
2 Tbs. sugar
1 cup milk - bringing the milk just below a boil, so it begins to form
     film on top
1 cup water
2 Tbs. Mazola oil
2 tsp. salt

In a large bowl, dissolve the yeast with the sugar in the *warm* water.

Scald the milk by bringing it to just below a boil—just until it begins to form a film on top. Add the scalded milk and all the rest of the ingredients to the yeast mixture.

Mix together and turn the dough out onto a lightly floured surface. Knead for about three minutes, until the dough smooths out as you push it away from yourself and fold it in over toward you.

Shape the dough into a ball.

Put it in a large oiled bowl. Cover with a towel.

Let the dough rise in a warm spot. You can preheat the oven to 200°, turn it off, and put the bowl in with the door left open a crack. It takes about an hour for the bread to rise to about double its size.

Now punch the dough down and form into two loaves. Put in oiled bread pans. Let it rise, covered, until it doubles in size again. Bake at 450° for ten minutes. Turn down to 350° for 35 minutes.

Remove when bread sounds hollow when you thump it with your knuckles.

Cool for five minutes before turning out on wire racks.

Spread butter over the top. Slice and eat *now* with butter. This makes the best toast or Cheese Rarebit, and it's wonderful for great big homemade sandwiches—if there's anything left when you get done having it warm right out of the oven!

*The truth is that even when it's NOT snowing, we never know what Granny is baking, cooking or trying out now. When friends come over, she'll often pop down with some fresh little treat, and we all indulge ourselves. And knowing this, Bill will often call from work to make sure that I put some aside for him, although, I **always** save him some anyway.*

Worry is like a rocking chair:
It gives you something to do,
but doesn't get you anywhere.

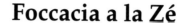

Foccacia a la Zé

🐾 *This wonderful recipe is from a restaurant no longer in business because its Chef/Owner, Dayton Azavedo, was offered such a great job—with more money and more time to spend with his family and friends—that he closed down, much to everyone's loss in Martinez, California. Our friends and family will always remember our fabulous meals there and try to get over to his new place across the bay. Thank heavens I was lucky enough to get this recipe, because it can't be replaced by anyone else's!*

For a large party, you will need a large restaurant size sheet pan (for at home use two large sheets and divide the dough in between).

1 oz. regular or fast-acting yeast
3-1/4 lbs. bread flour
1 Tbs. oregano
1 Tbs. salt
1/3 cup+ Extra Virgin olive oil (the darker green ones have better taste)
6–8 garlic cloves, minced or crushed and marinated in olive oil
6–8 green onions, green stalks chopped fine
Parmesan cheese, grated
Salt and black pepper to taste

♥ Dough

Proof the yeast in one quart of warm water. Bubbles will form—it takes about five minutes.

Mix together the flour, oregano, salt and 1/3 cup olive oil.

Add the yeast to the dry ingredients:

Turn out the dough onto a floured board and knead it for ten minutes by hand or about five minutes in a Hobart/Kitchen Aid with dough hook.

Put the dough in an olive-oiled bowl. Cover the bowl with a cloth and let it rise in a warm place until it doubles in bulk. Or turn the oven on until it reaches 200°, then turn it off and put in the covered bowl and leave the oven door open while it rises. This will take about two hours.

Punch the dough down and roll it out to a sheet pan size(s).

Flip onto olive-oiled sheet pan.

Brush the top of the dough with the minced garlic that has marinated in olive oil—using some of the oil as well. You can put in shallow finger holes or dimples over the top first if you want.

Lightly salt and black pepper the top.

Sprinkle the finely chopped green onions over the surface.

Dust with Parmesan cheese.

Cover the whole thing with plastic wrap and allow it to rise a second time for about an hour or so.

Remove the plastic and drizzle olive oil all over the top.

Bake in a preheated oven at 425° for 25 to 30 minutes.

Allow to cool before cutting in squares and serving. Put out a small container of olive oil for dipping.

We like to serve the bread warm, so we wrap it in foil and heat it in the oven for six minutes or so before serving it.

Sometimes we add some chopped, sun-dried tomatoes and prosciutto on the top for the last two minutes, for a very nice added treat—although I must say it's true that nothing else is needed with this wonderful recipe.

It's *addictive*.

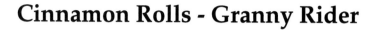

Cinnamon Rolls - Granny Rider

1 cup milk
2 Tbs. fast-acting yeast
1/4 cup sugar
3 cups flour
1 tsp. salt
2 large eggs, beaten
1/4 cup Mazola oil
4 Tbs. butter, melted
3 Tbs. cinnamon
3 Tbs. plus 1/2 cup dark brown sugar
1/4 cup water

Scald the milk. When lukewarm, add the yeast, sugar, and *1-1/2 cups* of the flour.

When bubbly, add: the salt, eggs, oil and remaining flour.

Mix well. Put on floured board and knead well.

Let rise in a warm place, covered, until it doubles in size.

Punch the dough down and turn it out onto a counter or board.

Roll it into a 1/4" thick oblong shape.

Spread three tablespoons of butter over the top, and sprinkle it with the cinnamon and three tablespoons of the brown sugar.

Roll up lengthwise and cut in circles.

Place in Baker's Joy-sprayed 9" x 13" pan.

Mix the 1/2 cup brown sugar, remaining tablespoon of melted butter and 1/4 cup water, and pour it over the top of the rolls.

Let the rolls rise until double in size again.

Preheat the oven to 350° and bake for 35 minutes.

If you ask her very nicely, Granny will make these rolls to take to work or to take to friends. Sometimes she makes them "just because" they sound good on a cold, gray morning. We don't put raisins or nuts in our cinnamon rolls, as the kids like them plain. But who's to complain when they are hot and ready to butter the moment you roll out of bed on the weekends, because Granny's left them on the counter in the knowledge that you're just getting up!

♥ *Helpful Hint*

Trouble with yeast dough rising? Put on medium temperature of heating pad.

Muffins and Biscuits

- ♥ Coarse texture is from insufficient stirring and cooking at too low a temperature.

- ♥ Over-mixing causes peaks in center and a soggy texture.

- ♥ Bake at correct temperature for perfect results.

- ♥ Muffins will slide right off of pans if you first place the hot pan on a wet, cold towel. I spray my baking pans beforehand with Baker's Joy and never have a problem.

- ♥ Lumpy biscuits are from not enough mixing.

- ♥ Dry biscuits are from baking in too slow an oven and from handling too much.

- ♥ Uneven browning is from rolling too thin, temperature too high, and from not using smooth-bottomed pans with bright finishes.

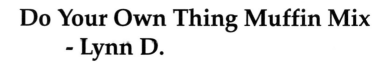

Do Your Own Thing Muffin Mix - Lynn D.

These are Lynn's fast and easy basics for making muffins. You can add nuts, raisins, and flavorings of your choice.

Preheat the oven to 425°.

♥ Batter

1-1/2 cups flour
1/2 cup sugar
2 tsp. baking powder
1/4 tsp. salt
1/2 cup milk
1/4 cup Mazola oil
1 large egg

Sift together all the dry ingredients.

Beat together the milk, oil, and egg and add to the dry ingredients.

♥ Variations

Now add whatever you thought would taste good today:

Chopped fruit: 1/2 cup fresh or 1 cup dried
Chopped nuts: 1/2 cup walnuts, pecans, etc.
Flavoring: 1/2 tsp. vanilla, rum, orange, almond, etc.

Spoon the batter into sprayed muffin tins. (I even spray my Teflon with Baker's Joy).

Bake for 15 to 20 minutes.

Remove to wire racks to cool. Dust with powdered sugar for an added touch.

Keep when cooled in Ziploc bags.

Sweet Holiday Muffins - Robbie T.

2 cups flour
2/3 cup sugar
1 Tbs. baking powder
1/2 tsp. salt
3/4 cup eggnog
1/2 cup dark rum
1/2 cup dark raisins or currents
5 Tbs. butter, melted
1 large egg, beaten
1/2 tsp. fresh grated nutmeg
Chopped walnuts (optional)
Powdered sugar to dust

Preheat the oven to 400°.

In a small bowl, soak the raisins in the rum.

In Cuisinart or mixing bowl, combine the flour, sugar, baking powder and salt.

Add the eggnog, butter, egg and nutmeg. Blend well.

Add the rum, then the raisins and chopped nuts. If using a Cuisinart, take care not to chop up the raisins too much.

Pour into Baker's Joy-sprayed muffin tins 3/4 full.

Bake for 20 minutes.

When cool, remove it from the pan and dust it with powdered sugar.

Bran Muffins - Robin R.

1 cup Kellogg's Bran Buds
2 cups Kellogg's All Bran
1/2 cup Crisco
1-1/3 cups sugar
2 large eggs, beaten
2 cups buttermilk
2 cups flour
2-1/2 tsp. baking soda
1 tsp. salt

Preheat the oven to 400°.

Soak the Bran Buds in one cup of *boiling* water. Set aside and cool.

Cream together the Crisco and sugar.

Add the eggs and buttermilk.

Sift together and add the flour, soda and salt.

Add both the All Bran and the cooled Bran Buds. Mix well.

Spray muffin tins with Baker's Joy and fill them 2/3 full.

Bake for 15 minutes.

This makes five dozen small, or three dozen large muffins.

In airtight containers, the batter will keep up to two or three weeks in refrigerator, so you can make them fresh and hot on special mornings when something warm from the oven is just what you need to start the day.

♥ *Variation*

Add raisins, nuts, chopped apples, or fruits and berries of your choice.

♥ ♥ ♥

Zoo-hire Sweet Pancakes

1 cup 2% milk
2 Tbs. butter
1/2 cup flour
1 tsp. baking powder
1/8 tsp. salt
Powdered sugar, fresh blueberries and/or strawberries
Syrup(s) of your choice

In a microwave or saucepan, heat together the milk and butter. If using a microwave, put it in a 16-oz. glass measuring cup.

Let the mixture cool slightly.

In a bowl, combine the flour, baking powder and salt, and add the milk mixture.

Whisk until smooth. I let it rest for a few minutes, because it always is so lumpy! Then rewhisk the batter just before pouring it into the pan.

Pour into a heated small skillet (6" or 8") or griddle with a dab of melted butter in it. (Yes, we use stick-free skillets, but I love the added touch of a bit more butter!)

Watch for the bubbles, and turn. Serve right away. They probably would keep in the oven on warm, but I just serve each person off the grill, while the pancakes are *hot, hot hot!*

♥ *Sweet Variations*

For Jamey we do fresh blueberries and powdered sugar. Micha brings us homemade blueberry syrup, from Anderson Island. We combine both, dust with powdered sugar, and sprinkle a few fresh berries across the top. Me... I like Mrs. Butterworth's—heated. For Bill and Todd, I do strawberries. And we always serve these with regular or Canadian bacon, or sausage. Rarely do I serve eggs with these—don't think they need it. Yes, sometimes Jamey wants them, so of course I do them. Then Dad joins him. Todd and I watch. Where do they *put* it all, I wonder?

♥ ♥ ♥

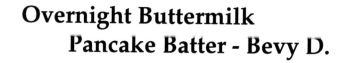

Overnight Buttermilk
Pancake Batter - Bevy D.

1-3/4 cup to 2 cups flour
Quart of buttermilk
2 tsp. baking soda
4 large eggs, separated
1-1/2 tsp. salt
1-1/2 tsp. baking powder
6 Tbs. butter, melted
1/3 cup sugar

Put the buttermilk and flour in a large covered container and shake well.

Add the soda and let sit out on the counter for at least two hours.

Beat the egg yolks until lemony in color. Keep separate from whites.

In a separate bowl, beat the egg whites until stiff.

Melt the butter, and blend it into the sugar until creamy.

Add the egg yolks, salt and baking powder to the buttermilk mixture in a large bowl. Then add the butter/sugar mixture.

Fold in the egg whites last. Let it rest for a half hour before cooking.

Pour the leftover batter in a Tupperware container and refrigerate for the next day or so. Batter lasted for three days when we didn't have company.

For company it's so nice because you can spend time over coffee while you put strips of bacon* on a cookie sheet and bake at 375° until brown, bring out the batter, warm the grill, set out the toppings of your choice. Pretty soon—and without any apparent effort—away you can go: with dollar sized pancakes, bacon and fresh fruit garnish.

*Oven-baked bacon should take about ten minutes. For six people or more, I always cook at least a pound— lean, and I always remember to check it so it doesn't burn.

French Toast - Jamey, with Joanie's help

3 large eggs
Drop of vanilla
Sprinkle of cinnamon - about 1/8 tsp.
Cinnamon bread or other bread of your choice
Dab of butter

Whisk the eggs, vanilla and cinnamon until blended in a medium flat-shaped bowl that you can lay your bread in. *This will do about 4 slices of bread.*

Take one piece of bread and dip it into the batter.

Cover both sides completely. *Don't get the bread too soggy or it will fall apart.*

Fry the battered bread on a flat grill or in a large frying pan with a dab of butter. Repeat until all the bread is done. Serve the toast hot, with syrups.

I always add a drop of water to the batter, too, but *they* don't. If you don't have enough mix, add another egg, or two, a dash more vanilla, another sprinkle of cinnamon, etc.

We don't like our French toast soggy, so we cook it on medium-heat, then it cooks through, without burning.

♥ *Variations*

Toss in a splash of orange liqueur, or what ever you have on hand for an added treat. But not too much.

A dab of cheese grated and bacon pieces cooked crisp in the batter is good. I throw in some chopped chives—if I'm using white bread and Jamey isn't around!

A splash of Tabasco, a few chopped jalapeno's, chopped white/red onions, ham pieces in the batter are also good. There are *so* many things you can do: drizzle some hot salsa over the top. *Why not?*

Slice your own bread, make a pocket and stuff it with pieces of Brie (without the rind) and smoked salmon, Brie and a dollop of berry jam, and melted jam on top with powdered sugar.

...Oh, you want to know what Joanie does in this recipe? She adds the splash of vanilla.

Stuffed French Toast
- Auntie Marie King

🐾 *Good friends are like a fine wine: they just improve with age. We go back a good many years—me and this delightful little lady, who hails from Plentywood, Montana. We used to enjoy this toast at Archie's, a restaurant in Bothell where Marie was part owner and I, for a time, was her weekday waitress. It's still a pleasure for me and the family to drop by and see her at work, for even though she promises to come on up to the house, we usually have to rely on phones for a chance to visit. Thank heaven for phones—and for this wonderful brunch recipe.*

8-oz pkg cream cheese, softened
1/ 4 cup Grand Marnier
12-oz. jar orange marmalade
1 tsp. vanilla
1/2 cup chopped walnuts (*plus more for topping), toasted in butter
1 large loaf unsliced French bread—soft crust
4 large eggs, beaten
1 cup whipping cream
Powdered sugar for dusting

In a mixer or Cuisinart put the cream cheese, marmalade, *1/8 cup* Grand Marnier, and *1/2 teaspoon* of the vanilla and mix together well. Add the 1/2 cup of nuts. If using a Cuisinart, be sure to add the nuts last and don't chop them too much.

Slice the bread in 1-1/2" to 2" widths and cut a pocket in the sides—not all the way through.

Stuff the slices with the cream cheese mixture and set them aside.

In a separate bowl mix: the beaten eggs, whipping cream, another 1/2 teaspoon vanilla and the remaining (1/8 cup) Grand Marnier.

Heat a large grill to medium. Spray it with Mazola oil, lightly so the bread won't stick. I add butter and Mazola mixed, too.

Dip the stuffed bread in the egg mixture, coating both sides, and fry on grill until lightly brown.

Remove and dust with powdered sugar, a touch of Orange Marmalade, a sprinkling of fresh berries and nuts. We like it with Canadian Bacon, sausage, or ham on the side.

Serve with a glass of champagne, with bitters and a lemon twist, or with orange juice.

Choriso and Egg Tortillas - Larry

 This dish is from the Waldorf Wilkerson, on Lake Tullock, where every summer we have the time of our lives trying other people's cooking masterpieces, while enjoying the pleasure of family, good friends, lively conversation, and crusin' the lake on the Party Barge with usually 10 or more people. This is sure to be a favorite with you, as it has been for us. You can have it for breakfast like Larry serves it, or for dinner. Either way it's great! (You can now get the recommended Carmalita brand of choriso in your grocery stores. (They have beef, too, but I don't like it as well.)

1 pkg. Carmelita brand chorizo (pork sausage) (3)
1 large yellow onion, finely chopped
1 dozen large eggs
1 pkg. flour tortillas
Mayonnaise
Grated Cheddar and Monterey Jack cheese
Condiments (see below)

Have the tortillas ready—keep warm on low in the oven. Remove skins from the sausage. Cook in a large sauté pan, until it loses its pink, breaking it into pieces.

Add the chopped onion and a splash of water and cook until limp.

Crack the eggs and whisk them together, then pour over the meat and onion. Stir until there is still some moisture, but the eggs are done.

Put a tablespoon of mayonnaise down the center of tortilla. Layer the Choriso/eggs over the mayonnaise with a sprinkling of the grated cheese.

♥ Condiments

Serve with condiments on the table of sour cream, black olives, salsa, chopped green onions, chopped green chiles/Jalapenos, avocado slices, and some tomatoes. Larry serves his with *peronchinis*— mild Greek peppers— on the side.

♥ ♥ ♥

Desserts and Delectables

Have Courage for the great sorrows of life,
and Patience for the small ones.
And when you have finished
your daily tasks,
Go to sleep in peace…
God is Awake.

Cake Making Hints

♥ Coarse-grained cake is caused by:
   (1) Too little mixing
   (2) Too much baking powder
   (3) Using shortening that's too soft or
   (4) Baking at too low a temperature

♥ A heavy cake is usually the result of:
   (1) Too much sugar or
   (2) Baking for too short a time

♥ A dry cake is caused by:
   (1) Too much flour
   (2) Too little shortening
   (3) Too much baking powder or
   (4) Cooking at too low a temperature

♥ Cracks and uneven surfaces are caused by:
   (1) Too much flour
   (2) Too hot an oven or
   (3) Starting from a cold oven

♥ Uneven browning is caused from:
   (1) Cooking at too high a temperature
   (2) Crowding the shelf and not allowing at least 2" around the cake pans or
   (3) Not using bright finish and smooth-bottomed pans

♥ Cakes that are uneven in color are not mixed well. Mix thoroughly, but *do not over-mix.*

♥ To keep icings moist and to prevent cracking, add a pinch of baking soda to icing.

♥ Do *not* grease the sides of cake pans. Grease only the bottoms.

♥ Eggs should be at least three days old before using in cakes. 1 egg = 4 Tbs. of liquid, 4 to 5 whole eggs = 1 cup, 7 to 9 whites = 1 cup, 12 to 14 yolks = 1 cup.

♥ When you take a cake from the oven, place it for a very few moments on a cloth wrung out of cold water. The pan will empty out without cake sticking.

♥ When adding fruit to cakes or in baking, dust in a little flour first and it will keep it from settling on the bottom. Also, add fruit last.

Old Country Applesauce Fruitcake - Bevy D.

*The first time I made this for the holidays, I didn't realize I hadn't bought **pitted** dried fruit. So, with my trusty Cuisinart, I just chopped it all up! Not until about three months later did someone comment about having bitten into some "shells from the nuts." Well, I **knew** I didn't have any shells in my nuts! So I got out the half sack of fruit I had left, and **read** the label on the package. Boy, was I mortified! Bevy had made this fruitcake so often that it didn't occur to her that I might need this dose of my own advice: Always read your recipes through—and your package labels carefully! Pitted!*

2-1/2 cups unsweetened applesauce, *heated*
1 cup (2 sticks) butter, softened
2 cups sugar
1 tsp. vanilla
4-1/2 cups flour
5 tsp. baking soda
1/2 tsp. baking powder
1 tsp. each: cinnamon, cloves, and allspice
2 tsp. cocoa
1 cup raisins or currents, soaked in brandy (optional)
1/2 cup chopped dates
1 cup chopped walnuts
1 cup (approximately) dried fruit*, pitted and chopped
Powdered sugar for dusting (optional)

*I use about two cups for more oomph. You might want to try it both ways. The one with more fruit is heavier and denser.

Preheat the oven to 325°.

Blend the hot applesauce with the butter. Add the sugar and vanilla.

Sift together the flour, soda, baking powder, spices and cocoa.

Add the dry ingredients to the applesauce mixture.

Fold in the raisins or currents, dates, walnuts and dried fruit.

Pour in a sprayed 9" x 13" pan and bake for 45 to 55 minutes. Test. In smaller pans bake for 25 minutes and test.

Dust with powdered sugar or make a cream cheese frosting with a touch of nuts, brandy-soaked raisins and some of the dried fruit cut up in it.

This is a great-tasting cake. You can make it in smaller pans and wrap it for gifts, like I have, or bake it in a 9" x 13" pan as recommended here. Just remember to cut down on the cooking time when doing smaller sizes. Test!

Pina Colada Cake - Jean M.

1 Duncan Hines yellow cake mix
1/4 cup Mazola oil
3/4 cup water
3/4 cup dark rum
2 large eggs, beaten
1 can Coconut Creme
1 15-oz. carton Cool Whip
2 cups shredded coconut

*I have been known to add a tad bit more rum and less water...

Preheat the oven to 350°.

Pour Mazola in a 9" x 13" pan and rub oil on the sides, too.

In the pan, combine the cake mix, water, rum, and eggs. It will be lumpy.

Bake for 30 to 35 minutes. Test and remove it from the oven.

While it is *still hot* from the oven, poke holes all over the top and pour on the Coconut Creme.

Let the cake sit for a few hours to marry the flavors.

Top with Cool Whip and the shredded coconut.

Refrigerate any leftovers, but bring it back to room temperature before you serve again, so the flavors will come out.

Carrot Cake - Nancy V.

 *I got this recipe from a woman I met at a cooking class at Magnolia Kitchens. She also took me to a chef's demonstration class at her club, and we kept touch for a while. Though busy lives and schedules have kept us apart, this recipe of Nancy's is— for me—a warm reminder of our acquaintance as well as a wonderful cake to serve to guests and family.*

4 large eggs
2 cups sugar
1/2 cup Mazola oil
2 cups flour
2 tsp. baking powder
1-1/2 tsp. baking soda
1/4 tsp. salt
1 tsp. cinnamon
2 cups grated carrots
20-oz. can crushed pineapple, drained
1/4 cup chopped walnuts

Preheat oven to 350°.

In a mixer or large Cuisinart, blend the eggs, sugar and oil.

Sift together the flour, baking powder, baking soda, salt and cinnamon.

Add the flour mixture, the grated carrots, and crushed pineapple to the mixing bowl or Cuisinart.

Mix well. Add the chopped walnuts and use the off/on switch. Leave in chunks.

Spray three 8" cake pans with Baker's Joy. Pour in the batter, evenly.

Bake for 35 to 40 minutes. Test. Let cool five minutes before removing to cake rack.

Let cool completely and spread with Cream Cheese Frosting *(see next page)*.

Women do have a sense of humor—look at the men they marry.

Cream Cheese Frosting

1 stick butter
8-oz. pkg. cream cheese
1 tsp. vanilla

1 lb. powdered sugar
Lemon or orange juice to thin*

*You could also use pineapple juice, but the lemon or orange will cut the
    sweetness and give it a bit of contrast.

Cream together the butter and cream cheese. Add the vanilla, and whisk in the
powdered sugar until the frosting is of spreading consistency.

Chocolate Buttercream Frosting - JoAnne M.

1/4 cup whipping cream
1/4 cup butter
2 oz. unsweetened Hershey's cocoa

1 tsp. vanilla
2-1/2 cups powdered sugar

In a saucepan heat the cream.   Add the butter, bringing just to a boil.

Remove from heat and stir in the cocoa and vanilla.

Whisk in the powdered sugar until smooth and spread it on your creation.

Chocolate Sour Cream Frosting

6-oz. pkg. chocolate chips
4 Tbs. butter
1/2 cup sour cream
1 tsp. vanilla

1/4 tsp. salt
1 tsp. cinnamon
Powdered sugar

Mix chocolate chips and butter over low heat.

Blend in sour cream, vanilla, salt, and cinnamon.

Slowly add in powdered sugar until the frosting reaches a spreading consistency.

Mix in well and then spread over cake in pan.

Black Russian Cake

 ....The most asked for dessert I've ever made for company!

1 box Duncan Hines Devil's Food cake mix
4-oz. pkg. Jell-O instant chocolate-flavored pudding mix
4 large eggs, beaten
1 cup Mazola oil
1-1/4 cup Black Russian mix or 3/4 cup vodka to 1/2 cup Kahlua
1 cup chopped toasted almonds, pistachios, or nuts of your choice

Preheat oven to 350°.

I put all the ingredients—*except* the nuts in my Cuisinart and blend.

Add nuts last to chop *just a little*.

Pour into a Baker's Joy-sprayed Bundt pan.

Bake for 50 minutes. Test.

Remove from oven and dust top with powdered sugar.

Let sit five minutes, then turn out on cake plate and dust it with powdered sugar again—all over.

Now, some of my friends like to poke holes in it and pour added liqueur into it. I think it's strong enough as it is. But.... they use different liqueurs. Go for it.

I like to drizzle mine with Chocolate Buttercream Frosting. (It takes only half of the recipe.)

This is *sooo good* with a Bailey's Coffee.

♥ ♥ ♥

Grandpa Gleasen's Brandy Apple-Raisin Chocolate Cake

2 sticks butter
2 cups sugar
3 cups flour
1 tsp. cinnamon
1 tsp. fresh grated nutmeg
2 tsp. baking soda
2 cups applesauce—fresh, if possible
1 tsp. vanilla
1 cup dark raisins plumped in hot brandy
3/4 cup chopped walnuts

Preheat oven to 325°.

Spray a Bundt pan with Baker's Joy.

In Cuisinart or mixer, cream together the butter and sugar until light and fluffy.

In a separate bowl, sift together the flour, cinnamon, nutmeg, and baking soda and add it to the creamed butter/sugar mixture.

Add the applesauce, vanilla, chopped walnuts and the raisins—throw both the raisins *and* the brandy in! Blend everything together gently and not for too long.

Pour into sprayed cake pan.

Bake for 1-1/4 hours until tester comes out clean. Remove from oven.

Let rest ten minutes. Remove to wire rack.

Dust with powdered sugar. Or melt some chocolate chips and drizzle on cake top, dusting with chopped nuts.

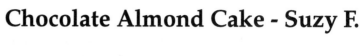

Chocolate Almond Cake - Suzy F.

1 tsp. instant Kava or other instant coffee
2 Tbs. hot water
8 oz. semisweet chocolate
3 large eggs, separated
1/2 cup + 1 Tbs.* butter
3/4 cup sugar
2 oz. almond paste, crumbled up
1/2 cup flour

Preheat the oven to 350°.

Dissolve coffee in *hot* water.

In a double boiler melt *four ounces* of the chocolate, saving the other four ounces for the glaze. Add the coffee mixture.

Whip egg whites until they form *stiff peaks*.

In a separate bowl, cream the *1/2 cup* butter and sugar well.

Add the crumbled almond paste, egg yolks, melted chocolate/coffee mixture and flour. Mix well.

Fold in the egg whites, in three parts, and carefully—this makes the cake lighter.

Spray an 8" heart-shaped pan with Baker's Joy and dust with cocoa.

Pour in the cake batter. Smooth the top.

Bake for 30 minutes until lightly brown. Test. Remove from oven.

Let the cake rest for ten minutes before removing from pan to cake plate. Dust with powdered sugar and top with a chocolate glaze:

♥ *Chocolate Glaze*

Melt the remaining four ounces of chocolate and *tablespoon of butter in a double boiler over boiling water whisking until glossy/shiny. Drizzle over the top of cake.

(I sometimes melt white and semisweet chocolate—separately, then drizzle in a zigzag pattern over the cake top, or make a fancy design on top of the cake with cut-out patterns my friend Marilyn brought me from a trip to Germany.)

Chocolate Sauerkraut Cake
- Grandma Gleasen

1/2 cup butter
1-1/2 cups sugar
3 large eggs
1 tsp. vanilla
2 cups flour
1 tsp. baking powder
2 cups or 1 #2 can sauerkraut
1 tsp. baking soda
1/4 tsp. salt
1/2 cup cocoa
1 cup water
1 cup chopped nuts of your choice, optional

Rinse the sauerkraut thoroughly, drain and squeeze dry. Set aside for Cuisinart. If you're using a mixer, first chop the sauerkraut up *fine*.

Preheat oven to 350°.

In Cuisinart or mixer, cream butter and sugar.

Add in eggs one at a time.

Add vanilla.

In a separate bowl, sift flour, baking powder, salt, soda, and cocoa together. Add to creamed mixture—alternately—with water.

Add sauerkraut. If using a Cuisinart, chop the sauerkraut up fine.

Add in nuts and chop a bit only.

Pour into a 9" x 13" pan. Bake for 40 to 45 minutes. Test.

Top with Chocolate Sour Cream Frosting.

Thanksgiving and Christmas Day Pumpkin Cream Cheese Roll
- Robin R.

You know, I don't care much for pumpkin pie, but I just love to bite into this. There's something about all the different spices that come out with each bite of the cream cheese and nuts that is just delectable. I think I'm also guilty of adding a touch more spice than I suggest for you here!

3 large eggs, slightly beaten
1 cup sugar
2/3 cup canned solid-packed pumpkin
3/4 cup flour
1 tsp. baking powder
2 tsp. ground cinnamon
1 tsp. pumpkin pie spice
1/2 tsp. ground nutmeg
1/2 tsp. salt
Powdered sugar
1 cup chopped walnuts, pecans, or hazelnuts

Preheat oven to 375°.

In Cuisinart or mixer, beat the eggs and sugar until thick and fluffy.

Add pumpkin.

Stir in all the dry ingredients *except* the powdered sugar and nuts.

Spray a jelly roll pan, line it with wax paper, respray and pour in the batter. Bake for 15 minutes.

Test, remove from oven and loosen the cake around edges with knife.

Dust a clean damp towel with powdered sugar and place it over the top of the pan. Invert the pan and flip it over to remove the warm cake.

Peel off the wax paper.

Roll up the cake into the powdered sugar-dusted towel from the short end (some do it the long way—whatever!).

Cakes

Place seam side down on wire rack to cool.

When cooled, unroll the cake carefully. (Don't worry about slight tears. The filling will cover them.)

Trim 1/4" from the edges.

Spread it evenly with the cream cheese filling.

Roll it back up and spread the remainder of the cream cheese mixture on top. Sprinkle on some chopped nuts.

Refrigerate until ready to serve.

Serve with brandy in coffee for a treat, and add whipped cream on top if you want to get carried away!

♥ *Cream Cheese Filling*

1 cup sifted powdered sugar
8 oz. cream cheese, softened
6 Tbs. butter, softened
1 tsp. vanilla

Beat together all these ingredients* until smooth.

*You could also dress this filling up with some rum-soaked raisins. Or brandy, as of course I do!

♥ *Helpful Hint*
Keeping your spices in alphabetical order will make them easier to locate and easier to reorder when you run out.

Happiness grows at our own firesides,
and is not to be picked in strangers' gardens.

Douglas Terrold

251

Chocolate Zucchini Cake - Sara T.

1/2 cup butter
1-3/4 cups sugar
4 Tbs. cocoa
2 large eggs, beaten
1 tsp. vanilla
1/2 cup sour milk
2-1/2 cups flour
1/2 tsp. cinnamon
1 tsp. baking soda
1/2 tsp. salt
1/2 tsp. baking powder
1/2 tsp. cloves
2 cups shredded zucchini—leave on green skin and wash well
1/2 cup chopped nuts
6-oz. pkg. small chocolate chips

Preheat oven to 325°.

Cream together the butter, sugar and cocoa.

Add the eggs, vanilla and sour milk.

Sift together the flour, cinnamon, soda, salt, baking powder and cloves.

Fold in the shredded zucchini, nuts and chocolate chips.

Pour into sprayed 9" x 13" dish.

Bake for 40 to 45 minutes.   Test. Remove from the oven to cool.

Frost or dust with powdered sugar.

True friends:
They are kind to each other's hopes;
they cherish each other's dreams.

Henry Thoreau

Harvey Wallbanger Cake
- Granny Rider's Favorite

1 box Duncan Hines yellow cake mix
1 4-oz. pkg. Instant Vanilla Pudding
1/2 cup Mazola oil
4 large eggs, beaten
1/4 cup vodka
1/4 cup Galliano
3/4 cup orange juice
Chopped nuts of choice or toasted pecans (optional)

Preheat oven to 350°.

Put all ingredients in the Cuisinart or a mixer and blend well.

Spray a Bundt pan with Baker's Joy and pour in the batter.

Bake for 50 minutes. Test. Remove from oven.

Dust with powdered sugar, wait five minutes, then remove from pan to cake dish and dusted with the powdered sugar again.

♥ Variation

This cake—like the Black Russian—can certainly stand on its own. But for a variation with a flourish you could top it off with a mixture of cream cheese and a touch of orange juice and grated orange peel.

In any form the Harvey Wallbanger cake is a great party treat—for you as well as your company—as all ingredients go in one bowl and you can dress while it cooks! And no one usually wants only one piece, *right, Granny! ?*

Peace of mind lies in not wishing for things we don't have:
but what else is there to wish for?

Milky Way Cake - Angie

6 Milky Way bars, chopped up—plus one more to top cake with
2 cups sugar
3 sticks butter
2-1/2 cups flour
1/2 tsp. baking soda
4 large eggs, beaten
1 tsp. vanilla
1/4 cup buttermilk
1 cup pecans, medium chopped —plus 1/2 cup more for topping

Preheat oven to 350°.

In a small heavy saucepan, melt candy bars, sugar and butter over low heat. Set aside to cool.

Mix the remaining ingredients in a large bowl.

Pour the melted candy bar mixture into the bowl and stir in well.

Spray a 9" x 13" pan with Baker's Joy and pour in the batter.

Bake 40 minutes, remove from oven and let cool.

♥ *Icing*

16 oz. powdered sugar
1 stick butter
8-oz. pkg. cream cheese

Mix together and spread on cake.

Top with finely chopped candy bar and add some more chopped up pecans.

A woman's work is never done,
especially the part she asks her husband to do.

Mississippi Mud Cake
- Angie's Sister

1/2 cup flour
2 sticks butter
2 cups sugar
4 large eggs
1/2 cup cocoa
1 cup chopped pecans
1 7-oz. jar Marshmallow Creme

Melt the butter and mix it with all the remaining ingredients, *except* Marshmallow Creme.

Pour into 13" x 9" sprayed pan.

Bake at 350° for 30 to 35 minutes. Test.

Remove from oven and spread Marshmallow Creme on the cake while it's still hot.

Let cool and slather it with the following icing:

♥ *Icing*

1 stick butter, softened
16 oz. powdered sugar
1/2 cup cocoa
1/2 cup evaporated milk
1 tsp. vanilla

Mix butter, sugar, vanilla, and cocoa.

Add milk, a little at a time, until the consistency is as thick as you wish. You may not need all the milk, as it depends on whether you like your frosting thick or slightly runny.

♥ ♥ ♥

Peanut Butter Cake - Wendy M.

1/2 cup butter
1/2 cup sugar
1/2 cup brown sugar (I use dark.)
1 large egg, beaten
1/3 cup peanut butter
1/2 tsp. baking soda
1/4 tsp. salt
1/8 tsp. vanilla extract
1/4 cup flour
1/2 cup whole wheat flour
1/4 cup wheat germ
1 cup rolled oats
1 cup chopped walnuts
6-oz. pkg. semisweet chocolate chips

Preheat the oven to 350°.

Cream together butter and *both* sugars.

Add the egg, peanut butter, soda, salt, and vanilla.

Combine the flour, wheat germ, and oats. Stir into above.

Mix in the nuts and chocolate chips.

Divide between two sprayed 9" cake pans.

Bake 20 to 25 minutes. Test. Remove from oven.

Spread frosting over warm cake and cut when cool.

♥ *Peanut Butter Frosting*

1/2 cup powdered sugar
1/4 cup peanut butter
2 to 4 Tbs. evaporated milk or cream

Combine powdered sugar, peanut butter, and enough evaporated milk or cream to achieve the degree of runniness you wish. Swirl it over the warm cake and let it melt in.

Pecan Cake

3-1/4 cup flour
1-1/2 tsp. nutmeg
1 tsp. baking powder
1/2 tsp. baking soda
Bourbon (or other liquor of choice, such as rum, brandy, or cream
    sherry)
1 cup raisins
2 sticks butter, softened
2 cups sugar
1/4 cup dark brown sugar
5 large eggs
1 cup buttermilk
2 cups pecans, chopped (You do know not to over-chop!)
Powdered sugar

Pour enough bourbon or other liquor over the raisins to cover them and let marry for 1/2 hour.

Preheat the oven to 325°.

Mix together the flour, nutmeg, baking powder, and soda.

In a large, separate bowl, cream the softened butter, sugar, and brown sugar until light and fluffy.

Add the five eggs, one at a time.

Stir in the flour mix, alternating with the cup of buttermilk.

Stir in the bourbon-soaked raisins.

Add the coarsely chopped pecans.

Fold the mixture into sprayed tube or Bundt pan.

Bake for 1-1/4 hours. Test.

Dust with powdered sugar. Let sit five minutes, then remove to cake rack.

♥ ♥ ♥

Christmas Morning
Brunch Cake - Granny Rider

🐾 *On Christmas morning—with little sausages, strawberries, a cup of Kava—we begin the ritual of the Zoo-hires, opening the rest of our presents. The house smells of turkey cooking, the cinnamon in this cake, the crunch of the sausages that are dipped in catsup. The house is filled with laughter and love, and the rest of the day is filled with friends stopping by to share the bounty of our table, which we are so fortunate to be able to provide. It is, to me, the **best** day of my life; I have it **all**: good food, great friends, and peace and contentment for all who enter here. And yes: cats, cats, cats! (with allergy tablets handy for all our dearest who suffer!)—Hey, it's the kitties' day **too**!*

♥ Cake Batter

1 cup sugar
2 large eggs, beaten
1-1/2 cups flour
2 tsp. baking powder
1/4 tsp. salt
1/2 cup milk
1/4 cup butter

Preheat oven to 375°. Spray a square or oblong pan with Baker's Joy.

In a mixer or Cuisinart, mix all the batter ingredients together and set aside.

♥ Topping

3/4 cup chopped walnuts
1-1/2 Tbs. flour
3/4 cup packed dark brown sugar
1-1/2 tsp. cinnamon
2 Tbs. butter

Melt the butter in a sauce pan. Mix in the chopped walnuts and toast them in the butter for a minute or two. Add the flour, brown sugar, and cinnamon, and mix well.

Put half of the nut topping in the bottom of the sprayed pan. Pour over the batter. Top with rest of the nuts.

Bake at 375° for 30 minutes. Serve hot, cut into squares and topped with more melted butter.

Washington Apple Cake/Pie

I've always loved serving this dessert for family and friends. I changed the original recipe a bit by pouring some caramel topping over the apples before pouring the batter—which cooks up to a crunchy crust with a cake-like filling underneath down to the apples. Just delicious!

3 large eggs
2 cups sugar
3/4 cup oil
2 cups flour
2 tsp. cinnamon
1 tsp. baking soda
1 tsp. vanilla
1 cup coarsely chopped walnuts
3 apples or about 1-1/2 lbs., peeled and cored, sliced thin
Powdered sugar for dusting cake top
1 lb., 3 oz. jar Smucker's Butterscotch Caramel-flavored topping
Whipped cream to top off the cake itself!

Preheat the oven to 350°.

In a large bowl with electric mixer beat the eggs until they are light and fluffy.

In a small bowl stir together the sugar and oil, then beat the sugar mixture into the eggs until the mixture is well combined.

In another bowl whisk together the flour, cinnamon, and the baking soda, then add to the egg mixture.

Beat in the vanilla and—lastly—the walnuts until they are combined.

Arrange the sliced apples in the bottom of a butter-greased 9" x 13" baking dish.

Pour the Butterscotch Caramel over the top of the apples to your taste (I used half the jar).

Spread the batter evenly over the apple/caramel topping.

Bake on the middle rack of the oven for 50 to 60 minutes, until tester comes out clean.

Let it cool on a rack for 15 minutes and dust with the powdered sugar. Serve warm with a dollop of whipped cream.

Turtle Cake - Robbie T.

On Sara's son Robbie's first visit to Europe, he came across this recipe at a country inn, in Germany. He liked it so much, he asked for the recipe and brought it back to share with us. We've been making it ever since—always at Halloween, along with molded chocolates and the Black Bottom Cupcakes you'll find elsewhere in here! This is a taste treat the all kids—big and little—seem to **love**!

1 box of chocolate cake mix (two layers)*
3/4 cup melted butter
2/3 cup evaporated milk
1 pkg. of at least 50 caramels
12-oz. pkg. chocolate chips
1 cup chopped walnuts (or pecans or blanched almonds)

***They used German chocolate; I use Devil's Food by Duncan Hines,
    with pudding. It's *soooo* rich!**

This recipe is *very easy* to do. But since it is done in several parts, I suggest you read it through so you can have a better sense of coordination before beginning!

Preheat the oven to 350°.

♥ *Part One*

Mix together the chocolate cake mix, melted butter, and *1/3* cup of the evaporated milk. Pour *half* of the mixture into a sprayed 9" x 13" pan.

Bake for six minutes.

♥ *Part Two*

While the cake is baking, unwrap the caramels, and put them in a bowl.

Add the remainder of the milk (1/3 cup) and melt the mixture in a double boiler, *or* microwave it for at least four minutes—until the caramels are melted and can be stirred into the milk. Test. And watch—as each microwave is different. Don't let it burn! (Yes, I've done it!)

♥ *Part Three*

When the cake is done, remove it from the oven, and while it's still warm, sprinkle it with the chocolate chips. Spread carefully with spatula to cover.

Immediately sprinkle the chopped nuts over the melted chocolate.

Pour the hot caramel mixture over top of chocolate and nuts.

Now drop the *rest* of the cake batter over the top.

Put the cake *back* in the oven, and bake for another 15 to 20 minutes until done.

Remove and let cool completely until firm.

Cut into bars, or large squares, and serve with a scoop of ice cream.

Contentment is the art of keeping your tastes below your neighbor's income.

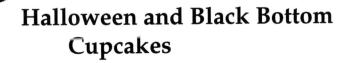

Halloween and Black Bottom Cupcakes

There are some special food items that I only make on certain holidays. This one fits the mood for Halloween, and boy, did those kids love it when they were little! Halloween is so much more fun when there are children around. There is something so special about the way those little eyes light up when they know it's treat time, and that you've made something "just for them". My sons enjoyed everything I made, and these cupcakes were gone in seconds!

8-oz. pkg. cream cheese
1 large egg
1/3 cup sugar
1/8 tsp. salt
6 oz. semisweet chocolate chips
1-1/2 cups flour
1 cup sugar
1/4 tsp. cocoa
1 tsp. baking soda
1/2 tsp. salt
1 cup water
1/3 cup Mazola oil
1 Tbs. apple cider vinegar
1 tsp. vanilla

Preheat the oven to 350°.

Combine the cream cheese, egg, sugar and salt, and beat well.

Stir the chocolate chips into mixture and set the bowl aside.

Sift together the flour, sugar, cocoa, soda and salt.

Add the water, Mazola oil, cider vinegar and vanilla.

Fill cupcake liners 1/3 full with batter.

Top each cup with one tablespoon of the chocolate chip/cream cheese mixture. Sprinkle top with nuts if you like—I do.

Bake for 30 to 35 minutes.

Makes about two dozen.

Amaretto Cookies - Joan D.

1 cup plus 2 Tbs. blanched almonds
3/4 cup plus 3 Tbs. powdered sugar
3/4 tsp. almond extract or Amaretto liqueur
1 tsp. flour
2 large egg whites, room temperature
1/3 cup sugar

Preheat oven to 300°.

In your Cuisinart grind the almonds and 1/4 cup powdered sugar to a fine powder. Put aside in another bowl.

Stir the remaining 1/2 cup plus 3 Tbs. powdered sugar and the flour into the nut mixture.

In a separate bowl, beat the egg whites until soft peaks form.

Gradually add the sugar to the egg whites and continue to beat until stiff and shiny.

Fold the nut mixture into the whites in three batches, adding the almond extract with the last addition. The egg whites will deflate due to the heaviness of the nuts, but *don't despair.*

Transfer the batter to a pastry bag fitted with a 1/2" plain tip.

On parchment lined, lightly buttered baking sheets, pipe mounds about one and a half inches high, and one and a half inches apart. (If you want a smaller size, cook less time, of course.)

Smooth the top of each cookie with a damp finger, to round them off.

Bake for 35 minutes until lightly brown.

Turn off the oven and let the cookies dry in the oven for 30 minutes to give them a crunchy bite.

Remove with a spatula to wire racks. Cool. Store in airtight containers.

♥ *Helpful Hint*

When rolling out cookie dough, sprinkle the counter with powdered sugar instead of flour. Too much flour makes the dough heavy. When freezing cookies with frosting, place them in freezer unwrapped for two hours on cookie sheet, then remove and combine carefully in plastic bag.

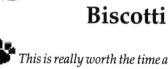

Biscotti

🐾 *This is really worth the time and takes very little effort. For though it's done in several steps, it isn't hard to make these hard Italian cookies that are ideal for dipping in your coffee! You can serve them plain, or dip them in melted chocolate. I like to dip mine plain.*

1 cup all-purpose flour
1 tsp. baking powder
1 tsp. cinnamon
1/2 tsp. cloves
1/8 tsp. nutmeg
2 cups chopped almonds or filberts
1 cup sugar
2 large eggs, lightly beaten
1/4 cup Mazola oil

Preheat the oven to 350°.

Sift the flour, baking powder, cinnamon, cloves and nutmeg in a Cuisinart or mixing bowl.

Blend the sugar, eggs and oil together in another bowl until fluffy.

Add this mixture to the sifted ingredients and add the nuts. Mix well. If using a Cuisinart, just flick the on/off switch a couple of times so the nuts will remain chunky.

This will make a sticky dough. So turn it out onto a lightly floured board. Then divide the dough into two or three pieces. Lightly knead the pieces into a long French bread loaf shape, but don't knead it too much—just enough to shape it.

Gently place the dough on a *greased* cookie sheet.

Bake for 25 minutes until the biscotti are firm—*but not hard.*

Remove the long cookies from the oven and the baking sheet. Cut them into small finger slices.

Put the slices *back* on the cookie sheets and then bake them on one side for about five minutes.

Turn the pieces over and them bake the other side for about five minutes—or until both sides are a nice, golden brown.

Remove and cool completely on wire racks. Store in an airtight container.

Cheesecake Squares - Connie A.

5 Tbs. butter
1/3 cup dark brown sugar
1 cup flour, sifted
1/4 cup chopped walnuts
1/2 cup white sugar
8-oz. pkg. cream cheese, softened
1 large egg, beaten
2 Tbs. milk
1 Tbs. lemon juice
1/4 tsp. vanilla

Preheat the oven to 350°.

Cream together the butter and brown sugar.

Add the flour and nuts and mix well. Set aside one cup of this mixture for the topping.

Press the remaining mix into *ungreased* bottom of an 8" x 8" pan.

Bake for 12 to 15 minutes until light brown. Remove, leaving oven on for the cake part.

Blend together the white sugar and cream cheese until smooth.

Add the egg, milk, lemon juice and vanilla. Mix well and pour over the baked crust.

Sprinkle with the cup of reserved crust topping and return to oven to bake for 25 more minutes.

Cool, chill and cut in squares.

Serve alone or with fresh fruit over top.

Or, top with some thawed, puréed berries with a touch of vanilla and some whole berries mixed in.

I add a splash of liqueur in the berries for added zip.

♥ ♥ ♥

Chocolate Chip Pudding Cookies
- Krysy B.

Krysy is like a daughter to us. Bubbling and bouncing—sometimes serious— she is so endearing. Always dropping in and out of our lives, she arrives with hugs and kisses and stays to entertain us with accounts of her latest adventure's on life's pathways. So very special to us, we particularly miss her when she isn't around at Christmas time, for that's when we often made candy and other treats together. She loves chocolate, she loves to eat, and she loves these particular cookies. And just to make sure we'll make them while she's there, she's been known to bound into our house with a brown bag containing all the ingredients!

2-1/4 cups flour
1 tsp. baking soda
1 cup butter, softened
3/4 cup packed dark brown sugar
1/4 cup sugar
3-oz. pkg. small Jell-O instant chocolate-flavored pudding mix
1 tsp. vanilla
2 large eggs
12-oz. pkg. Nestlé mint chocolate *or* peanut butter chips
1 cup chopped walnuts, pecans, hazelnuts and/or pistachios

Preheat the oven to 350°.

Mix the flour with the baking soda.

In another bowl, combine the butter, sugars, pudding mix and vanilla. Mix until smooth.

Beat in the eggs.

Gradually add the flour mixture.

Stir in the chocolate chips and nuts. The batter will be stiff.

Drop in heaping tablespoons onto *ungreased* cookie sheets about two inches apart. Bake for eight to ten minutes.

Remove to wire rack to cool. Store in airtight container.

Chocolate Meltaway Bars/Balls

This is my own variation of a recipe I liked in the "Readers Write In" section of Better Homes and Gardens. *I made it for a special dessert one night and everyone just loved it.*

2 8-oz. Hershey's chocolate bars with almonds
1 8-oz. carton of Cool Whip, thawed
1 Tbs. Chambord (optional)
1/2 cup chopped toasted almonds
2/3 to 1 cup crushed chocolate wafer cookies for coating

Break the chocolate bars into pieces and melt them over low heat in a double boiler. Let cool to room temperature. It should be a little runny—not firm. Add the Chambord, if you're using it.

Fold the chocolate mixture into the Cool Whip and add the nuts. Refrigerate overnight, covered.

Spread the crushed chocolate wafers on a large plate.

With an ice cream scoop or large spoon, dip out about 1/4 cup per serving and roll in the chocolate wafer crumbs. Do this fast, as it melts quickly in handling.

Place the balls on wax-papered cookie sheet or in foil-lined muffin papers, and freeze, covered, until ready to serve.

You can serve these "plain" or with a dab of Cool Whip flavored with liqueur—such as Raspberry, with a few fresh raspberries to go over top—and a smattering of chopped nuts.

♥ Variations

You could add a bit of cinnamon and sugar to chocolate wafer crumbs.

Or, spoon the chocolate filling into a baked and cooled pie crust of Oreo cookies and butter. In which case you would freeze it, covered, and cut it into wedges to serve.

Chocolate Waffle Cookies - Myrt J.

Myrt used to come for lunch at Archie's, where I was working, every Friday, and what a pleasure it was to wait on her. If I could have my own restaurant—doing it homestyle, with lots of love—I would particularly love for Myrt to come and make the desserts. Because, as her daughter says, when it comes to baking, she's "the best"!

1 cup butter
3 squares of bitter chocolate or 3/4 cup cocoa
4 large eggs, beaten
1-1/2 cups sugar
2 tsp. vanilla
2 cups flour
1/2 cup chopped nuts (optional)

Slowly melt the butter and chocolate or cocoa.

Mix together the beaten eggs, sugar and vanilla and combine it with the melted chocolate mixture.

Add the flour, mixing in well.

Add the chopped nuts.

Pour the batter onto a medium hot waffle iron either in droplets—like small cookies, or in long bar shapes.

Bake for approximately one minute, five seconds.

Frost with your favorite frosting, or peanut butter, or just dust it with powder sugar.

*When you see the odd shapes of some human beings,
it's hard to believe that they all come from the same pattern.*

Lemon Bars - Phil S.

Preheat oven to 350°.

♥ *Crust*

1 cup butter
2 cups flour
1/2 cup powdered sugar

Combine the butter, flour and sugar, and stir well in your Cuisinart/ mixing bowl until it holds together like a pie dough.

Pat the mixture into 9" x 13" pan.

Bake for 20 minutes, until it starts to slightly brown around the edges. Remove it from the oven.

♥ *Topping*

4 large eggs
1-3/4 cups sugar
1/3 cup flour
1/2 tsp. baking powder
1/3 cup fresh lemon juice
Powdered sugar for dusting

Combine the eggs, sugar, flour, baking powder and lemon juice, and mix well.

Pour this mixture into the baked base in the 9" x 13" pan.

Bake at 350° for 25 minutes until lightly golden brown.

Remove and dust with powdered sugar.

Cool completely, and sprinkle once again with powdered sugar. If you like a more tart taste, don't dust it right out of oven.

Cut into bars or squares.

Macadamia Nut Bars

7-oz. can plain or Kona-covered Macadamia nuts, chopped
3 cups cake flour
3/4 cup powdered sugar
1-1/4 cup butter or 2-1/2 sticks butter, softened
12-oz. pkg. Nestlé chocolate chips or 2 cups of good chocolate pieces*

*You can go overboard and use white chocolate to be fancy, fancy.
    Well, why not?

Preheat oven to 325°.

In Cuisinart:

Combine the cake flour, sugar and butter until it starts to hold together.

Add the nuts last so they don't get too crushed up. Save a few for the top.

Pat this mixture into a 9" x 13" pan. Bake for 30 minutes, until golden brown. Watch carefully.

Remove and immediately sprinkle with the chocolate chips and/or pieces, smoothing them around as they melt.   Like I said, a few shavings of white chocolate is Mmmmm!

Put a few leftover chopped nuts on top.

Cool at least 30 minutes before cutting.

Happiness adds and multiplies as we divide it with others.

Good Old Refrigerator Cookies - Granny Rider

🐾 *My mom **always** has treats around. It's her middle name. We are always wondering how a woman with such a sweet tooth can stay so tiny. I really am not a sweet eater. But there are times when I want some thing to nibble on. These cookies, cooked crunchy just for me, are—even today—such a nice little surprise, especially when Granny gets carried away and makes two batches, as the boys—and Bill, too—like theirs soft. Bobba liked them with his tea, which was served every afternoon when he was at home. I thought for years that the world stopped at 4:00 for teatime.*

3 cups flour
1 tsp. baking soda
1/2 tsp. cream of tartar
1/2 tsp. salt
1 cup butter
1 cup dark brown sugar
1 cup white sugar
2 large eggs, beaten
2 tsp. vanilla
2/3 cup chopped walnuts

Preheat the oven to 375°.

Mix the flour, soda, cream of tartar and salt together.

Cream the butter, brown sugar and white sugar together and add to the flour mixture.

Add the beaten eggs and vanilla. Mix together well.

Fold in the chopped nuts.

Roll into logs, wrap in plastic and chill in refrigerator.

Cut in circles or—like Granny does—in oblong squares. Place on cookie sheets 1" apart.

Bake for 12 minutes.

Remove to wire rack, then to an airtight container.

Hazelnut Shortbread

1/3 cup chopped filberts/hazelnuts
2 cups flour
1 cup cornstarch
1-1/4 cups butter
1/2 cup sugar
2-1/2 sticks butter, softened

In Cuisinart, chop nuts to a medium consistency. Remove to bowl and set aside.

Mix the flour, cornstarch, and ground nuts together.

In Cuisinart bowl—dusted out of nut dust—beat the butter and sugar until fluffy and light.

Add flour mixture until just blended.

Preheat the oven to 325°.

On a *lightly* floured surface, with *lightly* floured hands, knead the dough until it's well blended and smooth. This should take just a few turns. Don't use a lot of flour—that will make the dough tough.

Roll the dough out carefully to form an oblong square—about 1/4" thick.

Place the rolled out dough on an *ungreased* cookie sheet.

Mark each piece with a knife—*but not all the way through*—to form squares or wedges that you will cut later on. Prick the dough all over with fork prongs.

Bake for 30 minutes, until light brown.

Remove the cookie sheet to a wire rack to cool. Cut into the shortbread when it's cool.

Store in airtight container.

I just can't leave this alone when I first make it after an absence. So rich and light, it just melts in your mouth. It also makes an easy and excellent gift.

Pie Making Hints

♥ *Common Problems*

Tough: Over-mixing, is not like bread just treat lightly

Too much water, drop in gradually until it starts to hold together

Too much flour added in when rolling out, just lightly dust work space

Not enough fat, or not a good product - Use Crisco, although some like Fluffo

Crumbly: Too much fat, some products are just better than others!

Not enough water, must hold it together

Shrinks: Stretched when put in pan, not rolled a bit oversized and you can cut off.

Over-handled and thumped around like bread dough is a No No!

Rolled too thin causing to break, crack and dry out

Blistered: Not pricked enough on bottom and sides

Baked at too low a temperature

♥   To cut pie into five equal pieces, slice a "Y" in the pie and then slice the two larger pieces in half.

♥   To cut pie into six or eight equal pieces, cut pie in half and divide each half, matching the other side to first half cuts.

♥   At kitchen and restaurant supply stores they have a metal barred toothed form, in a circle, with knob to hold on to as you press that marks the pieces for even cutting per slice.

♥   If you run out of nuts for a pecan pie, substitute crushed cornflakes.

♥   Sprinkle powdered sugar over crust of cream pie to prevent it becoming soggy.

♥   When baking fruit pies from which the juice runs over, sprinkle with salt and they'll burn to a crisp and can be easily scraped up with a spatula.

♥   For Never Fail/weep meringue, add a teaspoon of cornstarch to the sugar before beating it into the egg whites. Cover pie with plastic or wax paper coated in margarine for no sticking.

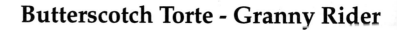

Butterscotch Torte - Granny Rider

This is something that will impress the guests. And it's not that hard. There's just a few steps required to make it festive.

Preheat the oven to 325°.

♥ Cake

6 large eggs, separated
1-1/2 cups sugar
1 tsp. baking powder
2 tsp. vanilla
2 cups graham crackers, crushed
1 cup chopped nuts of your choice—walnuts, almonds, hazelnuts, or
    pecans

Beat the egg whites until stiff and set aside.

In a separate bowl, beat the egg yolks, and add the sugar, baking powder, and vanilla.

Fold in the stiffly beaten egg whites, the crushed crackers and the nuts.

Pour into two 9" lined pans sprayed with Baker's Joy.

Bake for 30 to 35 minutes. Test.

Remove from oven and cool for 1/2 hour.

Remove from the pans and cut each half in half, for a four-layer cake.

♥ Frosting

Beat together :

2 cups whipped cream
3 Tbs. powdered sugar

Spread this frosting on each layer of the cake, stack the layers one on top of other, frost the sides and refrigerate.

♥ Topping

Combine and cook the following ingredients until thick:

1/4 cup butter
1/4 cup water
1 cup dark brown sugar
1 large egg, well beaten
1/2 tsp. vanilla.

Let this mixture cool, and then drizzle it all over the cake.

Return the torte to the refrigerator until ready to serve.

Strawberry Cream Cheese Pie - Aunt June

8 oz. cream cheese, softened
1 cup powdered sugar
1/2 pint heavy whipping cream
1 tsp. vanilla
1 9" baked pie crust
1 pint fresh strawberries, dusted in sugar to taste or 10 oz. frozen strawberries, thawed
    and drained

Blend the cream cheese with the sugar.

Whip the cream until stiff and mix in the vanilla.

Fold into the cream cheese mix.

Pour into the baked pie shell and top with the strawberries.

Cool in the refrigerator—not the freezer—for at least two hours to firm it up.

I usually do it in layers—cream, strawberries, cream, strawberries etc.—because I like it that
way.

I particularly love to make this pie when the strawberries are *just ripe*, and oh so sweet!

Lemon Cloud - Tom B.

 *My friend (and chef) Tom Bannister used to make this for brunch banquets. Every time he made this the other waitresses and I would just pray that there would be some left over when the festivities were over! As for my share: I gave it to my dear friend, Helen. It was her favorite! I've adapted the recipe for a smaller group. It's done in layers, but the steps are easy and the time it takes for the parts to cool should be well worth it when you see the pleasure everyone will derive from diving into this delectable dessert.*

♥ Crust

Preheat the oven to 350° and spray a large 9" x 13" pan with Baker's Joy. Mix together:

2 cups flour
1/2 lb. butter
1/2 cup chopped nuts

Press into the pan and bake for ten minutes, until lightly brown. Cool.

♥ Filling

2 8-oz. pkgs. cream cheese
2 cups powdered sugar
2 cups whipped cream or Cool Whip

Whip together the cream cheese and sugar.

Fold in the whipped cream or Cool Whip, pour the mixture over the baked crust and refrigerate until firm.

♥ Topping

1 large box Jell-O lemon-flavored pudding mix
2 cups Cool Whip
1 cup shredded coconut, toasted
1/2 cup additional nuts (optional)

Following instructions on the box, make the pudding and mix it with the 2 cups of Cool Whip.

Mix together the toasted coconut and nuts sprinkle the mixture over the rest of the "cloud".

Refrigerate until firm, then cut into squares and serve.

Baked Pecan Pastry Shell

9" pie pan - for bottom crust only
1 cup flour
3 Tbs. finely ground pecans
2 Tbs. powdered sugar
1/2 cup *unsalted* butter - *cold*
1 large egg yolk, beaten

Combine the flour, pecans, and sugar in medium bowl.

Cut in the butter until the mixture resembles coarse crumbles.

Stir in the egg yolk with a fork until well mixed.

(I like to make this crust in my Cuisinart, adding in the nuts last so they don't over chop. But don't mix the dough too much or it becomes tough. As soon as the mixture starts to hold together, take it out and form into crust.)

Press the crust evenly into the pie pan bottom and sides.

Refrigerate for one hour, *uncovered*.

Preheat the oven to 425°.

Bake the crust until golden brown—about eight minutes. Watch carefully.

Cool completely before putting in filling of your choice.

This crust is excellent for Peanut Butter, Pumpkin, and Glazed Strawberry pies, among others!

♥ ♥ ♥

Chambord Cheesecake

♥ *Crust*

1/3 cup melted butter
1 package of chocolate wafer cookies
Dash of salt
1/4 tsp. of cinnamon
1/2 cup ground or crushed nuts of choice

Mix all the ingredients together well.

Press on the bottom and up the sides of a 9" buttered springform pan.

♥ *Filling*

1 lb. bittersweet chocolate squares or pieces
2 Tbs. soft butter
1-1/2 lb. cream cheese, softened
4 large eggs
1 cup sugar
3 Tbs. unsweetened cocoa
Dash salt
3 Tbs. Chambord
3/4 cup sour cream
1 Tbs. vanilla

Put the bittersweet chocolate in a double broiler, and add the butter. Melt carefully over simmering water so you don't dry the mixture out with too much heat.

In Cuisinart or large mixing bowl, beat the sugar and eggs until fluffy for one minute.

Combine and add all the rest of ingredients *except* the melted chocolate and butter.

Now add chocolate mix, mixing in well, but not too much.

Pour the cheesecake filling into the crust. Make the top level as possible.

Bake at 350° in the middle of the oven for ten minutes. Turn down to 325° and bake 35 minutes more. Test. The cake should be firm, but don't over cook or it cracks. It will tighten up as it cools off.

Turn off the oven and let the cake sit for one hour in the oven. Let it cool down and then put in the refrigerator overnight.

Serve in a puddle of raspberry purée made with 1 Tbs. or more of Chambord. Top with a few fresh berries and sprinkle on some grated sweet chocolate.

Macadamia Nut Pie

3 large eggs, beaten
1 Tbs. vanilla
2/3 cup sugar
1 stick butter, melted
1 cup *dark* corn syrup
2 Tbs. of Kahlua
10-oz. can Macadamia nuts, chopped
2 unbaked pie shells

Preheat the oven to 350°.

Mix the eggs, vanilla, sugar, butter, corn syrup and Kahlua in Cuisinart or mixer. Blend well.

Add the nuts, but don't chop them up too fine.

Pour into pie shell bottoms. Smooth tops as well as you can.

Bake for 30 to 40 minutes. Should be nice and golden brown.

Let the pies sit to firm up before cutting into slices.

Serve with whipped cream flavored with Kahlua, French Vanilla or coffee-flavored ice cream, or Cool Whip.

Lemon Pie - Nanny for Phil S.

The filling for this pie goes into a prebaked 9" pie crust—so do first! Use an egg wash to seal the crust so it won't get soggy. Let the crust cool while you're preparing the filling.

♥ *Filling*

1/4 cup cornstarch
1 cup sugar
Dash of salt
1-1/ 2 cups *boiling* water
1 Tbs. butter, softened
1 tsp. grated lemon rind
6 Tbs. lemon juice
3 large eggs, separated
2 Tbs. milk

In a small bowl, beat the egg yolks with the milk and set it aside.

In a heavy saucepan or double boiler, mix together the cornstarch, sugar and salt.

Add the boiling water gradually, stirring constantly.

Cook this mixture slowly, until it's clear—about five to six minutes.

Add the butter, lemon rind and juice.   Cook on low to medium heat for two minutes.

Remove the filling from the heat and let it cool slightly, then add the egg yolk/milk mixture.

Return to the stove and bring the filling to a boiling point, then remove it from the heat and let it cool slightly.

Pour into prebaked crust.

♥ *Meringue*

3 large egg whites
6 Tbs. sugar
1 tsp. lemon juice

Beat egg whites, adding the sugar *gradually* while beating. Add the lemon juice. Beat the mixture until it forms stiff peaks—but isn't dry. Spread in a design over the lemon filling.

Bake the pie at 350° for 15 minutes until top starts to get light brown.

Remove, refrigerate, and serve well chilled.

Lemon Curd - Roy and Ann McKay

Ann brought a tray of these tarts to our Open House one Christmas, and my husband Bill stood at the counter next to them, until I noticed that he had nearly eaten them all—and chased him away. The next year, Ann and Roy brought some for our guests—along with an extra tin—just for Bill. They are just the dearest people.

3 to 4 large lemons - rind only and their juice
1/4 lb. (1/2 stick) butter
2 cups sugar
6 large eggs, well beaten

Grate the lemon rinds and both the "zest" and the juice.

Cream the butter and sugar until light and fluffy.

Put in double boiler and add the grated lemon rind and the juice. Mix well.

Add the beaten eggs. Stir well, and cook over simmering water until thickened—about 35 minutes. Stir *constantly*.

Pour into your *prebaked* tart shells. Or save the curd in sealed jars for later use.

Refrigerate.

Almond Puff

 *Don't let this recipe scare you. It's actually very easy, and the taste is absolutely wonderful!*

1 cup (two sticks) butter
3 cups flour
2 Tbs. plus 1 cup of water
1 tsp. almond extract
3 large eggs
1 cup or more chopped almonds
Powdered sugar

Preheat the oven to 350°.

♥ Part 1

Cut the *first* stick of butter into *one cup* of flour as you would for a pie crust.

Sprinkle the two tablespoons of water over the mixture. Mix with a fork. Round into a ball. Divide in half.

On an *ungreased* baking sheet, pat each half into a strip—an oblong, 12" x 3" shape—three inches apart.

♥ Part 2

In a medium saucepan, heat the *second* stick of butter and the one cup of water to a rolling boil.

Remove the pan from the heat and quickly stir in the almond extract and the *second* cup of flour.

Put the pan back on burner and stir vigorously over low heat until the mixture forms a ball—in about one minute.

Remove the pan from the heat again. Beat in the eggs, *all at one time*, until the mixture is smooth. Divide it in half.

♥ Part 3

Spread each half of the almond mixture on the strips of dough on the cookie sheet as evenly as possible, covering them completely.

Bake for one hour or until the topping is crisp and brown. Cool.

♥ *Powdered Sugar Glaze*

1-1/2 cups powdered sugar
2 Tbs. butter, softened
1-1/2 tsp. vanilla
1–2 Tbs. warm water
Finely chopped or ground nuts

Mix the powdered sugar, butter, vanilla and water until smooth. Spread over the almond puff and sprinkle with nuts.

♥ ♥ ♥

Grandmother's Raspberry Pie - Suzy M.

4 to 5 cups (depending on their size) of fresh raspberries
3/4 cup water
4 Tbs. cornstarch
1 cup sugar
1 tsp. lemon juice
1 prebaked 8" or 9" pie shell - egg washed to seal

Reserve one cup of the raspberries to sprinkle on the bottom of the pie shell.

Simmer the rest of the raspberries and the water together for three to four minutes:

Mix together the cornstarch and sugar and add it to the raspberry mixture. Cook until the mixture is clear—*stirring constantly.*

Add the lemon juice and remove the filling from the heat. Let it cool a bit before pouring it into the crust.

Sprinkle the reserved raspberries evenly in the bottom of the pie shell.

Pour the cooled berry mixture on top of the fresh berries.

Refrigerate until firm. Then cut.

Top with whipped cream.

Elegant Layered Dessert:
The Boys' Favorite - Anytime!

It may seem weird the way these puddings go together, but it is a taste treat you will make over and over, as it's easy, pretty fast, and consistently gets rave reviews! Read the recipe through: the ingredients and steps are presented in parts...

♥ *Layer 1:*

l cup flour
1/2 cup butter
1/2 cup chopped walnuts

Preheat over to 350°.

Mix and pat into an *ungreased* 9" x 13" oblong pan.

Bake for 15 to 20 minutes until lightly brown.

♥ *Layer 2:*

8 oz. cream cheese
l cup powdered sugar
l cup Cool Whip*

*You will need more for topping, so get a large container.

Cream together and pour over baked, cooled crust.

♥ *Layer 3:*

4-oz. pkg. Instant Vanilla pudding
4-oz. pkg. Jell-O instant chocolate-flavored pudding mix
3 cups milk
Chopped nuts of choice and chocolate sprinkles (optional)

Mix together and pour carefully over the top of the cream cheese.

Top the whole thing carefully with more Cool Whip mixed with chopped nuts. Or, sprinkle chocolate sprinkles...

Put in the refrigerator—*not* the freezer—for one hour to firm up.

Thanksgiving Pecan Pie

1-1/2 cups slightly chopped pecans
1 Tbs. flour
1/4 cup sugar
1 cup dark brown sugar
1 Tbs. cream
1/2 cup butter, melted
3 large eggs, beaten
1-1/ 2 tsp. vanilla
2 Tbs. brandy
1 prepared pie crust (of course you made it?)

Preheat oven to 350°.

In Cuisinart or mixer, combine sugars, cream, eggs and melted butter.

Add vanilla and brandy.

Add pecans, but if you're using a Cuisinart, don't over-chop.

Pour into prepared crust.

Bake for one hour.

I like this pie made with crushed chocolate wafers or ginger snaps and butter—with a touch of cinnamon— for a crust. Ready-made chocolate crusts (Keebler's, for one) are available in most supermarkets.

Conversation is the art of hearing as well as being heard.

Crunchy Apple Pie

In cookbooks from back East you hear of their Grapenut puddings, cakes, and pies. Well, I don't know where Mom got this one, but I must agree with my friend Sara: this one is great for a change.

♥ *Crust*

1-1/2 cups flour
2 Tbs. sugar
1 tsp. salt
1/2 cup Mazola oil
2 tsp. cream

Mix all these ingredients together to form a crust and lay in a 9" pie pan. Make a pretty edge.

♥ *Filling*

2/3 cup sugar
1/4 cup flour
1 tsp. cinnamon
1/2 cup sour cream
4 cups peeled, cored and sliced Granny Smith or Golden Delicious apples

Mix all these together and pile it on top of the crust.

♥ *Topping*

1/2 cup Grapenuts flakes
1/2 cup flour
1/3 cup dark brown sugar
1/2 tsp. nutmeg
1/2 tsp. cinnamon
1/4 cup butter, softened

Mix all these together and sprinkle it over the top.

Bake at 375° for 35 minutes, until it is nice, bubbly and brown on top.

Let it sit for a bit—if you can—before cutting into it, so it will hold together.

Ice cream is nice on top.

Frozen Chocolate Frango Pie
- Julie B.

1 cup butter
2 cups sifted powdered sugar
4 squares *unsweetened* chocolate, melted
4 large eggs
3/4 tsp. peppermint extract or 1/4 tsp. peppermint oil
2 tsp. vanilla
1-1/2 cups ground pecans
Cupcake papers or baked pie shell of choice
Whipped cream and cherries for topping

Using electric mixer, beat the butter and sugar until light and fluffy.

Add the melted chocolate and continue beating.

Add eggs one at a time.

Add the peppermint and vanilla.

Beat until smooth.

Sprinkle the ground pecans to cover the surface of a prebaked, cooled pie crust or the bottoms of cupcake cups.

Spoon in filling.

Freeze until firm.

Serve with whipped cream and a cherry on top. Or a sprinkle of nuts.

Fortune favors the bold, but abandons the timid.

Latin Proverb

Soda Cracker Dessert - Phyllis S.

My friend Phyllis lives in the home she inherited from her parents over on Whidby Island, in the Puget Sound. There is a slight lilt to her voice that —along with the whitish blond hair and blue eyes, her love for the outdoor sports, and her domestic delight in sharing a family recipe—is strongly indicative of her Scandinavian heritage. This is a dessert that her Aunt Milly taught to her mom and which her mom in turn used to make every year for Phyllis' birthday at her request. And now, thankfully, we can enjoy it—any time—too!

3 egg whites
1 cup sugar
14 crushed soda crackers
1/2 tsp. baking powder
Dash vanilla
1/2 cup chopped walnuts
Whipped cream for topping

Preheat the oven to 300°.

Beat the egg whites until stiff.

Mix together all the other ingredients except the whipped cream, and fold gently into the egg whites.

Pour into an ungreased 9" x 9" pan or pie pan.

Bake for 20 to 25 minutes.

Serve with *real* whipped cream on top.

It's bad manners to talk with your mouth full,
except when you're praising your hostess'
cooking.

Hungarian Rugola - Lotsz

There are so many little treats—sweet and savory—that you can make with one, simple pastry recipe for the foundation. This one makes four 10" circles for filling. Or you can cut into smaller, bite-sized sizes (2" x 2") as well....

♥ *Pastry*

2 cups flour
2 sticks butter, softened
8 oz. pkg. cream cheese

Combine the flour, butter and cream cheese. Roll the pastry out as you would a pie crust, and cut it into circles.

♥ *Fillings*

For *sweet treats*, fill with a dollop of jam or jelly, cream cheese, cinnamon and sugar, or slices of fruit.

For *savory appetizers*, you might try some of the following fillings (I always throw in a dash of Morton's, but by now you probably know that!):

- ♥ Sautéed mushrooms, onion, spinach, with cream sherry and chopped cooked crisp bacon.
- ♥ Smoked Salmon and cream cheese.
- ♥ Sautéed sausage with some chopped red pepper. Throw in a bit of grated cheese of your choice.
- ♥ Chopped ham with grated Swiss cheese—mixed with a dab of Dijon hot mustard.
- ♥ Shrimp, cream cheese, chopped onion, with a squeeze of lemon and a drop of Tabasco.
- ♥ Crab, cream cheese, a dab of milk, with a touch of curry.

Whatever filling you use, don't use too much, as you need to roll and/or seal the rugola up into half moons, pinwheels, or whatever shape you'd like.

Bake at 375° for 15 to 20 minutes on *ungreased* cookie sheets. Watch for light brown color.

You can also press the pastry into little muffin pans or small fancy metal molds, put in your filling of choice, and seal or leave it open.

This dough keeps in the refrigerator for two weeks in a Ziploc bag. So nice to have on hand.

The Very Best Ever Chocolate Peanut Butter Pie - Michael's Mom

Every now and then someone simply passes through your life, leaving you with brief but happy, wonderful memories. And, when you see them once again, after a long time, you're just so glad for the few special occasions that bring you together to share time with that person again. Michael—one of the many bosses I had in the restaurant chain for which I once worked—was one of these. He brought this pie to Bill's surprise 40th birthday party, and it was so good that all the men stood around eating it with spoons right out of the pan—without even bothering to use a plate. There are just not enough stars around to rank this ten-star plus recipe!

8-oz. pkg. cream cheese, softened
14-oz. can *sweetened condensed* milk
1/4 cup lemon juice
1 tsp. vanilla
4-1/2 oz. Cool Whip
1 cup crunchy peanut butter
Shaved chocolate for topping (optional)

Mix together the cream cheese, condensed milk, lemon juice, vanilla, and Cool Whip.

Fold in the peanut butter, until the mixture is as smooth as crunchy can get and pour either in pie pan or baked crust.

Put the pie in the refrigerator with topping of shaved chocolate, or do it just before serving. (But it sticks on better if you sprinkle it on beforehand.)

♥ Variations

Michael serves his without a crust. But to be fancy, fancy, use chocolate wafers, gingersnaps, baked shortbread, or pecan crust, if you want.

You could also add crumbles of chocolate bar to make this a *chocolate* peanut butter pie. But, first try it Mike's way. Again—there are just not enough stars for this one!

♥ ♥ ♥

A Proper Tea for Sonia

This is so wonderful with pies and pastries that I must put this here! When Sonia lived with us off and on for about four years when she was in her early twenties, we would often find ourselves discussing life's problems, the solutions, the things to consider in the paths ourselves and others had followed over a lovely cup of tea. We didn't always have a treat, but would curl up on the love seat and couch with much shared love of a wonderful old custom. When I gave her the first, handwritten version of this cookbook, she asked me to include this Proper Tea, as it meant so much to us. Bobba and Mom always had tea around 4:00 with pie, cake, or whatever taste treat she had made for that time of day. I'm happy to include this ceremony here because I agree with Sonia that it's too bad we have become too busy to stop for tea. It revives, relaxes, and makes a hassled world recede for a few minutes.

Bring water to a boil in large-sized teapot.

Take off burner immediately.

Pour into a fancy glass teapot of your choice and the cups for yourself or guests.

Reheat leftover water, adding fresh and bring once again to boil.

Put tea of choice into pot and let steep—that is, sit—to whatever strength you like your tea. Five minutes is the usual length of time.

Pour cooling water from the glass teapot and cups into a waiting pan and proceed to pour the hot tea into the glass teapot and serve with warmed cups right away.

Serve with slices of lemon, milk, and sugar for those who wish it.

A nice tray of sandwiches cut in squares, circles, rectangles with no crusts, cookies, cake or fancy breads—banana, zucchini, lemon, etc.—with pats of butter and jam is a lovely way to bring a long day to a end.

Wild Blackberry Pie

1-1/ 2 cups sugar
1/3 cup flour
1 tsp. cinnamon
2 Tbs. butter pieces
2 oz. cream cheese pieces*
4 cups fresh tiny blackberries or marionberries

*Buy 3-oz. package and use leftover in crust.

Preheat the oven to 425°.

Make two pie crusts (see below). Roll and fold one crust into pie pan bottom.

Mix all the listed ingredients well with the berries.

Pour the berry mixture into the prepared pie crust.

Add the top crust, seal the edges, cut in design and put on a pie drip pan or cookie sheet—because berry pies *always* drip.

Bake for 40 to 45 minutes.

♥ *Crust*

2 cups flour
1 tsp. salt
2/3 cup + 2 Tbs. Crisco*
1/4 cup cold water

*Sometimes I replace the 2 Tbs. Crisco with 1 oz. of cream cheese)

I put all ingredients, except the water, into the Cuisinart and mix for a minute to blend, then add the water. Don't over mix! *Just* mix it until it begins to come together.

Remove the pie dough, divide it in half, and roll each between two lightly floured sheets of wax paper. Make the bottom crust a bit larger so it will fill up to the top of the edges and be sealed with the top crust after you've poured the berries.

Bread Pudding - Don B.

1 16-oz. loaf Sun Maiden or other raisin bread, cut in cubes
1/2 qt. of Half and Half
1/2 qt. whipping cream
3 large eggs, beaten
1-1/2 cups sugar
2 Tbs. vanilla
1/4 cup brandy
3/4 cup chopped toasted nuts of your choice (optional)
Powdered sugar to dust (optional)

Preheat the oven to 325°.

Butter a 9" x 13" pan and put in the bread cubes.

Mix the rest of the ingredients together, and pour it over the bread. I always stir it in to make sure all the bread is covered.

Let sit in refrigerator for 1 hour to marry all ingredients—covered.

Bake for 50 minutes in a larger pan with 1/2" water in it, so it will steam. (But don't let the water come up too far on the sides or it may boil over and could ruin the pudding.

I dust with powdered sugar when it comes out.

Serve with whipped cream flavored with liqueur, or vanilla.

Bread pudding should be served warm, although some people prefer it at room temperature. It can be reheated in a microwave or conventional oven.

Yesterday is a Cancelled Check;
Tomorrow is a Promissory Note;
Today is the only Cash you have - so spend it wisely.

Burnt Cream

1 pint whipping cream
4 large egg yolks
1/2 cup sugar
1 Tbs. vanilla
White and dark brown sugar to cover top of custards

Preheat your oven to 350°.

Heat the whipping cream in small, heavy long-handled saucepan over *low* heat until bubbles form around the edge of pan.

In a medium bowl whisk together the egg yolks and sugar until the mixture is thick and a lemony color.

Gradually, beat in the warm whipping cream—not too fast or you'll curdle the eggs!

Add the vanilla.

This should make about six nice six-ounce servings. So pour into *ungreased* custard cups or small oval baking dishes of your choice.

Place in large baking pan that has about 1/2 inch of water in the bottom.

Bake for 45 minutes until set. Check. Should not brown on top.

Remove from water bath and refrigerate on a tray. Cover in plastic—carefully.

♥ To Serve

Mix about four tablespoons of white sugar to one teaspoon of dark brown sugar to cover tops of custard. (You might need to make more, since you'll want to cover the custard well—so that when it melts, it makes a nice "burnt crust" that cracks with each bite and gets down to combine with the custard.)

Now sprinkle the sugar mixture all over the top of the custard.

Place the custard cups on oven rack directly under the broiler and cook until the topping is medium brown. *Watch!* They burn easily and fast!

Some people follow all the above steps and then re-refrigerate and serve cold. But from waitressing I have found that most people like the top done just before it's served.

Mexican Flan - Micha E.

14-oz.can sweetened condensed milk
1 can of water (use same can as the milk)
1/2 tsp. vanilla
3 large eggs
1/3 cup water
1 cup sugar

Preheat oven to 325°.

In a large bowl, whisk together the condensed milk, can of water, vanilla and eggs:

Combine the remaining (1/3 cup) water and the sugar in a heavy saucepan or long-handled frying pan, and heat it over medium heat.

Stir and blend until it becomes a caramel color.

Pour into the caramel mixture into round flan or similar baking dish of your choice, and let the syrup cool and harden to form a crust that will cover the custard itself, when you turn it over later.

It takes about five minutes at most for the syrup to harden.

Over hardened caramel coating, carefully pour the milk and egg mixture.

Place the flan dish in a larger pan and carefully pour 1/2 inch water around the outer side of the flan dish. (*No water in the flan dish!* This is called cooking in a water bath.)

Carefully place in the oven and bake for 50 minutes to an hour. When it's done, the flan should be firm in the center, but not cracking or browning.

Remove from oven, and let sit for ten minutes to firm up a bit. Carefully run a knife around the edges of the flan to loosen it for easier removal.

Now: Place a large plate over the flan dish and gently flip it over—and out.

Cover and refrigerate until serving.

This can be done individually in smaller dishes, following the same directions, although the cooking time may vary.

Candy Making

There are two different methods of determining when candy has been cooked to the proper consistency. My way is with a candy thermometer, and I recommend that you get the best you can buy, because it pays for itself if you don't ruin batch after batch. The other way is by using the classic cold water test, and I hope my version of this chart will be helpful for you. But I love my thermometer and have noted in a couple of the following recipes where I believe it is essential.

When you use the cold water method, use a fresh cup of cold water for *each* test. Remove the candy from the heat and pour about 1/8 tsp. or less—just a drop—of candy into the cold water. Pick the candy up in your fingers and roll into a ball if possible.

Soft Ball Test Candy will roll into a soft ball which quickly loses its shape when removed from the water.

Firm Ball Test Candy will roll into a firm but not hard ball. It will flatten out a few minutes after being removed from water.

Hard Ball Test Candy will roll into a hard ball which has lost almost all plasticity and will roll around on a plate on removal from the water.

Soft Crack Test Candy will form brittle threads which will soften on removal from the water.

Hard Crack Test Candy will form brittle threads in the water which will remain brittle after being removed from the water.

Caramelized. The sugar first melts, then becomes a golden brown. It will form a hard brittle ball in cold water.

Candy Type	*Consistency/Temperature Range*
Fudge, Fondant	Soft ball: 234°–240°
Divinity, Caramels	Firm ball: 244°–248°
Marshmallows	Hard ball: 250°–266°
Taffy, Nougat	Soft crack : 270°–290°
Peanut Brittle	Hard crack: 300°–310°
Caramelized Sugar	Caramelized: 320°–350°

One Final Note

You'll notice that heavy saucepans are recommended throughout this section for making candy. This is very important. I use Club Aluminum long-handled saucepans for all my candy-making and can't recommend them highly enough for this purpose. A three-quart size is the most useful.

Aplets

2 envelopes unflavored gelatin
3-oz. pkg. lemon-flavored Jell-O
1-1/4 to 1-1/2 cups cooled, unsweetened fresh or store-bought
    applesauce
2 cups sugar
1/2 tsp. vanilla
1/2 tsp. lemon juice
1/2 to 1 cup chopped walnuts
Powdered sugar and cornstarch, to dust candy in.

In a bowl, dissolve the unflavored gelatin and Jell-O in 1/2 cup applesauce. Set aside.

In a heavy saucepan, bring to boil remaining applesauce and sugar.

Stir in the gelatin mixture and simmer 20 minutes.

Remove from heat and add vanilla, lemon juice and walnuts.

Pour into Pam-sprayed 9" x 9" pan.

Refrigerate at least 24 hours before cutting into squares.

Dust with powdered sugar, with just a touch cornstarch in it to make the sugar stick to the candy.

Store in Ziploc bags.

Misery loves company,
But Happiness throws more parties!

Almond Roca - Robin R.

The family favorite! A few years ago, I got my picture on the front page of the North End paper. They wrote a lovely story about how I decorate my house, our Open Door Policy, and my own winning recipe of Almond Roca—which had made the story possible in the first place. Then, one afternoon, we went over to my friend Robin's, after she had just finished making her own Almond Roca, and my son Todd announced that her Almond Roca was much better than mine! "Get her recipe, Mom!" he urged. I did, and so shall you. Because it's easy, and (I must confess) the best!

You will need a candy thermometer for this recipe.

8 oz. sliced almonds
1 big (8-oz.) Hershey's milk chocolate almond bar
1 lb. butter*
2 cups sugar

> *** Don't buy cheap butter. Butter freezes; get it on sale, and make this candy anytime.**

In Cuisinart, chop up nuts to crumbles. Put in a bowl.

Chop up chocolate bar to crumbles. Put in another bowl.

Cover a large cookie sheet in foil, including the sides.

Put half the nuts over the bottom and half the chocolate on top of nuts.

Cut the butter into 2" pieces. Use a good brand or you'll find out—as I did—that it can break down, ruining the recipe, and you'll have to start *all over*.

In a large heavy saucepan, melt butter with the sugar over *medium* heat, stirring constantly to mix together well. You also have to keep stirring and not let it sit or it burns, ruining the taste.

Put in candy thermometer and cook, stirring occasionally, until it reads 300°.

Don't let it burn. This takes about 20 minutes or more.
Pour the candy—remember, it's very hot!—over the nuts and chocolate.

Spread out with spatula. *Do this as quickly as possible*, so it doesn't harden and become unspreadable.

Top with the other half of the chocolate, smoothing it over the

surface with spatula.

Sprinkle on the rest of the nuts. Pat down lightly with a *clean* spatula, so they sink part way into the chocolate and cling.

Let sit at room temperature for one and a half hours to harden.

Or, refrigerate for one hour *uncovered* and then either break up or cover it. Refrigeration gives it more of a toffee consistency.

Break into pieces to serve, of course, and store in Ziploc bags. *Yum!*

Fancy Fudge - for Granny Rider

1/2 stick butter
12-oz. pkg. Nestlé semisweet chocolate chips
12-oz. can sweetened condensed milk
1 tsp. salt
1 tsp. almond extract
2 Tbs. chopped golden raisins
1/3 cup chopped candied (glazed) cherries or mixed fruit
1/3 cup chopped pecans

In double boiler, with water *just simmering* underneath:

Melt chocolate chips and butter, *stirring constantly*.

Add milk, almond extract, and salt. Stir until smooth.

Add raisins, cherries and pecans.

Pour into 6" x 6" buttered pan. Or, drop into little foil cups. If pouring in a pan, remember to line it first with buttered plastic wrap for easier removal from the pan to cut after it's chilled.

Refrigerate until firm then cut into pieces, wrap them in plastic, and put in Ziploc bags to keep fresh. (I cut into three big pieces to give as gifts and/or to cut into smaller pieces for separate occasions at home later on.)

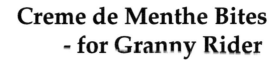

Creme de Menthe Bites
- for Granny Rider

24 marshmallows, large
2/3 cup creme de menthe
1/2 pint whipping cream, whipped
1/2 cup toasted chopped almonds
6 oz. chocolate bar, melted for topping*

*I use Hershey's, some like Nestlé—or use the expensive chocolate, if you
    have it. Sometimes I do; sometimes, I don't! My friend, candymaker
    Suzanne M., uses only Cadbury milk chocolate or Guittard.

In a double boiler over simmering water, melt the marshmallows in the creme
de menthe.

Remove from heat and fold in nuts and then fold in whipped cream.

In a small muffin pan put foil cups. Spoon in marshmallow mix to near the top.

Melt the chocolate bar. Drizzle over the marshmallow/creme de menthe cups. Sprinkle with
a few more nuts if you want, like we do.

Freeze until firm, or ready to serve. Cover so they don't pick up other smells.

You can use any liqueur flavor you like for this treat—for example Amaretto, Frangelico, or a
strawberry liqueur. By any other name, these bites are just as good!

♥ *Helpful Hint*

When cream will not whip, add an egg white to the cream and chill it. It will whip!

Chocolate Raspberry Cups

Now this recipe is for someone with a very sweet tooth. It's too rich for me to eat, but my mom, Aunt Dorothy, Auntie Jean and Mac just love this one. And it's so easy to make!

16 oz. bittersweet chocolate, grated
1 cup whipping cream
4 Tbs. unsalted butter, cut in pieces
4 large egg yolks
1 cup powdered sugar
1/2 cup Chambord or raspberry liqueur of choice—though Chambord has
      such a wonderful taste, I think, that it's really worth the additional
      cost.
Fresh or frozen raspberries for purée base

In a double boiler, over simmering water, melt grated chocolate and butter. Cream together with whisk for about ten minutes. Stirring occasionally.

Remove from heat.

Mix in egg yolks—one at a time, with whisk, then gradually whisk in the powdered sugar until dissolved.

Add Chambord. Mix in completely.

Pour into small foil candy cups, foil-lined small muffin pans, or any medium-sized clam or scallop molds lined with plastic wrap so you can remove the candy in one piece. Always cover *completely* and put in refrigerator to firm up.

You can also pour this candy into a loaf pan and cut in squares later on, to be real simple. Just remember to put in a layer of buttered plastic wrap, first, so you can get it out in one piece. Cover, refrigerate to firm and later make into slices. *It must be kept chilled*, though, or it will get melty, and won't hold its shape.

When ready to serve, purée some raspberries with dash of Chambord, and lay a puddle down on a saucer. Center your candy on the dish, drizzle some purée on top, and add a few whole berries. To make it more festive, you can swirl some melted white chocolate over on top of that.

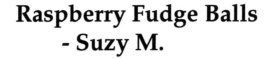

Raspberry Fudge Balls
- Suzy M.

For that someone special on your list with a sweet tooth! We make these at Christmas, and boy, are they a hit! Very, very rich. The nice thing is: they don't take long, and they aren't cooked per sé, so they're not time-consuming. Just done it parts.

8-oz. pkg. cream cheese, soft
6-oz. pkg. semisweet chocolate chips
3/4 cup vanilla wafer crumbs
1/4 cup raspberry preserves, seedless
1/3 cup finely chopped almonds or nuts of your choice
Cocoa and ground nuts (optional) to roll the balls in

Melt the chocolate chips in a double boiler or microwave and combine it with the cream cheese.

Stir in the vanilla wafer crumbs, raspberry preserves and nuts.

Put in the refrigerator—*not* the freezer—and let firm up. This takes at least 1 hour.

Take one tablespoon pieces and shape them into balls. Roll in cocoa (and nuts, if used) on a flat saucer or plate. (Note: They melt fast on your hands: a good candy store has plastic gloves, which might help.)

Put in little paper cups or foil cups. Cover and *keep refrigerated* until ready to serve.

♥ Variations

Could shape into a log and cut off pieces, then cut in designs with small cutters, but you must keep it chilled, or it gets mushy.

For a really festive dessert, cut into small fancy designs and serve on a bed of puréed raspberries with Chambord.

Chocoholics *love* this one. So just remember to serve this treat in small pieces, as they tend to overindulge!

Favorite Fudge - Molly C.

2 cups sugar
6-oz. can evaporated milk
7-oz. jar Marshmallow Creme
12-oz. Nestlé semisweet chocolate chips
1 Tbs. butter
Pinch of salt
1 cup chopped walnuts or other nuts of your choice (optional)

In a heavy saucepan, bring sugar and milk to a boil.

Boil for five minutes on medium, *stirring constantly.*

Remove from heat and add the Marshmallow Creme, chocolate chips, butter, and salt, mixing together well.

Add the chopped nuts.

Pour into a pan brushed with melted butter over bottom and sides, pour in fudge. Or, line with buttered plastic wrap before pouring. This makes it so easy to remove and cut.

Refrigerate covered in plastic.

When firm, I have Billie cut it into three big squares for me to wrap and store in Ziploc bags to keep fresh in the refrigerator. We cut the fudge into bite-sized pieces just before serving.

This is a very creamy, smooth fudge—unless of course you add the nuts! It takes so little time to make that I usually do two batches—one plain, one with nuts.

It's also a great gift to give someone, as you can whip it up in an hour and a half, go out the door and take it to a special friend. (I'm on my way, Molly dear...!)

God made Woman Beautiful and Foolish:
Beautiful, that man might love her; and
Foolish, that she might love him.

Peanut Brittle - Jana G.

Now this is a 10-star recipe that I like to make for special people at special request. No, It's not hard and on holidays it's must for some: Right, Uncle Lu!? I usually make Almond Roca and the Peanut Brittle, only, during the holidays, because we all gain so much weight on it! Well... They eat the whole batch, if I don't get it out of the house right away!

This is another recipe that begs for a Candy Thermometer! It's also better to have two people available to help you pull it apart—although I have done it on my own. I also have a large glass of boiling hot water nearby to drop in candy thermometer so it cleans easier. Soak pan in hot water when done and it will dissolve the sugar candy coating. For ingredients, you will need:

2 large cookie sheets, well buttered on bottom and sides
1/2 cup water
2 cups sugar
1 cup light corn syrup
Dash of salt (I tried this without it and it just was blah!)
3 cups raw Spanish peanuts
1/2 cube butter, premeasured and ready to go!
1 tsp. pure vanilla extract, premeasured
2 tsp. of baking soda, premeasured

In a *large* heavy saucepan with long handle, combine the water, sugar, corn syrup and salt. Put the water in *first* and mix well so the sugar won't stick to the bottom.

Using medium heat, bring the mixture to boil until sugar is dissolved, with pan lid *on*. This takes about five minutes or so.

Take off the lid; the sugar and water should be combined and *clear*.

Put in candy thermometer. Add peanuts and *stir* so peanuts don't burn.

Cook uncovered, stirring occasionally, until it reaches 280°, then add the butter and vanilla extract.

Stir constantly until the mixture reaches 290°—this takes a few minutes—then add the baking soda and stir constantly until it turns to a caramel color. (Sometimes, it may look this terrible greenish shade and seem as if it's never going to come to caramel, but it will fool you and turn out—if you just keep stirring it!) But don't panic: It will turn out fine!

Pour half batches onto buttered cookie sheets, and pull apart to spread out with two forks. Do this *fast*, as this hardens quickly. I try to have some one home when I do it. But, often this is impossible. You may just have a bit thicker brittle than if someone is right on top of it— to stretch—as you pour.

Let the candy set until hardened (about one-half hour), break into pieces, and store in Ziploc bags until ready to use.

♥ ♥ ♥

Marzipan - for Granny Rider

Only 100 calories per tablespoon!

1-1/2 cups blanched whole almonds
1-1/2 cups powdered sugar
1 large egg white
1-1/4 tsp. almond extract
1/4 tsp. salt

In the Cuisinart finely grind almonds, 1/2 cup at a time.

Add remaining ingredients, blending to make a *stiff paste*.

Divide into sections and add drops of coloring, appropriate for whatever you wish to form (apples, oranges, lemons, strawberries, etc.), mixing in well.

Form into shapes and let dry for 30 minutes, or more before serving.

Put leftovers in Ziploc bag and refrigerate to use later.

This can keep up to six weeks. (It doesn't last for even a week with my Mom!)

Marzipan is a wonderful gift for Christmas or birthdays. Get a cute little basket, some colored plastic straw and lay in your creative pieces Cover/seal in plastic.

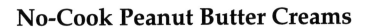

No-Cook Peanut Butter Creams

4 cups or 1 lb. powdered sugar
1-1/2 cups creamy peanut butter
1/3 cup milk
1/4 cup honey
1/2 tsp. salt
1/2 tsp. vanilla
6-oz. pkg. Nestlé semisweet chocolate chips

Combine all ingredients, except the chocolate chips, in large bowl. Mix together well.

Remove and knead until smooth.

Pat into *ungreased* 9" pan.

In a double boiler, melt chocolate chips over low heat.

Spread over mixture.

Let chocolate harden and firm up for about 30 minutes, and cut into squares.

My friend Robin takes little foil candy cups and forms the mixture into balls, pouring the chocolate over the top. You also can dip the balls first, put them on wax paper to dry, and then put them in foil cups.

You could also stuff them with an M & M or a hazelnut, almond, pecan to be fancy. Just mold the peanut mixture around nut and then dip in your chocolate.

♥ *To Make into Bars:*

Use squares of store-bought or homemade shortbread.

Flatten peanut mix on top of shortbread and carefully dip into or pour over chocolate. Let dry on rack over wax paper.

Decorate top of warm chocolate with shaved chocolate bar and/or peanut crumbles, sprinkled over top immediately. Or make zigzags of white melted chocolate.

Need I say, keep in Ziploc bags, airtight cannisters, or jars?

Helpful Hints

There are Faith, Hope and Love, these Three:
But the Greatest of these is Love.

Corinthians 1:13

♥ *Tips for Working with Fats/Oils*

To strain cooking oil after deep frying, place a paper coffee filter in the funnel used to pour the oil back into its container. Then just throw the filter and crumbs away.

When you need butter and it's frozen, strip it off with your vegetable peeler. It thaws almost instantly and is spreadable.

Drop a lettuce leaf into a pot of homemade soup to absorb excess grease from top. Best if soup is refrigerated until fat hardens on the top. Place of piece of wax paper over the top, touching, and it can all be peeled off.

Add a cup of water to bottom portion of broiling pan before putting in oven will absorb smoke and grease.

Any dish that is dipped in flour or flour/egg coating will stick better if left to sit chilled in refrigerator for one hour, laid out on a sprayed cookie sheet, lightly covered so it doesn't take on refrigerator smells.

♥ *Gardening Tips*

When your hands get badly stained from gardening, add a teaspoon of sugar to the soapy lather you wash them in.

Marigolds will repel rodents in your garden.

Plant a few springs of dill near your tomato plants to prevent tomato worms on your plants.

Use hair spray on a bee in the house to immobile and remove harmlessly.

♥ *Laundry Tips*

Soak colored cottons overnight in strong salt water and they will not fade.

To dry drip-dry garments faster and with fewer wrinkles, hang garment over the top of a dry cleaner's plastic bag.

To remove burned-on starch from your iron, sprinkle salt on a sheet of waxed paper and slide iron back and forth several times. Then polish it with silver polish until roughness or stain is removed.

To whiten laces, wash them in sour milk.

♥ *Cleaning Made Easy*

Use large or small powder puffs for polishing your silverware, copper and brass.

Dip a new broom in hot salt water before using. This toughens the bristles and makes it last longer.

Keep a toothbrush around the kitchen sink to clean rotary beaters, graters, choppers and similar utensils like your Cuisinart blades.

You can clean darkened aluminum pans easily by boiling in them 2 tsp. cream of tartar mixed in a quart of water for ten minutes.

Spray garbage sacks with ammonia to prevent dogs from tearing the bags before pickup day.

To clean your blender, fill it halfway with hot water and add a drop of detergent. Cover and turn it on for a few seconds. Drain, rinse and dry.

Always oil your grater before using for a fast cleanup.

To clear a sink or basin drain, pour 1/2 cup baking soda followed by a cup of vinegar down the drain and let the mixture foam, then run hot water. When the drain is clogged with grease, pour a cup of salt and a cup of baking soda followed by a kettle of boiling water.

If one glass is stuck inside of another, simply fill the top one with cold water and dip the bottom one in hot water. They will come apart without breaking. A handful of dry laundry detergent scattered in garbage cans after cleaning will help repel flies and other insects.

For garbage disposal smells, drop orange or lemon rinds in and grind a few minutes.

If you scorch the inside of one of your pans, just fill pan halfway with water and 1/4 cup soda. Let boil and it will loosen and float to the top.

Never put a cover on anything that is cooked in milk. You could spend wasted minutes cleaning up, as it will always boil over.

Wax your ashtrays. Ashes won't cling, odors won't linger and they can be wiped clean with a paper towel. This saves daily washing.

Keep a mint plant in rooms where odors are a problem. They absorb stale odors and keep your home smelling sweet.

Silver will shine after a rubbing with damp baking soda on a soft cloth.

If a cracked dish is boiled for 45 minutes in sweet milk, the crack will be so welded together that it will hardly be visible, and so strong it will stand the same usage as before.

♥ *Stains*

Alcohol. Sponge right away with cold water, then cold water and glycerine. Rinse with white vinegar for a few seconds it, stains remain. Wash with detergent/water.

Blood. Pre-soak in cold water for at least 30 minutes. If the stain persists, add three Tbs. ammonia in 1 gallon of water. Rinse. Wash in detergent/water which has been worked into the stain.

Candle Wax. Scrape off with dull knife as much wax as possible. Place fabric between two blotters—good stationary store will have—or facial tissues and press with warm iron. If, color stain, sponge with *nonflammable* dry cleaning solvent. Wash with detergent in the hottest water safe for fabric.

Chewing gum. Rub area with ice, then scrape off with *dull* blade. Sponge with dry cleaning solvent; allow to air dry. Wash in detergent and hottest water safe for fabric. Turpentine will work on different materials. Test small spot, first.

Chocolate and Cocoa. Pre-soak stain in cold water. Wash in hot water with detergent. Remove any grease stains with dry cleaning solvent. If, color remains, sponge with hydrogen peroxide, and wash again.

Coffee. Sponge off or soak with cold water as soon as possible. Wash, using detergent and bleach safe for fabric. Remove cream grease stains with nonflammable dry cleaning solvent. Wash again.

Crayon. Scrape with *dull* blade. Wash in hottest water safe for fabric, with detergent and 1-1/2 cups of baking soda. If, your full load is crayon stained, due to crayons in that "little" pocket...take to cleaners or coin-operated dry cleaning machines.

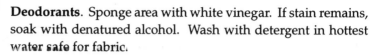

Deodorants. Sponge area with white vinegar. If stain remains, soak with denatured alcohol. Wash with detergent in hottest water safe for fabric.

Dye. If, dye transfers from a noncolorfast item during washing, immediately bleach discolored items. Repeat as necessary *before* drying. On whites, use color remover. CAUTION: Do not use color remover in washer, or around washer or dryer as it may damage the finish.

Egg. Scrape with *dull* knife. Pre-soak in cold or warm water for at least 30 minutes. Remove grease with dry cleaning solvent. Wash in hottest water safe for fabric, with detergent.

Fruit and Fruit Juices. Sponge with cold water. Pre-soak in cold or warm water for at least 30 minutes. Wash with detergents and bleach safe for fabric.

Grass. Pre-soak in cold water for at least 30 minutes. Rinse. Pre-treat with detergent. Wash, using detergent, hot water, and bleach safe for fabric. On acetate and colored fabrcs, use part of alcohol to two parts water.

Grease, Oil and Tar. (1) Use powder or chalk absorbents to remove as much grease as possible Pretreat with detergent or nonflammable dry cleaning solvent, or liquid shampoo. Wash in hottest water safe for fabric, using plenty of detergent. (2) Rub spot with lard and sponge with nonflammable dry cleaning solvent. Wash in hottest water and detergent safe for fabric.

Ink. (1) Ball-Point: Pour *denatured alcohol* through stain. Rub in petroleum jelly. Sponge with nonflammable dry cleaning solvent. Soak in detergent solution. Wash with detergent and cleach safe for fabric. (2) Fountain Pen: Run cold water through stain until no more color will come out. Rub in lemon juice and detergent. Let stand five minutes. Wash. If a yellow stain remains, use a commercial rut remover or Oxalic Acid, as for rust stains. CAUTION: Never use Oxalic Acid or any Rust Remover around washer and dryer as it can damage the finish. Such chemicals may also remove permanent press fabric finishes. (3) *Keep poisonous removers away from children's reach.*

Lipstick. Loosen stain with a nonflammable dry cleaning solvent. Rub detergent in until stain outline is gone. Wash in hottest water and detergent safe for fabric.

Meat Juices. Scrape with dull knife blade. Pre-soak in cold or warm water for 30 minutes. Wash with detergent and bleach safe for fabric.

Mildew. Pre-treat clothing as soon as possible with detergent. Wash. If any stain remains, sponge with lemon juice and salt. Dry in the sun. Wash, using hottest water, detergent and bleach safe for fabric. I have found bleach and water or Tilex, if you have it, works great for walls, ceilings, etc. But leave a window open.

Milk, Cream, Ice cream. Pre-soak in cold or warm water for 30 minutes. Wash. Sponge any grease spots with nonflammable dry cleaning solvent. Wash again.

Nail Polish. Sponge with polish remover or banana oil. Wash. If, stain remains, sponge with denatured alcohol to which a few drops of ammonia have been added. Wash again. CAUTION: do not use polish remover on acetate or triacetate fabrics.

Paint Splashes. Equal parts of ammonia and turpentine will remove spots no matter how long they have been dried. Saturate the spots several times, then wash out with warm soap suds.

Perspiration. Sponge fresh stain with ammonia; old stain with white vinegar. Pre-soak in cold or warm water. Rinse. Wash in hottest water safe for fabric. If, fabric is yellowed, use bleach. If, stain still remains, dampen and sprinkle with meat tenderizer or Pepsin. Let stand one hour. Brush off and wash. For persistent odor, sponge with colorless mouthwash.

Scorch. Wash with detergent and bleach safe for fabric. On heavier scorching, cover stain with cloth dampened with hydrogen perixide. Cover this with dry cloth and press with hot iron. Rinse well. CAUTION: Severe scorching cannot be removed because of fabric damage.

Soft Drinks. Sponge *immediately* with cold water and alcohol. *Heat and detergent may set stain.*

Tea. Sponge or soak with cold water as soon as possible. Wash using detergent and bleach safe for fabric.

Window Cleaner. Pour car windshield solvent in a spray bottle and use instead of expensive brands of household window cleaner.

Wine, Red. Pour over spill with white wine, let soak in, cover with paper towels and blot up as much as you can by stepping on them. Wash with detergent/water and pat up with paper towels once again. Some people have luck with Club Soda.

Equivalents Chart

♥ *Liquid Measure Volume Equivalents*

Dash/dab/tad = less than 1/8 tsp.
1 coffee spoon = 1/4 tsp.
3 tsp. = 1 Tbs.
2 tsp. = 1/3 cup = 1 fl. oz.
4 Tbs. = 1/4 cup
8 Tbs. = 1/2 cup
16 Tbs. = 1 cup
5 Tbs. + 1 tsp. = 1/3 cup
12 Tbs. = 3/4 cup
5/8 cup = 1/2 cup + 2 Tbs.
7/8 cup = 3/4 cup + 2 Tbs.

1 jigger = 1-1/2 fl. oz. or 3 Tbs.
1 oz. = 2 Tbs. fat or liquid
2 oz. = 1/4 cup
4 oz. = 1/2 cup
8 oz. = 1 cup
16 oz. = 1 lb.

1 cup = 1/2 pint
2 cups = 1 pint
2 pints = 1 quart
4 cups = 1 quart
4 quarts = 1 gallon
8 quarts = 1 peck
4 pecks = 1 bushel
1 pound = 16 oz. = 454 grams

♥ *Equivalents for Common Ingredients*

All purpose flour	1 pound = 4 cups
Cake flour	1 pound = 4-1/2 cups
Unsifted whole wheat flour	1 pound = 3-1/2 cups
Butter	1 stick = 1/2 cup or 8 Tbs.
	1/2 pound = 2 sticks
	1 pound = 2 cups or 4 sticks
	1 stick = 8 Tbs.
	1/2 stick = 4 Tbs.
	1/4 stick = 2 Tbs.
Grated cheese	1/4 pound = 1 cup

Equivalents and Substitutions for Common Ingredients

Cheese	1 pound = 2-2/3 cup
Shredded American cheese	1 pound = 4 cups
Crumbled blue cheese	1/4 lb. = 1 cup
Lemon	1 whole = 3 Tbs. juice
Orange	1 whole = 1/3 cup juice
Granulated sugar	2 cups = 16 oz. or 1 lb.
Unsifted powdered sugar	3-1/2 - 4 cups = 16 oz. or 1 lb.
Packed brown sugar	2-1/4 cups = 16 oz. or 1 lb.
Uncooked macaroni	4 oz. = 1 to 1-1/4 cup = 2 cups cooked
Spaghetti	7 oz. = 4 cups cooked
Uncooked noodles	4 oz. = 1-1/2 to 2 cups = 2 cups cooked
Saltine crackers	28 = 1 cup crumbs
Graham crackers	14 square = 1 cup crumbs
Vanilla Wafers	22 = 1 cup crumbs
Cracker crumbs	3/4 cup = 1 cup
Chocolate	1 square = 1 oz. = 4 Tbs. grated
Bread slices	4 dry = 1 cup crumbs
Soft bread	1 slice = 1/4 cup
Dry bread	1 slice = 1/3 cup
Coconut fine grated	1 cup = 3-1/2 oz.
Coconut flaked	1-1/3 cups = 3-1/2 oz.
Active dry yeast	1 pkg. = 1 cake compressed yeast = 1 Tbs.
Instant minced onion	1 Tbs. rehydrated = 1 small onion

♥ Substitutions for Common Ingredients

Thickening agents	1 Tbs. cornstarch = 2 Tbs. flour
Herbs	1 tsp. dried herbs = 1 Tbs. fresh herbs
Mustard	1 Tbs. prepared = 1 tsp. dried
Garlic	1/8 tsp. garlic powder = 1 small pressed clove garlic
Semisweet Chocolate	1 oz. chocolate + 4 tsp. sugar = 1-2/3 oz.
Chocolate	3 Tbs. cocoa + 1 Tbs. fat = 1 oz. chocolate
Baking powder	1/4 tsp. baking soda + 1/2 tsp. cream of tartar
Sour milk (1 cup)	1 cup milk + 1 Tbs. vinegar or lemon juice or 1 cup buttermilk
Sweet milk (1 cup)	1 cup sour milk or buttermilk + 1/2 tsp. baking soda
Whole milk (1 cup)	1/2 cup evaporated milk + 1/2 cup water or 1 cup nonfat dry milk + 1 Tbs. butter

♥ *Large Parties*	25	50	100
Rolls	4 dozen	8 dozen	16 dozen
Bread	50 slices	100 slices	200 slices
	3-1 lb. loaves	6-1 lb. loaves	12-1 lb. loaves
Butter	1/2 lb.	3/4 to 1 lb.	1-1/2 lb.
Mayonnaise	1 cup	2 to 3 cups	4 to 6 cups
Crackers	1-1/2 lbs.	3 lbs.	6 lbs.
Cheese 2 oz. per	3 lbs.	6 lbs.	12 lbs.
Turkey/Chicken	13 lbs.	25/35 lbs.	50/75 lbs.
Fish - whole	13 lbs.	25 lbs.	50 lbs.
Fish - steak/fillets	7-1/2 lb.	15 lbs.	30 lbs.
Potato Salad	4-1/4 qts.	2-1/4 gallons	4-1/2 gallons
Spaghetti	1-1/4 gallons	2-1/2 gallons	5 gallons
Baked Beans	3/4 gallon	1-1/4 gallons	2-1/2 gallons
Lettuce	4 heads	8 heads	15 heads
Carrots - 1/2 cup	6-1/4 lbs.	12-1/2 lbs.	25 lbs.
Tomatoes	3-5 lbs.	7-10 lbs.	14-20 lbs.
Watermelon	37-1/2 lbs.	75 lbs.	150 lbs.
Cake	1 10x12 sheet	1 12x20 sheet	2 12x20 sheets
Coffee	1/2 lb.	1 lb.	2 lb.
Tea	1/12 lb.	1/6 lb.	1/3 lb.

♥ Notes

Coffee	1 lb. + 2 gallons of water = 40 cups
Punch	1 gallon of punch fills 40 punch cups
	Average guest drinks 3-4 cups
Wine	1 bottle of wine serves six 4-oz. wine glasses
Liquor	1 fifth = 16 1-1/2 oz. jiggers
	1 quart = 20 1-1/2 oz. jiggers
	1 jigger = 1-1/2 oz. which is the average drink measurement
	Average guest has 2-3 drinks
Hors d'oeuvres	Average 10 pieces per guest
Hot cocktails	Average 3 per guest
Cold cocktails	Average 4 per guest
Cheese	3 lbs. serves 25-30 generously

Index

A

Asparagus Spears, Spicy   23

B

Bacon-Wrapped Water Chestnuts   21
Baked Pecan Pastry Shell   277
Barbecue Sauce. *See* Sauces
Bean Dishes. *See* Vegetable Dishes
Beef Dishes. *See also* Casseroles
   Chile   115
   Chop Steak Hawaiian - Al Schilling   120
   Enchiladas - Lynn W. K.   107
   Everyday Roasts and Gravy   111
   Flank Steak, Mom's Good Old   109
   Galouskes - Beverly D.   104
   Hamburger Rice - Darlene M.   116
   Homemade Chili - Granny Rider   115
   Joe's Special   103
   Meatballs - Scotty T.   118
   Meatloaf Supremo   112
   Prime Rib Roast and Yorkshire Pudding   110
   Steak Bradford - Steve B.   108
   Swiss Steak - Granny Rider   114
   Tacos - Mom   106
   Tamale Pie   117
   The Best Stroganoff!   113
Bernaise Sauce/Blender   97
Beverages. *See also* Liqueurs and Party Drinks
Biscotti. *See* Cookies and Bars
Black-Eyed Peas - Billie Z.   69
Blue Cheese Dressing - Jim R.   86
Breads. *See* Sweet and Savory Quick Breads.
       See also Yeast Breads, Muffins and Rolls
Bread, Hot French. See Hot Hors D'Oeuvres
Bruschetta - Mom's Way   30
Butterscotch Torte 274

C

Cake Making Hints   241
Cakes. *See also* Frostings
   Black Russian Cake   246
   Brandy Apple-Raisin Chocolate Cake   247
   Carrot Cake   244
   Chocolate Almond Cake - Suzy F.   248
   Chocolate Sauerkraut Cake - Grandma Gleasen   249
   Chocolate Zucchini Cake - Sara T.   252
   Christmas Morning Brunch Cake - Granny Rider   258
   Harvey Wallbanger Cake   253
   Milky Way Cake - Angie   254
   Mississippi Mud Cake   255
   Old Country Applesauce Fruitcake - Bevy D.   242
   Peanut Butter Cake - Wendy M.   256

    Pecan Cake   258
    Pina Colada Cake - Jean M.   243
    Turtle Cake - Robbie T   260
    Washington Apple Cake/Pie   259
Canapés and Finger Foods
    Bacon-Wrapped Water Chestnuts - Dolores S.   21
    Deli Delights - Linda D.   26
    Deviled Eggs   28
    Egg Salad Sandwich   27
    Garlic Almonds   29
    "Hot" Dilly Beans - Bevy D.   24
    Meat Log - Via Ron   22
    Spicy Asparagus Spears - Doug and Lois B.   23
    Tuna Salad Sandwich   25
Candies and Confections
    Almond Roca - Robin R.   298
    Aplets   297
    Candy Making Hints   296
    Chocolate Raspberry Cups   301
    Creme de Menthe Bites   300
    Fancy Fudge   299
    Favorite Fudge - Molly C.   303
    Marzipan - for Edith   305
    No-Cook Peanut Butter Creams   306
    Peanut Brittle - Jana G.   304
    Raspberry Fudge Balls - Suzy M.   302
Candy Making Hints   296
Carrot Salad - Mauny K.   63
Casseroles   172
    Broccoli Casserole   169
    Chicken Casserole - Shay   133
    Corn Casserole   175
    French Green Bean Casserole   168
    Good Old Tuna   144
    Ham and Leek   121
    Hamburger Casserole   119
    Hash Brown Casserole   163
    Pork Chop and Rhubarb   126
    Potatoes Romanoff   159
    Scalloped Potatoes - Mom   164
    Spinach Casserole - Frances F.   173
    Sweet and Sour Bean Casserole   159
Cheesecake. See Pies and Pastries
Cheese Soup   57
Chicken Dishes. See Poultry and Game
Chocolate Almond Cake 248
Chocolate Peanut Butter Pie 290
Chocolate Sauerkraut Cake 249
Chocolate Zucchini Cake 252
Clam Chowder   58, 59
Clam Linguini 153
Coleslaw. See Salads
Condiments. See Dips and Spreads

Cookies and Bars
  Amaretto Cookies - Joan D.   263
  Biscotti   264
  Cheesecake Squares - Connie A.   265
  Chocolate Chip Pudding Cookies - Krysy B.   266
  Chocolate Meltaway Bars/Balls   267
  Chocolate Waffle Cookies - Myrt J.   268
  Hazelnut Shortbread   272
  Lemon Bars - Phil S.   269
  Macadamia Nut Bars   270
  Refrigerator Cookies - Granny Rider   271
Crab-Filled Won Ton - Jim R.   31
Crab Logs   42
Cranberry Dream Salad   72
Cream Puffs, Stuffed   44
Cucumbers   63
Cupcakes. *See* Holiday Treats
Custards
  Burnt Cream   294
  Mexican Flan   295

D

Deli Delights   26
Dips and Spreads. *See also* Sandwiches
  Baked Bean Dip - Mom's Way   6
  Baked Green Chili Dip - Melissa B.   5
  Fruit Dip Ida   71
  Hamet   20
  Hawaiian Cheese Roll - Liz B.   16
  Hot Pepper Jelly/Cream Cheese - Robin R.   10
  Hot Shrimp Dip - Lynn D.   9
  Hummos   7
  Jezebel Dip - Lynn D.   8
  Man Keeper Dip - Liz B.   11
  No Avocado Guacamole - Lynn D.   12
  Salmon Party Ball   17
  Salsa - Mark C,   14
  Spinach Dip - Marilyn A.   13
  Sweet and Sour Mustard - Robin R.   15
Drinks. *See* Liqueurs and Party Drinks

E

Eggs, Deviled   28
Egg Salad Sandwich   27
Elegant Layered Dessert   284
Enchiladas - Lynn K.   107

F

Finger Foods. *See* Canapés and Finger Foods
Fish dishes. *See* Seafood
Flan. *See* Custards
French Dressing - Uncle Freddy M.   87

French Toast. *See* Pancakes and French Toast
Frostings
   Chocolate Buttercream Frosting - JoAnne   245
   Chocolate Sour Cream   245
   Cream Cheese   245
Fruit Dip Ida   71
Fruit Salad. *See* Salads
Fruitcake. *See* Cakes
Fudge. *See* Candies and Confections

G

Galouske's - Bev. D.   104
Garlic Almonds   29
Granny Rider's Recipes
   Butterscotch Torte   274
   Cherry Salad Supreme   74
   Chicken Salad - Granny's Favorite   83
   Christmas Morning Brunch Cake   258
   Cinnamon Rolls   228
   Croissants   223
   Cucumbers   63
   Good Old Refrigerator Cookies   271
   Goulash Beans   158
   Green Salad   84
   Hamburger Casserole   119
   Homemade Chile   115
   Infallible Rice   173
   Lemon Pie   280
   Macaroni and Cheese   155
   Rice Salad   80
   Sweet and Sour Bean Casserole   159
   Swiss Steak   114
   Tamale Pie   117
   White Bread   224
Grape Leaves - Michael's 10 Star   18
Gravy
   Country Gravy - Steve B.   100
   Everyday Roasts and Gravy   111
Greek Bread   37
Green Salad - Granny Rider   84
Guacamole, No-Avocado   12

H

Ham. *See* Pork Dishes
Hamet   20
Holiday Treats
   Christmas Morning Brunch Cake   258
   Halloween Black Bottom Cupcakes   262
   New Year's Morning Fizz - Lynn D.   51
   Sweet Holiday Muffins   231
   Thanksgiving/Christmas Day Pumpkin Cream Cheese Roll   250
   Thanksgiving Pecan Pie   285

Hollendaise Sauce   98
Honey Mustard Dressing - Jim R.   88
Hot Hors d'oeuvres. *See also* Dips and Spreads
   Bruschetta - Mom's Way   30
   Chicken Wings - Gloria S.   43
   Crab Logs   42
   Crab-filled Won Tons - Jim R.   31
   Greek Bread   37
   Ham/Chicken Balls   46
   Hot French Bread - Bonnie   39
   Mexican Platter - Debbie and Tom B.   47
   Mushroom Squares   33
   Mushroom Turnovers   34
   Rolls and Breadsticks in the Tube   36
   Stuffed Cream Puffs   44
   Stuffed Mushrooms - Ellen H.   32
   Stuffed Sausage Bread - Linda D.   38
   Welsh Rarebit   45
Hummus   7
Hungarian Rugola 289
Hungarian Turos Juisa 155

I

Irish Cream 48

J

Joe's Special   103

L

Lamb Dishes
   Lamb Marinade - Duke's   128
   Roast Leg of Lamb   12
Lemon Cloud 276
Lemon Curd 281
Lemon Pie 280
Liqueurs and Party Drinks
   Easy Irish Cream   48
   Margaritas - Robin R.   51
   New Year's Morning fizz   51
   Orange Liqueur - Lynn D.   49
   Raspberry Liqueur - Bevy D.   50
   The Best Irish Cream   48
   The Snatch - Spiced Tea Pick-Me-Up   52

M

Macaroni Salad - Jeanie   68
Margaritas - Robin R.   51
Mayonnaise, Blender   95
Meat Log. *See* Canapés and Finger Foods
Meatballs. *See* Beef

Mexican Dishes
    Flan   295
    Mexican Platter   47
    Chorizo and Egg Tortillas   237
    Enchiladas - Lynn W.Kocher   107
    Tacos - Mrs. Z.   106
Muffins. *See* Yeast Breads, Muffins and Rolls
Mushrooms Squares   33
Mushrooms, Stuffed - Ellen   32
Mushroom Turnovers   34
Mustard, Sweet and Sour - Robin R.   15

N

New Year's Morning Fizz - Lynn D.   51

O

Orange Liqueur - Lynn D.   49
Oriental Salad - Debra B.   75

P

Pancakes and French Toast
    French Toast - Jamey   235
    Overnight Buttermilk Pancake Batter - Bevy D.   234
    Spinach Pancakes Deluxe   174
    Stuffed French Toast - Auntie Marie King   236
    Zoo-Hire Sweet Pancakes   233
Party Balls and Logs. *See* Dips and Spreads
Pasta Dishes
    Chicken Fettucini   147
    Clam Linguini   153
    Hungarian Turos Juisa - Oscar F.   155
    Lasagna - Robin R.   150
    Macaroni and Cheese   154
    Pasta Swirls   146
    Pesto Sauce   93
    Spaghetti Italiano - Mr. Onion's   152
    Spaghetti Sauce - Frances F.   151
    Spinach-Stuffed Shells   149
    Stuffed Manicotti - Nancy P.   148
Pastries. *See* Pies and Pastries
Pecan Chicken-Stuffed Tomatoes 138
Pesto Sauce - Mr. McCutchan   93
Pickles
    "Hot" Dilly Beans - Bevy D.   24
    Spicy Asparagus Spears   23
Pie Making Hints   273
Pies and Pastries   277
    Almond Puff   282
    Baked Pecan Pastry Shell   277
    Butterscotch Torte - Granny Rider   274

Chambord Cheesecake   278
Cheesecake Squares   265
Chocolate Peanut Butter Pie - Michael's Mom   290
Crunchy Apple Pie   286
Elegant Layered Dessert   284
Frozen Chocolate Frango Pie - Julie B.   287
Hungarian Rugola   289
Lemon Cloud - Tom B.   276
Lemon Curd - Roy and Ann McKay   281
Lemon Pie - Nanny for Phil S.   280
Macadamia Nut Pie   279
Mexican Flan   295
Raspberry Pie, Grandmother's - Suzy M.   283
Soda Cracker Dessert - Phyllis S.   288
Strawberry Cream Cheese Pie - Aunt Jane   275
Thanksgiving Pecan Pie   285
Washington Apple Cake/Pie   259
Wild Blackberry Pie - Janet   292
Pies, Savory   158
Green Tomato Pie   158
Quiche Zerhire   178
Pineapple Fluff - Auntie Jean W.   70
Pineapples, Scalloped   179
Pizza/Bread Sticks - Robin R.   40
Poppy Seed Dressing for Fruit   89
Pork Dishes   121
Baked Ham - Mom   121
Ham and Chicken Balls   46
Ham and Leek Casserole   121
Ham Hocks and Baby Lima Beans - Al S.   123
Ham with Rice and Bean Salad   80
Pork Chop and Rhubarb Casserole   126
Pork Chops and Gravy   125
Pork Chops, Bratwurst and Sauerkraut   124
Toad in the Hole   122
Potatoes, Fancy Baked - Nancy P.   162
Potatoes Romanoff   159
Potatoes, Scalloped   164
Poultry and Game. *See also* Pasta; Pasta Dishes
Baked Chicken   129
Chicken Breasts, Stuffed   131
Chicken Casserole - Shay   133
Chicken Salad - Granny's Favorite   83
Chicken Salad - Sue F.   82
Chicken Wings - Gloria S.   43
Cornish Game Hens - Julie   132
Cornish Game Hens - Pinky   130
Fancy Chicken - Lynn D.   134
Pecan Chicken Stuffed Tomatoes   138
Sweet and Sour Chicken - Sally C.   136
Turkey Stuffing - Micha E.   137
Puddings
Bread Pudding   293
Pumpkin Cheese Roll   250

Q

Quiche Zerhire   176

R

Raspberry Liqueur   50
Rice, Infallible   173
Rice Salad - Granny Rider   80
Rolls and Breadsticks in the Tube   36

S

Salad Dressings
   Blue Cheese Dressing - Jim R.   86
   French Dressing - Uncle Freddy   87
   Honey Mustard Dressing - Jim R.   88
   Poppy Seed Dressing for Fruit   89
Salads. *See also* Hors d'oeuvres: Canapés and Finger Foods
   Black-Eyed Peas - Billie   69
   Carrot Salad - Mauny K.   63
   Cherry Salad Supreme - Granny Rider   74
   Chicken Salad - Granny's Favorite   83
   Chicken Salad - Sue F.   82
   Chinese Green Salad - Judy Lindell   85
   Coleslaw - Bevy D.   64
   Cranberry Dream Salad   72
   Cucumbers - Granny Rider   63
   Curried Spinach Salad - Frances E.   77
   Double Duty Fruit Dish - Carol R.   71
   Greek-Style Green Salad - Kim B.   66
   Green Salad - Mom   84
   Ham with Rice and Bean Salad   80
   Hearts of Palm Salad - Micha E.   67
   Layered Salad - Dennis L.   65
   Macaroni Salad   68
   Oriental Salad - Debra B.   75
   Pea Salad   69
   Pineapple Fluff - Auntie Jean   70
   Rice Salad - Granny Rider   80
   Rice Salad Deluxe   81
   Special California Spinach Salad - Lynn D.   78
   Spinach Waldorf Salad   76
   Tuna Salad Deluxe - JoAnne M.   79
   Two Wedding Salads   73
Salmon Marinade and Barbeque Sauce   91
Salmon Party Ball   17
Salsas. *See* Dips and Spreads
Sandwiches. *See also* Dips and Spreads
   Egg Salad Sandwich   27
   Tuna Salad Sandwich   25
Sauces. *See also* Pasta Dishes
   Barbecue Sauce - Frances F.   92
   Barbecue Sauce - Jim R.   90
   Bernaise Sauce   97

Cucumber-Dill Sauce   139
Hollandaise Sauce   98
Mornay Sauce   97
Pesto Sauce - Mr. McCutchan   93
Salmon Marinade/Barbeque Sauce   91
Sweet and Sour Sauce - Frances F.   94
Tartar Sauce Deluxe - Mrs. Scott   94
Teriyaki Sauce - 10 Star!   99
White Sauces   96
Seafood. *See also* Pasta Dishes
Seafood Dishes
Baked Halibut - Steve's Way   141
Curried Shrimp, Alaska Style - Mike S.   140
Fancy Seafood Rolls   139
Good Old Tuna Casserole   144
Partytime Salmon - Gerard's   143
Scallops - Gary Michel   142
Sole - My Way   145
Shellfish. *See* Seafood
Shortbread. *See* Cookies and Bars
Side Dishes. *See* Casseroles; Vegetable Dishes
Snatch   52
Soufflés
Corn Soufflé   160
Soups
Cheese Soup   57
Clam Chowder - Browny's   59
Clam Chowder - Duke's   58
Cream of Broccoli or Asparagus Soup   60
Split Pea Soup - Rider/Zerhire   62
Tomato Soup - Armand M.   61
Spinach
California Spinach Salad   78
Curried Spinach Salad   77
Spinach Dip - Marilyn A.'s 10 Star   13
Spinach Waldorf   76
Spreads. *See* Dips and Spreads
Steak Bradford   108
Sweet and Savory Quick Breads
Avocado Bread   213
Blue Cheese Bread   215
Blueberry Bread   214
Hawaiian Nut Bread   216
Lemon Almond Bread   217
Old-fashioned Peach Bread   218
Pineapple-Carrot Bread   219
Rhubarb Bread - Sara T.   220
Strawberry Bread   221
Zucchini Bread - Jim R.   222
Sweet and Sour Sauce - Frances F.   94

T

Tacos - Mom   106

Tartar Sauce Deluxe 94
Teriyaki Sauce - 10 Star! - Jim R. 99
Thanksgiving Pumpkin Cream Cheese Roll 250
Toad in the Hole 122
Tomato/Cheese Soup - Armand 61
Tortes. *See* Pies and Pastries
Tuna Dishes
   Tuna Salad Deluxe 79
   Tuna Salad Sandwich 25

V

Vegetable Dishes. *See also* Casseroles
   Baked Beans – Mrs. G. 157
   Baked Onions 166
   Broccoli Casserole - Nancy P. 169
   Chili - Melly Belly's Way 161
   Eggplant Parmesan 170
   French Green Bean Casserole 168
   Fried Tomatoes - My Dad, Carl 167
   Good Old Baked Beans Deluxe 158
   Goulash Beans 158
   Green Tomato Pie - Joy M. 156
   Leeks Argentine Style - Micha E. 171
   Hot Dilly Beans 24
   Red Beans and Rice 178
   Spinach Casserole 171
   Sweet and Sour Red Cabbage - Katherine 172
   Yams - Micha E. 165
   Zucchini Bake 173
   Zucchini Fritters 179

W

Welsh Rarebit. *See* Hot Hors d'oeuvres
White Sauces 96

Y

Yak milk 53
Yeast Breads, Muffins and Rolls
   Bran Muffins - Robin R. 232
   Cinnamon Rolls - Granny Rider 228
   Do Your Own Thing Muffin Mix - Lynn D. 230
   Foccacia a la Zé 226
   My Mom's Yummy Croissants 223
   Sweet Holiday Muffins - Robbie T. 231
   White Bread - Granny Rider 224
Yorkshire Pudding. *See also* Beef Dishes; Toad

Z

Zucchini Dishes.
   Zucchini Bake 173
   Zucchini Fritters 179

In Parting…

I often think that people we have loved…
And who have loved us
Not only make us more human,
But become a part of us
And we carry them around all the time,
Whether we see them or not.
And, in some ways…
We are a sum total of
Those who have loved us,
And those we have given ourselves to,
So we are never alone.

I have a handwritten copy of this, torn and dog-eared in my wallet, because I love it so… I don't know where I got it from, so many years ago, but it expresses Exactly How I Feel.

Peace and God Bless you All.

Mom and the Cats